A History of A...

Leonard Woolsey Bacon

About Pyrrhus Press

Pyrrhus Press specializes in bringing books long out of date back to life, allowing today's readers access to yesterday's treasures.

Leonard Woolsey Bacon's *A History of American Christianity* traces the history of religion in the country from the European exploration of North America and all the way up into the 19th century. Along the way, Bacon looks at all the different branches of Christianity that were present in the colonies and country, especially Protestants, Catholics, and Quakers, and the important roles religion played in society.

A HISTORY OF AMERICAN CHRISTIANITY.

CHAPTER I. PROVIDENTIAL PREPARATIONS FOR THE DISCOVERY OF AMERICA—SPIRITUAL REVIVAL THROUGHOUT CHRISTENDOM, AND ESPECIALLY IN THE CHURCH OF SPAIN.

The heroic discovery of America, at the close of the fifteenth century after Christ, has compelled the generous and just admiration of the world; but the grandeur of human enterprise and achievement in the discovery of the western hemisphere has a less claim on our admiration than that divine wisdom and controlling providence which, for reasons now manifested, kept the secret hidden through so many millenniums, in spite of continual chances of disclosure, until the fullness of time.

How near, to "speak as a fool," the plans of God came to being defeated by human enterprise is illustrated by unquestioned facts. The fact of medieval exploration, colonization, and even evangelization in North America seems now to have emerged from the region of fanciful conjecture into that of history. That for four centuries, ending with the fifteenth, the church of Iceland maintained its bishops and other missionaries and built its churches and monasteries on the frozen coast of Greenland is abundantly proved by documents and monuments. Dim but seemingly unmistakable traces are now discovered of enterprises, not only of exploration and trade, but also of evangelization, reaching along the mainland southward to the shores of New England. There are vague indications that these beginnings of Christian civilization were extinguished, as in so many later instances, by savage massacre. With impressive coincidence, the latest vestige of this primeval American Christianity fades out in the very year of the discovery of America by Columbus.[2:1]

By a prodigy of divine providence, the secret of the ages had been kept from premature disclosure during the centuries in which, without knowing it, the Old World was actually in communication with the New. That was high strategy in the warfare for the advancement of the kingdom of God in the earth. What possibilities, even yet only beginning to be accomplished, were thus saved to both hemispheres! If the discovery of America had been achieved four centuries or even a single century earlier, the Christianity to be transplanted to the western world would have been that of the church of Europe at its lowest stage of decadence. The period closing with the fifteenth century was that of the dense darkness that goes before the dawn. It was a period in which the lingering life of the church was chiefly manifested in feverish complaints of the widespread corruption and outcries for "reformation of the church in head and members." The degeneracy of the clergy was nowhere more manifest than in the monastic orders, that had been originally established for the express purpose of reviving and purifying the church. That ancient word was fulfilled, "Like people, like priest." But it was especially in the person of the foremost official representative of the religion of Jesus Christ that that religion was most dishonored. The fifteenth century was the era of the infamous popes. By another coincidence which arrests the attention of the reader of history, that same year of the discovery by Columbus witnessed the accession of the most infamous of the series, the Borgia, Alexander VI., to his short and shameful pontificate.

Let it not be thought, as some of us might be prone to think, that the timeliness of the discovery of the western hemisphere, in its relation to church history, is summed up in this, that it coincided with the Protestant Reformation, so that the New World might be planted with a Protestant Christianity. For a hundred years the colonization and evangelization of America were, in the narrowest sense of that large word, Catholic, not Protestant. But the Catholicism brought hither was that of the sixteenth century, not of the fifteenth. It is a most one-sided reading of the history of that illustrious age which fails to recognize that the great Reformation was a reformation of the church as well as a reformation from the church. It was in Spain itself, in which the corruption of the church had been foulest, but from which all symptoms of "heretical pravity" were purged away with the fiercest zeal as fast as they appeared,—in Spain under the reign of Ferdinand and Isabella the Catholic,—that the demand for a Catholic reformation made itself earliest and most effectually felt. The highest ecclesiastical dignitary of the realm, Ximenes, confessor to the queen, Archbishop of Toledo, and cardinal, was himself the leader of reform. No changes in the rest of Christendom were destined for many years to have so great an influence on the course of evangelization in North America as those which affected the church of Spain; and of these by far the most important in their bearing on the early course of Christianity in America were, first, the purifying and quickening of the miserably decayed and corrupted mendicant orders,—ever the most effective arm in the missionary service of the Latin Church,—and, a little later, the founding of the Society of Jesus, with its immense potency for good and for evil. At the same time the court of Rome, sobered in some measure, by the perilous crisis that confronted it, from its long orgy of simony, nepotism, and sensuality, began to find time and thought for spiritual duties. The establishment of the "congregations" or administrative boards, and especially of the Congregatio de Propaganda Fide, or board of missions, dates chiefly from the sixteenth century. The revived interest in theological study incident to the general spiritual quickening gave the church, as the result of the labors of the Council of Trent, a well-defined body of doctrine, which nevertheless was not so narrowly defined as to preclude differences and debates among the diverse sects of the clergy, by whose competitions and antagonisms the progress of missions both in Christian and in heathen lands was destined to be so seriously affected.

An incident of the Catholic Reformation of the sixteenth century—inevitable incident, doubtless, in that age, but none the less deplorable—was the engendering or intensifying of that cruel and ferocious form of fanaticism which is defined as the combination of religious emotion with the malignant passions. The tendency to fanaticism is one of the perils attendant on the deep stirring of religious feeling at any time; it was especially attendant on the religious agitations of that period; but most of all it was in Spain, where, of all the Catholic nations, corruption had gone deepest and spiritual revival was most earnest and sincere, that the manifestations of fanaticism were most shocking. Ferdinand and Isabella the Catholic were distinguished alike by their piety and their part in the promotion of civilization, and by the horrors of bloody cruelty perpetrated by their authority and that of the church, at the instigation of the sincere and devout reformer Ximenes. In the memorable year 1492 was inaugurated the fiercest work of the Spanish Inquisition, concerning which, speaking of her own part in it, the pious Isabella was able afterward to say, "For the love of Christ and of his virgin mother I have caused great misery, and have depopulated towns and districts, provinces and kingdoms."

The earlier pages of American church history will not be intelligently read unless it is well understood that the Christianity first to be transplanted to the soil of the New World was the Christianity of Spain—the Spain of Isabella and Ximenes, of Loyola and Francis Xavier and St. Theresa, the Spain also of Torquemada and St. Peter Arbues and the zealous and orthodox Duke of Alva.

CHAPTER II. SPANISH CONQUEST—THE PROPAGATION, DECAY, AND DOWNFALL OF SPANISH CHRISTIANITY.

It is a striking fact that the earliest monuments of colonial and ecclesiastical antiquity within the present domain of the United States, after the early Spanish remains in Florida, are to be found in those remotely interior and inaccessible highlands of New Mexico, which have only now begun to be reached in the westward progress of migration. Before the beginnings of permanent English colonization at Plymouth and at Jamestown, before the French beginnings on the St. Lawrence, before the close of the sixteenth century, there had been laid by Spanish soldiers, adventurers, and missionaries, in those far recesses of the continent, the foundations of Christian towns and churches, the stately walls and towers of which still invite the admiration of the traveler.

The fact is not more impressive than it is instructive. It illustrates the prodigious impetuosity of that tide of conquest which within so few years from the discovery of the American continents not only swept over the regions of South and Central America and the great plateau of Mexico, but actually occupied with military posts, with extensive and successful missions, and with a colonization which seemed to show every sign of stability and future expansion, by far the greater part of the present domain of the United States exclusive of Alaska—an ecclesiastico-military empire stretching its vast diameter from the southernmost cape of Florida across twenty-five parallels of latitude and forty-five meridians of longitude to the Strait of Juan de Fuca. The lessons taught by this amazingly swift extension of the empire and the church, and its arrest and almost extinction, are legible on the surface of the history. It is a strange, but not unparalleled, story of attempted coöperation in the common service of God and Mammon and Moloch—of endeavors after concord between Christ and Belial.

There is no reason to question the sincerity with which the rulers of Spain believed themselves to be actuated by the highest motives of Christian charity in their terrible and fatal American policy. "The conversion of the Indians is the principal foundation of the conquest—that which ought principally to be attended to." So wrote the king in a correspondence in which a most cold-blooded authorization is given for the enslaving of the Indians.[7:1] After the very first voyage of Columbus every expedition of discovery or invasion was equipped with its contingent of clergy—secular priests as chaplains to the Spaniards, and friars of the regular orders for mission work among the Indians—at cost of the royal treasury or as a charge upon the new conquests.

This subsidizing of the church was the least serious of the injuries inflicted on the cause of the gospel by the piety of the Spanish government. That such subsidizing is in the long run an injury is a lesson illustrated not only in this case, but in many parallel cases in the course of this history. A far more dreadful wrong was the identifying of the religion of Jesus Christ with a system of war and slavery, well-nigh the most atrocious in recorded history. For such a policy the Spanish nation had just received a peculiar training. It is one of the commonplaces of history to remark that the barbarian invaders of the Roman empire were themselves vanquished by their own victims, being converted by them to the Christian faith. In like manner the Spanish nation, triumphing over its Moslem subjects in the expulsion of the Moors, seemed in its American conquests to have been converted to the worst of the tenets of Islam. The propagation of the gospel in the western hemisphere, under the Spanish rule, illustrated in its public and official aspects far more the principles of Mohammed than those of Jesus. The triple alternative offered by the Saracen or the Turk—conversion or tribute or the sword—was renewed with aggravations by the Christian conquerors of America. In a form deliberately drawn up and prescribed by the civil and ecclesiastical counselors at Madrid, the invader of a new province was to summon the rulers and people to acknowledge the church and the pope and the king of Spain; and in case of refusal or delay to comply with this summons, the invader was to notify them of the consequences in these terms: "If you refuse, by the help of God we shall enter with force into your land, and shall make war against you in all ways and manners that we can, and subject you to the yoke and obedience of the church and of their Highnesses; we shall take you and your wives and your children and make slaves of them, and sell and dispose of them as their Highnesses may command; and we shall take away your goods, and do you all the mischief and damage that we can, as to vassals who do not obey and refuse to receive their lord; and we protest that the deaths and losses that shall accrue from this are your own fault."[8:1]

While the church was thus implicated in crimes against humanity which history shudders to record, it is a grateful duty to remember that it was from the church also and in the name of Christ that bold protests and strenuous efforts were put forth in behalf of the oppressed and wronged. Such names as Las Casas and Montesinos shine with a beautiful luster in the darkness of that age; and the Dominican order, identified on the other side of the sea with the fiercest cruelties of the Spanish Inquisition, is honorable in American church history for its fearless championship of liberty and justice.

The first entrance of Spanish Christianity upon the soil of the United States was wholly characteristic. In quest of the Fountain of Youth, Ponce de Leon sailed for the coast of Florida equipped with forces both for the carnal and for the spiritual warfare. Besides his colonists and his men-at-arms, he brought his secular priests as chaplains and his monks as missionaries; and his instructions from the crown required him to summon the natives, as in the famous "Requerimiento," to submit themselves to the Catholic faith and to the king of Spain, under threat of the sword and slavery. The invaders found a different temper in the natives from what was encountered in Mexico and Peru, where the populations were miserably subjugated, or in the islands, where they were first enslaved and presently completely exterminated. The insolent invasion was met, as it deserved, by effective volleys of arrows, and its chivalrous leader was driven back to Cuba, to die there of his wounds.

It is needless to recount the successive failures of Spanish civilization and Christianity to get foothold on the domain now included in the United States. Not until more than forty years after the attempt of Ponce de Leon did the expedition of the ferocious Menendez effect a permanent establishment on the coast of Florida. In September, 1565, the foundations of the oldest city in the United States, St. Augustine, were laid with solemn religious rites by the toil of the first negro slaves; and the event was signalized by one of the most horrible massacres in recorded history, the cold-blooded and perfidious extermination, almost to the last man, woman, and child, of a colony of French Protestants that had been planted a few months before at the mouth of the St. John's River.

The colony thus inaugurated seemed to give every promise of permanent success as a center of religious influence. The spiritual work was naturally and wisely divided into the pastoral care of the Spanish garrisons and settlements, which was taken in charge by "secular" priests, and the mission work among the Indians, committed to friars of those "regular" orders whose solid organization and independence of the episcopal hierarchy, and whose keen emulation in enterprises of self-denial, toil, and peril, have been so large an element of strength, and sometimes of weakness, in the Roman system. In turn, the mission field of the Floridas was occupied by the Dominicans, the Jesuits, and the Franciscans. Before the end of seventy years from the founding of St. Augustine the number of Christian Indians was reckoned at twenty-five or thirty thousand, distributed among forty-four missions, under the direction of thirty-five Franciscan missionaries, while the city of St. Augustine was fully equipped with religious institutions and organizations. Grave complaints are on record, which indicate that the great number of the Indian converts was out of all proportion to their meager advancement in Christian grace and knowledge; but with these indications of shortcoming in the missionaries there are honorable proofs of diligent devotion to duty in the creating of a literature of instruction in the barbarous languages of the peninsula.

For one hundred and fifteen years Spain and the Spanish missionaries had exclusive possession in Florida, and it was during this period that these imposing results were achieved. In 1680 a settlement of Scotch Presbyterians at Port Royal in South Carolina seemed like a menace to the Spanish domination. It was wholly characteristic of the Spanish colony to seize the sword at once and destroy its nearest Christian neighbor. It took the sword, and perished by the sword. The war of races and sects thus inaugurated went on, with intervals of quiet, until the Treaty of Paris, in 1763, transferred Florida to the British crown. No longer sustained by the terror of the Spanish arms and by subsidies from the Spanish treasury, the whole fabric of Spanish civilization and Christianization, at the end of a history of almost two centuries, tumbled at once to complete ruin and extinction.

The story of the planting of Christian institutions in New Mexico runs parallel with the early history of Florida. Omitting from this brief summary the first discovery of these regions by fugitives from one of the disastrous early attempts to effect a settlement on the Florida coast, omitting (what we would fain narrate) the stories of heroic adventure and apostolic zeal and martyrdom which antedate the permanent occupation of the country, we note the arrival, in 1598, of a strong, numerous, and splendidly equipped colony, and the founding of a Christian city in the heart of the American continent. As usual in such Spanish enterprises, the missionary work was undertaken by a body of Franciscan friars. After the first months of hardship and discouragement, the work of the Christian colony, and especially the work of evangelization among the Indians, went forward at a marvelous rate. Reinforcements both of priests and of soldiers were received from Mexico; by the end of ten years baptisms were reported to the number of eight thousand; the entire population of the province was reckoned as being within the pale of the church; not less than sixty Franciscan friars at once were engaged in the double service of pastors and missionaries. The triumph of the gospel and of Spanish arms seemed complete and permanent.

Fourscore years after the founding of the colony and mission the sudden explosion of a conspiracy, which for a long time had been secretly preparing, revealed the true value of the allegiance of the Indians to the Spanish government and of their conversion to Christ. Confounding in a common hatred the missionaries and the tyrannous conquerors, who had been associated in a common policy, the Christian Indians turned upon their rulers and their pastors alike with undiscriminating warfare. "In a few weeks no Spaniard was in New Mexico north of El Paso. Christianity and civilization were swept away at one blow." The successful rebels bettered the instruction that they had received from their rejected pastors. The measures of compulsion that had been used to stamp out every vestige of the old religion were put into use against the new.

The cause of Catholic Christianity in New Mexico never recovered from this stunning blow. After twenty years the Spanish power, taking advantage of the anarchy and depopulation of the province, had reoccupied its former posts by military force, the missionaries were brought back under armed protection, the practice of the ancient religion was suppressed by the strong hand, and efforts, too often unsuccessful, were made to win back the apostate tribes to something more than a sullen submission to the government and the religion of their conquerors. The later history of Spanish Christianity in New Mexico is a history of decline and decay, enlivened by the usual contentions between the "regular" clergy and the episcopal government. The white population increased, the Indian population dwindled. Religion as set forth by an exotic clergy became an object of indifference when it was not an object of hatred. In 1845 the Bishop of Durango, visiting the province, found an Indian population of twenty thousand in a total of eighty thousand. The clergy numbered only seventeen priests. Three years later the province became part of the United States.

To complete the story of the planting of Spanish Christianity within the present boundaries of the United States, it is necessary to depart from the merely chronological order of American church history; for, although the immense adventurousness of Spanish explorers by sea and land had, early in the sixteenth century, made known to Christendom the coasts and harbors of the Californias, the beginnings of settlement and missions on that Pacific coast date from so late as 1769. At this period the method of such work had become settled into a system. The organization was threefold, including (1) the garrison town, (2) the Spanish settlement, and (3) the mission, at which the Indian neophytes were gathered under the tutelage and strict government of the convent of Franciscan friars. The whole system was sustained by the authority and the lavish subventions of the Spanish government, and herein lay its strength and, as the event speedily proved, its fatal weakness. The inert and feeble character of the Indians of that region offered little excuse for the atrocious cruelties that had elsewhere marked the Spanish occupation; but the paternal kindness of the stronger race was hardly less hurtful. The natives were easily persuaded to become by thousands the dependents and servants of the missions. Conversion went on apace. At the end of sixty-five years from the founding of the missions their twenty-one stations numbered a Christian native population of more than thirty thousand, and were possessed of magnificent wealth, agricultural and commercial. In that very year (1834) the long-intended purpose of the government to release the Indians from their almost slavery under the missions, and to distribute the vast property in severalty, was put in force. In eight years the more than thirty thousand Catholic Indians had dwindled to less than five thousand; the enormous estates of the missions were dissipated; the converts lapsed into savagery and paganism.

Meanwhile the Spanish population had gone on slowly increasing. In the year 1840, seventy years from the Spanish occupancy, it had risen to nearly six thousand; but it was a population the spiritual character of which gave little occasion of boasting to the Spanish church. Tardy and feeble efforts had been instituted to provide it with an organized parish ministry, when the supreme and exclusive control of that country ceased from the hands that so long had held it. "The vineyard was taken away, and given to other husbandmen." In the year 1848 California was annexed to the United States.

This condensed story of Spanish Christianity within the present boundaries of the United States is absurdly brief compared with the vast extent of space, the three centuries of time, and what seemed at one time the grandeur of results involved in it. But in truth it has strangely little connection with the extant Christianity of our country. It is almost as completely severed from historical relation with the church of the present day as the missions of the Greenlanders in the centuries before Columbus. If we distinguish justly between the Christian work and its unchristian and almost satanic admixtures, we can join without reserve both in the eulogy and in the lament with which the Catholic historian sums up his review: "It was a glorious work, and the recital of it impresses us by the vastness and success of the toil. Yet, as we look around to-day, we can find nothing of it that remains. Names of saints in melodious Spanish stand out from maps in all that section where the Spanish monk trod, toiled, and died. A few thousand Christian Indians, descendants of those they converted and civilized, still survive in New Mexico and Arizona, and that is all."[15:1]

CHAPTER III. THE PROJECT OF FRENCH EMPIRE AND EVANGELIZATION—ITS WIDE AND RAPID SUCCESS—ITS SUDDEN EXTINCTION.

For a full century, from the discovery of the New World until the first effective effort at occupation by any other European people, the Spanish church and nation had held exclusive occupancy of the North American continent. The Spanish enterprises of conquest and colonization had been carried forward with enormous and unscrupulous energy, and alongside of them and involved with them had been borne the Spanish chaplaincies and missions, sustained from the same treasury, in some honorable instances bravely protesting against the atrocities they were compelled to witness, in other instances implicated in them and sharing the bloody profits of them. But, unquestionable as was the martial prowess of the Spanish soldier and adventurer, and the fearless devotion of the Spanish missionary, there appears nothing like systematic planning in all these immense operations. The tide of conquest flowed in capricious courses, according as it was invited by hopes of gold or of a passage to China, or of some phantom of a Fountain of Youth or a city of Quivira or a Gilded Man; and it seemed in general to the missionary that he could not do else than follow in the course of conquest. It is wholly characteristic of the French people that its entering at last upon enterprises of colonization and missions should be with large forecasting of the future and with the methods of a grand strategy.

We can easily believe that the famous "Bull of Partition" of Pope Alexander VI. was not one of the hindrances that so long delayed the beginnings of a New France in the West. Incessant dynastic wars with near neighbors, the final throes of the long struggle between the crown and the great vassals, and finally the religious wars that culminated in the awful slaughter of St. Bartholomew's, and ended at the close of the century with the politic conversion and the coronation of Henry IV.—these were among the causes that had held back the great nation from distant undertakings. But thoughts of great things to be achieved in the New World had never for long at a time been absent from the minds of Frenchmen. The annual visits of the Breton fishing-fleets to the banks of Newfoundland kept in mind such rights of discovery as were alleged by France, and kept attention fixed in the direction of the great gulf and river of St. Lawrence. Long before the middle of the sixteenth century Jacques Cartier had explored the St. Lawrence beyond the commanding position which he named Montreal, and a royal commission had issued, under which he was to undertake an enterprise of "discovery, settlement, and the conversion of the Indians." But it was not till the year 1608 that the first permanent French settlement was effected. With the coup d'œil of a general or the foresight of a prophet, Champlain, the illustrious first founder of French empire in America, in 1608 fixed the starting-point of it at the natural fortress of Quebec. How early the great project had begun to take shape in the leading minds of the nation it may not be easy to determine. It was only after the adventurous explorations of the French pioneers, traders, and friars—men of like boundless enthusiasm and courage—had been crowned by the achievement of La Salle, who first of men traversed the two great waterways of the continent from the Gulf of St. Lawrence to the Gulf of Mexico, that the amazing possibilities of it were fully revealed. But, whosesoever scheme it was, a more magnificent project of empire, secular and spiritual, has never entered into the heart of man. It seems to have been native to the American soil, springing up in the hearts of the French pioneer explorers themselves;[18:1] but by its grandeur, and at the same time its unity, it was of a sort to delight the souls of Sully and Richelieu and of their masters. Under thin and dubious claims by right of discovery, through the immense energy and daring of her explorers, the heroic zeal of her missionaries, and not so much by the prowess of her soldiers as by her craft in diplomacy with savage tribes, France was to assert and make good her title to the basin of the St. Lawrence and the lakes, and the basin of the Mississippi and the Gulf of Mexico. From the mouth of the St. Lawrence to the mouth of the Mississippi, through the core of the continent, was to be drawn a cordon of posts, military, commercial, and religious, with other outlying stations at strategic points both eastward and westward. The only external interference with this scheme that could be apprehended at its inception was from the Spanish colonies, already decaying and shrinking within their boundaries to the west and to the southeast, and from a puny little English settlement started only a year before, with a doubtful hold on life, on the bank of the James River. A dozen years later a pitiably feeble company of Pilgrims shall make their landing at Plymouth to try the not hopeful experiment of living in the wilderness, and a settlement of Swedes in Delaware and of Hollanders on the Hudson shall be added to the incongruous, unconcerted, mutually jealous plantations that begin to take root along the Atlantic seaboard. Not only grandeur and sagacity of conception, but success in achievement, is illustrated by the comparative area occupied by the three great European powers on the continent of North America at the end of a century and a half from the founding of Quebec in 1608. Dividing the continent into twenty-five equal parts, the French claimed and seemed to hold firmly in possession twenty parts, the Spanish four parts, and the English one part.[19:1]

The comparison between the Spanish and the French methods of colonization and missions in America is at almost every point honorable to the French. Instead of a greedy scramble after other men's property in gold and silver, the business basis of the French enterprises was to consist in a widely organized and laboriously prosecuted traffic in furs. Instead of a series of desultory and savage campaigns of conquest, the ferocity of which was aggravated by the show of zeal for the kingdom of righteousness and peace, was a large-minded and far-sighted scheme of empire, under which remote and hostile tribes were to be combined by ties of mutual interest and common advantage. And the missions, instead of following servilely in the track of bloody conquest to assume the tutelage of subjugated and enslaved races, were to share with the soldier and the trader the perilous adventures of exploration, and not so much to be supported and defended as to be themselves the support and protection of the settlements, through the influence of Christian love and self-sacrifice over the savage heart. Such elements of moral dignity, as well as of imperial grandeur, marked the plans for the French occupation of North America.

To a wonderful extent those charged with this enterprise were worthy of the task. Among the military and civil leaders of it, from Champlain to Montcalm, were men that would have honored the best days of French chivalry. The energy and daring of the French explorers, whether traders or missionaries, have not been equaled in the pioneer work of other races. And the annals of Christian martyrdom may be searched in vain for more heroic examples of devotion to the work of the gospel than those which adorn the history of the French missions in North America. What magnificent results might not be expected from such an enterprise, in the hands of such men, sustained by the resources of the most powerful nation and national church in Christendom!

From the founding of Quebec, in 1608, the expansion of the French enterprise was swift and vast. By the end of fifty years Quebec had been equipped with hospital, nunnery, seminary for the education of priests, all affluently endowed from the wealth of zealous courtiers, and served in a noble spirit of self-devotion by the choicest men and women that the French church could furnish; besides these institutions, the admirable plan of a training colony, at which converted Indians should be trained to civilized life, was realized at Sillery, in the neighborhood. The sacred city of Montreal had been established as a base for missions to the remoter west. Long in advance of the settlement at Plymouth, French Christianity was actively and beneficently busy among the savages of eastern Maine, among the so-called "neutral nations" by the Niagara, among the fiercely hostile Iroquois of northern New York, by Lake Huron and Lake Nipissing, and, with wonderful tokens of success, by the Falls of St. Mary. "Thus did the religious zeal of the French bear the cross to the banks of the St. Mary and the confines of Lake Superior, and look wistfully toward the homes of the Sioux in the valley of the Mississippi, five years before the New England Eliot had addressed the tribe of Indians that dwelt within six miles of Boston harbor."[21:1]

Thirty years more passed, bringing the story down to the memorable year 1688. The French posts, military, commercial, and religious, had been pushed westward to the head of Lake Superior. The Mississippi had been discovered and explored, and the colonies planted from Canada along its banks and the banks of its tributaries had been met by the expeditions proceeding direct from France through the Gulf of Mexico. The claims of France in America included not only the vast domain of Canada, but a half of Maine, a half of Vermont, more than a half of New York, the entire valley of the Mississippi, and Texas as far as the Rio Bravo del Norte.[21:2] And these claims were asserted by actual and almost undisputed occupancy. The seventy years that followed were years of "storm and stress" for the French colonies and missions. The widening areas occupied by the French and by the English settlers brought the rival establishments into nearer neighborhood, into sharper competition, and into bloody collision. Successive European wars—King William's War, Queen Anne's War (of the Spanish succession), King George's War (of the Austrian succession)—involved the dependencies of France and those of England in the conflicts of their sovereigns. These were the years of terror along the exposed northern frontier of English settlements in New England and New York, when massacre and burning by bands of savages, under French instigation and leadership, made the names of Haverhill and Deerfield and Schenectady memorable in American history, and when, in desperate campaigns against the Canadian strongholds, the colonists vainly sought to protect themselves from the savages by attacking the centers from which the murderous forays were directed. But each successive treaty of peace between England and France confirmed and reconfirmed the French claims to the main part of her American domain. The advances of French missions and settlements continued southward and westward, in spite of jealousy in European cabinets as the imposing magnitude of the plans of French empire became more distinctly disclosed, and in spite of the struggles of the English colonies both North and South. When, on the 4th of July, 1754, Colonel George Washington surrendered Fort Necessity, near the fork of the Ohio, to the French, "in the whole valley of the Mississippi, to its headsprings in the Alleghanies, no standard floated but that of France."[22:1]

There seemed little reason to doubt that the French empire in America, which for a century and a half had gone on expanding and strengthening, would continue to expand and strengthen for centuries to come. Sudden as lightning, in August, 1756, the Seven Years' War broke out on the other side of the globe. The treaty with which it ended, in February, 1763, transferred to Great Britain, together with the Spanish territory of Florida, all the French possessions in America, from the Arctic Ocean to the Gulf of Mexico. "As a dream when one awaketh," the magnificent vision of empire, spiritual and secular, which for so many generations had occupied the imagination of French statesmen and churchmen, was rudely and forever dispelled. Of the princely wealth, the brilliant talents, the unsurpassed audacity of adventure, the unequaled heroism of toil and martyrdom expended on the great project, how strangely meager and evanescent the results! In the districts of Lower Canada there remain, indeed, the institutions of a French Catholic population; and the aspect of those districts, in which the pledge of full liberty to the dominant church has been scrupulously fulfilled by the British government, may reasonably be regarded as an indication of what France would have done for the continent in general. But within the present domain of the United States the entire results of a century and a half of French Catholic colonization and evangelization may be summed up as follows: In Maine, a thousand Catholic Indians still remain, to remind one of the time when, as it is boldly claimed, the whole Indian population of that province were either converted or under Jesuit training.[23:1] In like manner, a scanty score of thousands of Catholic Indians on various reservations in the remote West represent the time when, at the end of the French domination, "all the North American Indians were more or less extensively converted" to Catholic Christianity, "all had the gospel preached to them."[23:2] The splendid fruits of the missions among the Iroquois, from soil watered by the blood of martyrs, were wasted to nothing in savage intertribal wars. Among the Choctaws and Chickasaws of the South and Southwest, among whom the gospel was by and by to win some of its fairest trophies, the French missionaries achieved no great success.[23:3] The French colonies from Canada, planted so prosperously along the Western rivers, dispersed, leaving behind them some straggling families. The abundant later growth of the Catholic Church in that region was to be from other seed and stock. The region of Louisiana alone, destined a generation later to be included within the boundaries of the great republic, retained organized communities of French descent and language; but, living as they were in utter unbelief and contempt of religion and morality, it would be an unjust reproach on Catholicism to call them Catholic. The work of the gospel had got to be begun from the foundation. Nevertheless it is not to be doubted that remote memories or lingering traditions of a better age survived to aid the work of those who by and by should enter in to rebuild the waste places.[24:1]

There are not a few of us, wise after the event, who recognize a final cause of this surprising and almost dramatic failure, in the manifest intent of divine Providence that the field of the next great empire in the world's history should not become the exclusive domain of an old-world monarchy and hierarchy; but the immediate efficient causes of it are not so obvious. This, however, may justly be said: some of the seeming elements of strength in the French colonization proved to be fatal elements of weakness.

1. The French colonies had the advantage of royal patronage, endowment,[24:2] and protection, and of unity of counsel and direction. They were all parts of one system, under one control. And their centers of vitality, head and heart, were on the other side of the sea. Subsisting upon the strength of the great monarchy, they must needs share its fortunes, evil as well as good. When, after the reverses of France in the Seven Years' War, it became necessary to accept hard terms of peace, the superb framework of empire in the West fell to the disposal of the victors. "America," said Pitt, "was conquered in Germany."

2. The business basis of the French colonies, being that of trade with the Indians rather than a self-supporting agriculture, favored the swift expansion of these colonies and their wide

influence among the Indians. Scattered companies of fur-traders would be found here and there, wherever were favorable points for traffic, penetrating deeply into the wilderness and establishing friendly business relations with the savages. It has been observed that the Romanic races show an alacrity for intermarriage with barbarous tribes that is not to be found in the Teutonic. The result of such relations is ordinarily less the elevating of the lower race than the dragging down of the higher; but it tends for the time to give great advantage in maintaining a powerful political influence over the barbarians. Thus it was that the French, few in number, covered almost the breadth of the continent with their formidable alliances; and these alliances were the offensive and defensive armor in which they trusted, but they were also their peril. Close alliance with one savage clan involved war with its enemies. It was an early misfortune of the French settlers that their close friendly relations with their Huron neighbors embattled against them the fiercest, bravest, and ablest of the Indian tribes, the confederacy of the Six Nations, which held, with full appreciation of its strategic importance, the command of the exits southward from the valley of the St. Lawrence. The fierce jealousy of the Iroquois toward the allies of their hereditary antagonists, rather than any good will toward white settlers of other races, made them an effectual check upon French encroachments upon the slender line of English, Dutch, and Swedish settlements that stretched southward from Maine along the Atlantic coast.

3. In one aspect it was doubtless an advantage to the French missions in America that the sharp sectarian competitions between the different clerical orders resulted finally in the missions coming almost exclusively under the control of the Jesuit society. This result insured to the missions the highest ability in administration and direction, ample resources of various sorts, and a force of missionaries whose personal virtues have won for them unstinted eulogy even from unfriendly sources—men the ardor of whose zeal was rigorously controlled by a more than martial severity of religious discipline. But it would be uncandid in us to refuse attention to those grave charges against the society brought by Catholic authorities and Catholic orders, and so enforced as, after long and acrimonious controversy, to result in the expulsion of the society from almost every nation of Catholic Europe, in its being stigmatized by Pope Benedict XIV., in 1741, as made up of "disobedient, contumacious, captious, and reprobate persons," and at last in its being suppressed and abolished by Pope Clement XIV., in 1773, as a nuisance to Christendom. We need, indeed, to make allowance for the intense animosity of sectarian strife among the various Catholic orders in which the charges against the society were engendered and unrelentingly prosecuted; but after all deductions it is not credible that the almost universal odium in which it was held was provoked solely by its virtues. Among the accusations against the society which seem most clearly substantiated these two are likely to be concerned in that "brand of ultimate failure which has invariably been stamped on all its most promising schemes and efforts":[26:1] first, a disposition to compromise the essential principles of Christianity by politic concessions to heathenism, so that the successes of the Jesuit missions are magnified by reports of alleged conversions that are conversions only in name and outward form; second, a constantly besetting propensity to political intrigue.[27:1] It is hardly to be doubted that both had their part in the prodigious failure of the French Catholic missions and settlements within the present boundaries of the United States.

4. The conditions which favored the swift and magnificent expansion of the French occupation were unfavorable to the healthy natural growth of permanent settlements. A post of soldiers, a group of cabins of trappers and fur-traders, and a mission of nuns and celibate priests, all together give small promise of rapid increase of population. It is rather to the fact that the French settlements, except at the seaboard, were constituted so largely of these elements, than to any alleged sterility of the French stock, that the fatal weakness of the French occupation is to be ascribed. The lack of French America was men. The population of Canada in 1759, according to census, was about eighty-two thousand;[27:2] that of New England in 1754 is estimated at four hundred and twenty-five thousand. "The white population of five, or perhaps

even of six, of the American provinces was greater singly than that of all Canada, and the aggregate in America exceeded that in Canada fourteenfold."[27:3] The same sign of weakness is recognized at the other extremity of the cordon of French settlements. The vast region of Louisiana is estimated, at fifty years from its colonization, at one tenth of the strength of the coeval province of Pennsylvania.[27:4]

Under these hopeless conditions the French colonies had not even the alternative of keeping the peace. The state of war was forced by the mother countries. There was no recourse for Canada except to her savage allies, won for her through the influence of the missionaries. It is justly claimed that in the mind of such early leaders as Champlain the dominant motive of the French colonization was religious; but in the cruel position into which the colony was forced it was almost inevitable that the missions should become political. It was boasted in their behalf that they had taught the Indians "to mingle Jesus Christ and France together in their affections."[28:1] The cross and the lilies were blazoned together as the sign of French dominion. The missionary became frequently, and sometimes quite undisguisedly, a political agent. It was from the missions that the horrible murderous forays upon defenseless villages proceeded, which so often marked the frontier line of New England and New York with fire and blood. It is one of the most unhappy of the results of that savage warfare that in the minds of the communities that suffered from it the Jesuit missionary came to be looked upon as accessory to these abhorrent crimes. Deeply is it to be lamented that men with such eminent claims on our admiration and reverence should not be triumphantly clear of all suspicion of such complicity. We gladly concede the claim[28:2] that the proof of the complicity is not complete; we could welcome some clear evidence in disproof of it—some sign of a bold and indignant protest against these crimes; we could wish that the Jesuit historian had not boasted of these atrocities as proceeding from the fine work of his brethren,[29:1] and that the antecedents of the Jesuits as a body, and their declared principles of "moral theology," were such as raise no presumption against them even in unfriendly minds. But we must be content with thankfully acknowledging that divine change which has made it impossible longer to boast of or even justify such deeds, and which leaves no ground among neighbor Christians of the present day for harboring mutual suspicions which, to the Christian ministers of French and English America of two hundred years ago and less, it was impossible to repress.

I have spoken of the complete extinction within the present domain of the United States of the magnificent beginnings of the projected French Catholic Church and empire. It is only in the most recent years, since the Civil War, that the results of the work inaugurated in America by Champlain begin to reappear in the field of the ecclesiastical history of the United States. The immigration of Canadian French Catholics into the northern tier of States has already grown to considerable volume, and is still growing in numbers and in stability and strength, and adds a new and interesting element to the many factors that go to make up the American church.

CHAPTER IV ANTECEDENTS OF PERMANENT CHRISTIAN COLONIZATION—THE DISINTEGRATION OF CHRISTENDOM— CONTROVERSIES—PERSECUTIONS.

We have briefly reviewed the history of two magnificent schemes of secular and spiritual empire, which, conceived in the minds of great statesmen and churchmen, sustained by the resources of the mightiest kingdoms of that age, inaugurated by soldiers of admirable prowess, explorers of unsurpassed boldness and persistence, and missionaries whose heroic faith has canonized them in the veneration of Christendom, have nevertheless come to naught.

We turn now to observe the beginnings, coinciding in time with those of the French enterprise, of a series of disconnected plantations along the Atlantic seaboard, established as if at haphazard, without plan or mutual preconcert, of different languages and widely diverse Christian creeds, depending on scanty private resources, unsustained by governmental arms or treasuries, but destined, in a course of events which no human foresight could have calculated, to come under the plastic influence of a single European power, to be molded according to the general type of English polity, and to become heir to English traditions, literature, and language. These mutually alien and even antagonistic communities were to be constrained, by forces superior to human control, first into confederation and then into union, and to occupy the breadth of the new continent as a solid and independent nation. The history reads like a fulfillment of the apocalyptic imagery of a rock hewn from the mountain without hands, moving on to fill the earth.

Looking back after the event, we find it easy to trace the providential preparations for this great result. There were few important events in the course of the sixteenth and early seventeenth centuries that did not have to do with it; but the most obvious of these antecedents are to be found in controversies and persecutions.

The protest of northern Europe against the abuses and corruptions prevailing in the Roman Church was articulated in the Augsburg Confession. Over against it were framed the decrees of the Council of Trent. Thus the lines were distinctly drawn and the warfare between contending principles was joined. Those who fondly dreamed of a permanently united and solid Protestantism to withstand its powerful antagonist were destined to speedy and inevitable disappointment. There have been many to deplore that so soon after the protest of Augsburg was set forth as embodying the common belief of Protestants new parties should have arisen protesting against the protest. The ordinance of the Lord's Supper, instituted as a sacrament of universal Christian fellowship, became (as so often before and since) the center of contention and the badge of mutual alienation. It was on this point that Zwingli and the Swiss parted from Luther and the Lutherans; on the same point, in the next generation of Reformers, John Calvin, attempting to mediate between the two contending parties, became the founder of still a third party, strong not only in the lucid and logical doctrinal statements in which it delighted, but also in the possession of a definite scheme of republican church government which became as distinctive of the Calvinistic or "Reformed" churches as their doctrine of the Supper. It was at a later epoch still that those insoluble questions which press most inexorably for consideration when theological thought and study are most serious and earnest—the questions that concern the divine sovereignty in its relation to human freedom and responsibility—arose in the Catholic Church to divide Jesuit from Dominican and Franciscan, and in the Reformed churches to divide the Arminians from the disciples of Gomar and Turretin. All these divisions among the European Christians of the seventeenth century were to have their important bearing on the planting of the Christian church in America.

In view of the destined predominance of English influence in the seaboard colonies of America, the history of the divisions of the Christian people of England is of preëminent importance to the beginnings of the American church. The curiously diverse elements that entered into the English Reformation, and the violent vicissitudes that marked the course of it, were all represented in the parties existing among English Christians at the period of the planting of the colonies.

The political and dynastic character of the movements that detached the English hierarchy from the Roman see had for one inevitable result to leaven the English church as a lump with the leaven of Herod. That considerable part of the clergy and people that moved to and fro, without so much as the resistance of any very formidable vis inertiæ, with the change of the monarch or of the monarch's caprice, might leave the student of the history of those times in doubt as to whether they belonged to the kingdom of heaven or to the kingdom of this world. But, however severe the judgment that any may pass upon the character and motives of Henry VIII. and of the councilors of Edward, there will hardly be any seriously to question that the movements directed by these men soon came to be infused with more serious and spiritual influences. The Lollardy of Wycliffe and his fellows in the fourteenth century had been severely repressed and driven into "occult conventicles," but had not been extinguished; the Bible in English, many times retouched after Wycliffe's days, and perfected by the refugees at Geneva from the Marian persecutions, had become a common household book; and those exiles themselves, returning from the various centers of fervid religious thought and feeling in Holland and Germany and Switzerland, had brought with them an augmented spiritual faith, as well as intensified and sharply defined convictions on the questions of theology and church order that were debated by the scholars of the Continent. It was impossible that the diverse and antagonist elements thus assembled should not work on one another with violent reactions. By the beginning of the seventeenth century not less than four categories would suffice to classify the people of England according to their religious differences. First, there were those who still continued to adhere to the Roman see. Secondly, those who, either from conviction or from expediency or from indifference, were content with the state church of England in the shape in which Elizabeth and her parliaments had left it; this class naturally included the general multitude of Englishmen, religious, irreligious, and non-religious. Thirdly, there were those who, not refusing their adhesion to the national church as by law established, nevertheless earnestly desired to see it more completely purified from doctrinal errors and practical corruptions, and who qualified their conformity to it accordingly. Fourthly, there were the few who distinctly repudiated the national church as a false church, coming out from her as from Babylon, determined upon "reformation without tarrying for any." Finally, following upon these, more radical, not to say more logical, than the rest, came a fifth party, the followers of George Fox. Not one of these five parties but has valid claims, both in its principles and in its membership, on the respect of history; not one but can point to its saints and martyrs; not one but was destined to play a quite separate and distinct and highly important part in the planting of the church of Christ in America. They are designated, for convenience' sake, as the Catholics, the Conformists, the Puritans or Reformists, the Separatists (of whom were the Pilgrims), and the Quakers.

Such a Christendom was it, so disorganized, divided, and subdivided into parties and sects, which was to furnish the materials for the peopling of the new continent with a Christian population. It would seem that the same "somewhat not ourselves," which had defeated in succession the plans of two mighty nations to subject the New World to a single hierarchy, had also provided that no one form or organization of Christianity should be exclusive or even dominant in the occupation of the American soil. From one point of view the American colonies will present a sorry aspect. Schism, mutual alienation, antagonism, competition, are uncongenial to the spirit of the gospel, which seeks "that they all may be one." And yet the history of the church has demonstrated by many a sad example that this offense "must needs come." No widely extended organization of church discipline in exclusive occupation of any country has ever long avoided the intolerable mischiefs attendant on spiritual despotism. It was a shock to the hopes and the generous sentiments of those who had looked to see one undivided body of a reformed church erected over against the medieval church, from the corruptions of which they had revolted, when they saw Protestantism go asunder into the several churches of the Lutheran and the Reformed confessions; there are many even now to deplore it as a disastrous set-back to the progress of the kingdom of Christ. But in the calmness of our long retrospect it is easy for us to recognize that whatever jurisdiction should have been established over an undivided Protestant church would inevitably have proved itself, in no long time, just such a yoke as neither the men of that time nor their fathers had been able to bear. Fifteen centuries of church history have not been wasted if thereby the Christian people have learned that the pursuit of Christian unity through administrative or corporate or diplomatic union is following the wrong road, and that the one Holy Catholic Church is not the corporation of saints, but their communion.

The new experiment of church life that was initiated in the colonization of America is still in progress. The new States were to be planted not only with diverse companies from the Old World, but with all the definitely organized sects by which the map of Christendom was at that time variegated, to which should be added others of native origin. Notwithstanding successive "booms" now of one and then of another, it was soon to become obvious to all that no one of these mutually jealous sects was to have any exclusive predominance, even over narrow precincts of territory. The old-world state churches, which under the rule, cujus regio ejus religio, had been supreme and exclusive each in its jurisdiction, were to find themselves side by side and mingled through the community on equal terms with those over whom in the old country they had domineered as dissenters, or whom perhaps they had even persecuted as heretics or as Antichrist. Thus placed, they were to be trained by the discipline of divine Providence and by the grace of the Holy Spirit from persecution to toleration, from toleration to mutual respect, and to coöperation in matters of common concern in the advancement of the kingdom of Christ. What further remains to be tried is the question whether, if not the sects, then the Christian hearts in each sect, can be brought to take the final step from mutual respect to mutual love, "that we henceforth, speaking truth in love, may grow up in all things into him, which is the head, even Christ; from whom all the body fitly framed and knit together through that which every joint supplieth, according to the working in due measure of each several part, shall make the increase of the body unto the building up of itself in love." Unless we must submit to those philosophers who forbid us to find in history the evidences of final cause and providential design, we may surely look upon this as a worthy possible solution of the mystery of Providence in the planting of the church in America in almost its ultimate stage of schism— that it is the purpose of its Head, out of the mutual attrition of the sects, their disintegration and comminution, to bring forth such a demonstration of the unity and liberty of the children of God as the past ages of church history have failed to show.

That mutual intolerance of differences in religious belief which, in the seventeenth century, was, throughout Christendom, coextensive with religious earnestness had its important part to play in the colonization of America. Of the persecutions and oppressions which gave direct impulse to the earliest colonization of America, the most notable are the following: (1) the persecution of the English Puritans in the reigns of James I. and Charles I., ending with the outbreak of the civil war in 1642; (2) the persecution of the English Roman Catholics during the same period; (3) the persecution of the English Quakers during the twenty-five years of Charles II. (1660-85); (4) the persecution of the French Huguenots after the revocation of the Edict of Nantes (1685); (5) the disabilities suffered by the Presbyterians of the north of Ireland after the English Revolution (1688); (6) the ferocious ravaging of the region of the Rhenish Palatinate by the armies of Louis XIV. in the early years of the seventeenth century; (7) the cruel expulsion of the Protestants of the archiepiscopal duchy of Salzburg (1731).

Beyond dispute, the best and most potent elements in the settlement of the seaboard colonies were the companies of earnestly religious people who from time to time, under severe compulsion for conscience' sake, came forth from the Old World as involuntary emigrants. Cruel wars and persecutions accomplished a result in the advancement of the kingdom of Christ which the authors of them never intended. But not these agencies alone promoted the great work. Peace, prosperity, wealth, and the hope of wealth had their part in it. The earliest successful enterprises of colonization were indeed marked with the badge of Christianity, and among their promoters were men whose language and deeds nobly evince the Christian spirit; but the enterprises were impelled and directed by commercial or patriotic considerations. The immense advantages that were to accrue from them to the world through the wider propagation of the gospel of Christ were not lost sight of in the projecting and organizing of the expeditions, nor were provisions for church and ministry omitted; but these were incidental, not primary.

This story of the divine preparations carried forward through unconscious human agencies in different lands and ages for the founding of the American church is a necessary preamble to our history. The scene of the story is now to be shifted to the other side of the sea.

CHAPTER V. THE PURITAN BEGINNINGS OF THE CHURCH IN VIRGINIA—ITS DECLINE ALMOST TO EXTINCTION.

There is sufficient evidence that the three little vessels which on the 13th of May, 1607, were moored to the trees on the bank of the James River brought to the soil of America the germ of a Christian church. We may feel constrained to accept only at a large discount the pious official professions of King James I., and critically to scrutinize many of the statements of that brilliant and fascinating adventurer, Captain John Smith, whether concerning his friends or concerning his enemies or concerning himself. But the beauty and dignity of the Christian character shine unmistakable in the life of the chaplain to the expedition, the Rev. Robert Hunt, and all the more radiantly for the dark and discouraging surroundings in which his ministry was to be exercised.

For the company which Captain Smith and that famous mariner, Captain Bartholomew Gosnold, had by many months of labor and "many a forgotten pound" of expense succeeded in recruiting for the enterprise was made up of most unhopeful material for the founding of a Christian colony. Those were the years of ignoble peace with which the reign of James began; and the glittering hopes of gold might well attract some of the brave men who had served by sea or land in the wars of Elizabeth. But the last thirty years had furnished no instance of success, and many of disastrous and sometimes tragical failure, in like attempts—the enterprises of Humphrey Gilbert, of Raleigh, of John White, of Gosnold himself, and of Popham and Gorges. Even brave men might hesitate to volunteer for the forlorn hope of another experiment at colonizing.

The little squadron had hardly set sail when the unfitness of the emigrants for their work began to discover itself. Lying weather-bound within sight of home, "some few, little better than atheists, of the greatest rank among them," were busying themselves with scandalous imputations upon the chaplain, then lying dangerously ill in his berth. All through the four months' passage by way of the Canaries and the West India Islands discontents and dissensions prevailed. Wingfield, who had been named president of the colony, had Smith in irons, and at the island of Nevis had the gallows set up for his execution on a charge of conspiracy, when milder counsels prevailed, and he was brought to Virginia, where he was tried and acquitted and his adversary mulcted in damages.

Arrived at the place of settlement, the colonists set about the work of building their houses, but found that their total number of one hundred and five was made up in the proportion of four carpenters to forty-eight "gentlemen." Not inadequately provisioned for their work, they came repeatedly almost to perishing through their sheer incapacity and unthrift, and their needless quarrels with one another and with the Indians. In five months one half of the company were dead. In January, 1608, eight months from the landing, when the second expedition arrived with reinforcements and supplies, only thirty-eight were surviving out of the one hundred and five, and of these the strongest were conspiring to seize the pinnace and desert the settlement. The newcomers were no better than the first. They were chiefly "gentlemen" again, and goldsmiths, whose duty was to discover and refine the quantities of gold that the stockholders in the enterprise were resolved should be found in Virginia, whether it was there or not. The ship took back on her return trip a full cargo of worthless dirt.

Reinforcements continued to arrive every few months, the quality of which it might be unfair to judge simply from the disgusted complaints of Captain Smith. He begs the Company to send but thirty honest laborers and artisans, "rather than a thousand such as we have," and reports the next ship-load as "fitter to breed a riot than to found a colony." The wretched settlement became an object of derision to the wits of London, and of sympathetic interest to serious minds. The Company, reorganized under a new charter, was strengthened by the accession of some of the foremost men in England, including four bishops, the Earl of Southampton, and Sir Francis Bacon. Appeals were made to the Christian public in behalf of an enterprise so full of promise of the furtherance of the gospel. A fleet of nine ships was fitted out, carrying more than five hundred emigrants, with ample supplies. Captain Smith, representing what there was of civil authority in the colony, had a brief struggle with their turbulence, and recognized them as of the same sort with the former companies, for the most part "poor gentlemen, tradesmen, serving-men, libertines, and such like, ten times more fit to spoil a commonwealth than either begin one or help to maintain one." When only part of this expedition had arrived, Captain Smith departed for England, disabled by an accidental wound, leaving a settlement of nearly five hundred men, abundantly provisioned. "It was not the will of God that the new state should be formed of these materials."[41:1] In six months the number of the colonists was reduced to sixty, and when relief arrived it was reckoned that in ten days' longer delay they would have perished to the last man. With one accord the wretched remnant of the colony, together with the latest comers, deserted, without a tear of regret, the scene of their misery. But their retreating vessels were met and turned back from the mouth of the river by the approaching ships of Lord de la Warr with emigrants and supplies. Such were the first three unhappy and unhonored years of the first Christian colony on the soil of the United States.

One almost shrinks from being assured that this worthless crew, through all these years of suicidal crime and folly, had been assiduous in religious duties. First under an awning made of an old sail, seated upon logs, with a rail nailed to two trees for a pulpit, afterward in a poor shanty of a church, "that could neither well defend wind nor rain," they "had daily common prayer morning and evening, every Sunday two sermons, and every three months the holy communion, till their minister died"; and after that "prayers daily, with an homily on Sundays, two or three years, till more preachers came." The sturdy and terrible resolution of Captain Smith, who in his marches through the wilderness was wont to begin the day with prayer and psalm, and was not unequal to the duty, when it was laid on him, of giving Christian exhortation as well as righteous punishment, and the gentle Christian influence of the Rev. Robert Hunt, were the salt that saved the colony from utterly perishing of its vices. It was not many months before the frail body of the chaplain sank under the hardships of pioneer life; he is commemorated by his comrade, the captain, as "an honest, religious, and courageous divine, during whose life our factions were oft qualified, our wants and greatest extremities so comforted that they seemed easy in comparison of what we endured after his memorable death." When, in 1609, in a nobler spirit than that of mere commercial enterprise, the reorganized Company, under the new charter, was preparing the great reinforcement of five hundred to go out under Lord de la Warr as governor of the colony, counsel was taken with Abbot, the Puritan Bishop of London, himself a member of the Virginia Company, and Richard Buck was selected as a worthy successor to Robert Hunt in the office of chaplain. Such he proved himself. Sailing in advance of the governor, in the ship with Sir Thomas Gates and Sir George Somers, and wrecked with them off the Bermudas, he did not forget his duty in the "plenty, peace, and ease" of that paradise. The ship's bell was rescued from the wreck to ring for morning and evening prayer, and for the two sermons every Sunday. There were births and funerals and a marriage in the shipwrecked company, and at length, when their makeshift vessel was ready, they embarked for their desired haven, there to find only the starving threescore survivors of the colony. They gathered together, a pitiable remnant, in the church, where Master Buck "made a zealous and sorrowful prayer"; and at once, without losing a day, they embarked for a last departure from Virginia, but were met at the mouth of the river by the tardy ships of Lord de la Warr. The next morning, Sunday, June 10, 1610, Lord de la Warr landed at the fort, where Gates had drawn up his forlorn platoon of starving men to receive him. The governor fell on his knees in prayer, then led the way to the church, and, after service and a sermon from the chaplain, made an address, assuming command of the colony.

Armed, under the new charter, with adequate authority, the new governor was not slow in putting on the state of a viceroy. Among his first cares was to provide for the external dignity of worship. The church, a building sixty feet by twenty-four, built long enough before to be now in need of repairs, was put into good condition, and a brave sight it was on Sundays to see the Governor, with the Privy Council and the Lieutenant-General and the Admiral and the Vice-Admiral and the Master of the Horse, together with the body-guard of fifty halberdiers in fair red cloaks, commanded by Captain Edward Brewster, assembled for worship, the governor seated in the choir in a green velvet chair, with a velvet cushion on a table before him. Few things could have been better adapted to convince the peculiar public of Jamestown that divine worship was indeed a serious matter. There was something more than the parade of government manifested by his lordship in the few months of his reign; but the inauguration of strong and effective control over the lazy, disorderly, and seditious crowd to be dealt with at Jamestown was reserved for his successor, Sir Thomas Dale, who arrived in May, 1611, in company with the Rev. Alexander Whitaker, the "apostle of Virginia."

It will not be possible for any to understand the relations of this colony to the state of parties in England without distinctly recognizing that the Puritans were not a party against the Church of England, but a party in the Church of England. The Puritan party was the party of reform, and was strong in a deep fervor of religious conviction widely diffused among people and clergy, and extending to the highest places of the nobility and the episcopate. The anti-Puritan party was the conservative or reactionary party, strong in the vis inertiæ, and in the king's pig-headed prejudices and his monstrous conceit of theological ability and supremacy in the church; strong also in a considerable adhesion and zealous coöperation from among his nominees, the bishops. The religious division was also a political one, the Puritans being known as the party of the people, their antagonists as the court party. The struggle of the Puritans (as distinguished from the inconsiderable number of the Separatists) was for the maintenance of their rights within the church; the effort of their adversaries, with the aid of the king's prerogative, was to drive or harry them out of the church. It is not to be understood that the two parties were as yet organized as such and distinctly bounded; but the two tendencies were plainly recognized, and the sympathies of leading men in church or state were no secret. The Virginia Company was a Puritan corporation.[44:1] As such, its meetings and debates were the object of popular interest and of the royal jealousy. Among its corporators were the brothers Sandys, sons of the Puritan Archbishop of York, one of whom held the manor of Scrooby. Others of the corporation were William Brewster, of Scrooby, and his son Edward. In the fleet of Sir Thomas Gates, May, 1609, were noted Puritans, one of whom, Stephen Hopkins, "who had much knowledge in the Scriptures and could reason well therein," was clerk to that "painful preacher," but not strict conformist, Master Richard Buck. The intimate and sometimes official relations of the Virginia Company not only with leading representatives of the Puritan party, but with the Pilgrims of Leyden, whom they would gladly have received into their own colony, are matter of history and of record. It admits of proof that there was a steady purpose in the Company, so far as it was not thwarted by the king and the bishops of the court party, to hold their unruly and ill-assorted colony under Puritan influences both of church and government.[45:1] The fact throws light on the remoter as well as the nearer history of Virginia. Especially it throws light on the memorable administration of Sir Thomas Dale, which followed hard upon the departure of Lord de la Warr and his body-guard in red cloaks.

The Company had picked their man with care—"a man of good conscience and knowledge in divinity," and a soldier and disciplinarian proved in the wars of the Low Countries—a very prototype of the great Cromwell. He understood what manner of task he had undertaken, and executed it without flinching. As a matter of course—it was the way in that colony—there was a conspiracy against his authority. There was no second conspiracy under him. Punishment was inflicted on the ringleaders so swift, so terrible, as to paralyze all future sedition. He put in force, in the name of the Company, a code of "Laws, Divine, Moral, and Martial," to which no parallel can be found in the severest legislation of New England. An invaluable service to the colony was the abolition of that demoralizing socialism that had been enforced on the colonists, by which all their labor was to be devoted to the common stock. He gave out land in severalty, and the laborer enjoyed the fruits of his own industry and thrift, or suffered the consequences of his laziness. The culture of tobacco gave the colony a currency and a staple of export.

With Dale was associated as chaplain Alexander Whitaker, son of the author of the Calvinistic Lambeth Articles, and brother of a Separatist preacher of London. What was his position in relation to church parties is shown by his letter to his cousin, the "arch-Puritan," William

Gouge, written after three years' residence in Virginia, urging that nonconformist clergymen should come over to Virginia, where no question would be raised on the subject of subscription or the surplice. What manner of man and minister he was is proved by a noble record of faithful work. He found a true workfellow in Dale. When this statesmanlike and soldierly governor founded his new city of Henrico up the river, and laid out across the stream the suburb of Hope-in-Faith, defended by Fort Charity and Fort Patience, he built there in sight from his official residence the parsonage of the "apostle of Virginia." The course of Whitaker's ministry is described by himself in a letter to a friend: "Every Sabbath day we preach in the forenoon and catechise in the afternoon. Every Saturday, at night, I exercise in Sir Thomas Dale's house." But he and his fellow-clergymen did not labor without aid, even in word and doctrine. When Mr. John Rolfe was perplexed with questions of duty touching his love for Pocahontas, it was to the old soldier, Dale, that he brought his burden, seeking spiritual counsel. And it was this "religious and valiant governor," as Whitaker calls him, this "man of great knowledge in divinity, and of a good conscience in all things," that "labored long to ground the faith of Jesus Christ" in the Indian maiden, and wrote concerning her, "Were it but for the gaining of this one soul, I will think my time, toils, and present stay well spent."

The progress of the gospel in reclaiming the unhappy colony to Christian civilization varies with the varying fortunes of contending parties in England. Energetic efforts were made by the Company under Sandys, the friend of Brewster, to send out worthy colonists; and the delicate task of finding young women of good character to be shipped as wives to the settlers was undertaken conscientiously and successfully. Generous gifts of money and land were contributed (although little came from them) for the endowment of schools and a college for the promotion of Christ's work among the white people and the red. But the course of events on both sides of the sea may be best illustrated by a narrative of personal incidents.

In the year 1621, an East India Company's chaplain, the Rev. Patrick Copland, who perhaps deserves the title of the first English missionary in India, on his way back from India met, probably at the Canaries, with ships bound for Virginia with emigrants. Learning from these something of the needs of the plantation, he stirred up his fellow-passengers on the "Royal James," and raised the sum of seventy pounds, which was paid to the treasurer of the Virginia Company; and, being increased by other gifts to one hundred and twenty-five pounds, was, in consultation with Mr. Copland, appropriated for a free school to be called the "East India School."

The affairs of the colony were most promising. It was growing in population and in wealth and in the institutions of a Christian commonwealth. The territory was divided into parishes for the work of church and clergy. The stupid obstinacy of the king, against the remonstrances of the Company, perpetrated the crime of sending out a hundred convicts into the young community, extorting from Captain Smith the protest that this act "hath laid one of the finest countries of America under the just scandal of being a mere hell upon earth." The sweepings of the London and Bristol streets were exported for servants. Of darker portent, though men perceived it not, was the landing of the first cargo of negro slaves. But so grateful was the Company for the general prosperity of the colony that it appointed a thanksgiving sermon to be preached at Bow Church, April 17, 1622, by Mr. Copland, which was printed under the title, "Virginia's God Be Thanked." In July, 1622, the Company, proceeding to the execution of a long-cherished plan, chose Mr. Copland rector of the college to be built at Henrico from the endowments already provided, when news arrived of the massacre which, in March of that year, swept away one half of the four thousand colonists. All such enterprises were at once arrested.

In 1624 the long contest of the king and the court party against the Virginia Company was ended by a violent exercise of the prerogative dissolving the Company, but not until it had established free representative government in the colony. The revocation of the charter was one of the last acts of James's ignoble reign. In 1625 he died, and Charles I. became king. In 1628 "the most hot-headed and hard-hearted of prelates," William Laud, became Bishop of London, and in 1633 Archbishop of Canterbury. But the Puritan principles of duty and liberty already planted in Virginia were not destined to be eradicated.

From the year 1619, a settlement at Nansemond, near Norfolk, had prospered, and had been in relations of trade with New England. In 1642 Philip Bennett, of Nansemond, visiting Boston in his coasting vessel, bore with him a letter to the Boston church, signed by seventy-four names, stating the needs of their great county, now without a pastor, and offering a maintenance to three good ministers if they could be found. A little later William Durand, of the same county, wrote for himself and his neighbors to John Davenport, of New Haven, to whom some of them had listened gladly in London (perhaps it was when he preached the first annual sermon before the Virginia Company in 1621), speaking of "a revival of piety" among them, and urging the request that had been sent to the church in Boston. As result of this correspondence, three eminently learned and faithful ministers of New England came to Virginia, bringing letters of commendation from Governor Winthrop. But they found that Virginia, now become a royal colony, had no welcome for them. The newly arrived royal governor, Sir William Berkeley, a man after Laud's own heart, forbade their preaching; but the Catholic governor of Maryland sent them a free invitation, and one of them, removing to Annapolis with some of the Virginia Puritans, so labored in the gospel as to draw forth the public thanks of the legislative assembly.

The sequel of this story is a strange one. There must have been somewhat in the character and bearing of these silenced and banished ministers that touched the heart of Thomas Harrison, the governor's chaplain. He made a confession of his insincere dealings toward them: that while he had been showing them "a fair face" he had privately used his influence to have them silenced. He himself began to preach in that earnest way of righteousness, temperance, and judgment, which is fitted to make governors tremble, until Berkeley cast him out as a Puritan, saying that he did not wish so grave a chaplain; whereupon Harrison crossed the river to Nansemond, became pastor of the church, and mightily built up the cause which he had sought to destroy.

A few months later the Nansemond people had the opportunity of giving succor and hospitality to a shipwrecked company of nine people, who had been cast away, with loss of all their goods, in sailing from the Bermudas to found a new settlement on one of the Bahamas. Among the party was an aged and venerable man, that same Patrick Copland who twenty-five years before had interested himself in the passing party of emigrants. This was indeed entertaining an angel. Mr. Copland had long been a nonconformist minister at the Bermudas, and he listened to the complaints that were made to him of the persecution to which the people were subjected by the malignant Berkeley. A free invitation was given to the Nansemond church to go with their guests to the new settlement of Eleuthera, in which freedom of conscience and non-interference of the magistrate with the church were secured by charter.[50:1] Mr. Harrison proceeded to Boston to take counsel of the churches over this proposition. The people were advised by their Boston brethren to remain in their lot until their case should become intolerable. Mr. Harrison went on to London, where a number of things had happened since Berkeley's appointment. The king had ceased to be; but an order from the Council of State was sent to Berkeley, sharply reprimanding him for his course, and directing him to restore Mr. Harrison to his parish. But Mr. Harrison did not return. He fulfilled an honorable career as incumbent of a London parish, as chaplain to Henry Cromwell, viceroy of Ireland, and as a hunted and persecuted preacher in the evil days after the Restoration. But the "poetic justice" with which this curious dramatic episode should conclude is not reached until Berkeley is compelled to surrender his jurisdiction to the Commonwealth, and Richard Bennett, one of the banished Puritans of Nansemond, is chosen by the Assembly of Burgesses to be governor in his stead.[51:1]

Of course this is a brief triumph. With the restoration of the Stuarts, Berkeley comes back into power as royal governor, and for many years afflicts the colony with his malignant Toryism. The last state is worse than the first; for during the days of the Commonwealth old soldiers of the king's army had come to Virginia in such numbers as to form an appreciable and not wholly admirable element in the population. Surrounded by such society, the governor was encouraged to indulge his natural disposition to bigotry and tyranny. Under such a nursing father the interests of the kingdom of Christ fared as might have been expected. Rigorous measures were instituted for the suppression of nonconformity, Quaker preachers were severely dealt with, and clergymen, such as they were, were imposed upon the more or less reluctant parishes. But though the governor held the right of presentation, the vestry of each parish asserted and maintained the right of induction or of refusing to induct. Without the consent of these representatives of the people the candidate could secure for himself no more than the people should from year to year consent to allow him. It was the only protection of the people from absolute spiritual despotism. The power might be used to repel a too faithful pastor, but if there was sometimes a temptation to this, the occasion was far more frequent for putting the people's reprobation upon the unfaithful and unfit. The colony, growing in wealth and population, soon became infested with a rabble of worthless and scandalous priests. In a report which has been often quoted, Governor Berkeley, after giving account of the material prosperity of the colony, sums up, under date of 1671, the results of his fostering care over its spiritual interests in these words: "There are forty-eight parishes, and the ministers well paid. The clergy by my consent would be better if they would pray oftener and preach less. But of all other commodities, so of this, the worst are sent us. But I thank God there are no free schools nor printing, and I hope we shall not have, these hundred years."

The scandal of the Virginia clergy went on from bad to worse. Whatever could be done by the courage and earnestness of one man was done by Dr. Blair, who arrived in 1689 with limited powers as commissary of the Bishop of London, and for more than fifty years struggled against adverse influences to recover the church from its degradation. He succeeded in getting a charter for William and Mary College, but the generous endowments of the institution were wasted, and the college languished in doing the work of a grammar school. Something was accomplished in the way of discipline, though the cane of Governor Nicholson over the back of an insolent priest was doubtless more effective than the commissary's admonitions. But discipline, while it may do something toward abating scandals, cannot create life from the dead; and the church established in Virginia had hardly more than a name to live. Its best estate is described by Spotswood, the best of the royal governors, when, looking on the outward appearance, he reported: "This government is in perfect peace and tranquillity, under a due obedience to the royal authority and a gentlemanly conformity to the Church of England." The poor man was soon to find how uncertain is the peace and tranquillity that is founded on "a gentlemanly conformity." The most honorable page in his record is the story of his effort for the education of Indian children. His honest attempt at reformation in the church brought him into collision not only with the worthless among the clergy, but also on the one hand with the parish vestries, and on the other hand with Commissary Blair. But all along the "gentlemanly conformity" was undisturbed. A parish of French Huguenots was early established in Henrico County, and in 1713 a parish of German exiles on the Rappahannock, and these were expressly excepted from the Act of Uniformity. Aside from these, the chief departures from the enforced uniformity of worship throughout the colony in the early years of the eighteenth century were found in a few meetings of persecuted and vilified Quakers and Baptists. The government and clergy had little notion of the significance of a slender stream of Scotch-Irish emigration which, as early as 1720, began to flow into the valley of the Shenandoah. So cheap a defense against the perils that threatened from the western frontier it would have been folly to discourage by odious religious proscription. The reasonable anxiety of the clergy as to what might come of this invasion of a sturdy and uncompromising Puritanism struggled without permanent success against the obvious interest of the commonwealth. The addition of this new and potent element to the Christian population of the seaboard colonies was part of the unrecognized preparation for the Great Awakening.

CHAPTER VI. THE NEIGHBOR COLONIES TO VIRGINIA—

MARYLAND AND THE CAROLINAS.

The chronological order would require us at this point to turn to the Dutch settlements on the Hudson River; but the close relations of Virginia with its neighbor colonies of Maryland and the Carolinas are a reason for taking up the brief history of these settlements in advance of their turn.

The occupation of Maryland dates from the year 1634. The period of bold and half-desperate adventure in making plantations along the coast was past. To men of sanguine temper and sufficient fortune and influence at court, it was now a matter of very promising and not too risky speculation. To George Calvert, Lord Baltimore, one of the most interesting characters at the court of James I., the business had peculiar fascination. He was in both the New England Company and the Virginia Company, and after the charter of the latter was revoked he was one of the Provisional Council for the government of Virginia. Nothing daunted by the ill luck of these companies, he tried colonizing on his account in 1620, in what was represented to him as the genial soil and climate of Newfoundland. Sending good money after bad, he was glad to get out of this venture at the end of nine years with a loss of thirty thousand pounds. In 1629 he sent home his children, and with a lady and servants and forty of his surviving colonists sailed for Jamestown, where his reception at the hands of the council and of his old Oxford fellow-student, Governor Pott, was not cordial. He could hardly have expected that it would be. He was a recent convert to the Roman Catholic Church, with a convert's zeal for proselyting, and he was of the court party. Thus he was in antagonism to the Puritan colony both in politics and in religion. A formidable disturbing element he and his company would have been in the already unquiet community. The authorities of the colony were equal to the emergency. In answer to his lordship's announcement of his purpose "to plant and dwell," they gave him welcome to do so on the same terms with themselves, and proceeded to tender him the oath of supremacy, the taking of which was flatly against his Roman principles. Baltimore suggested a mitigated form of the oath, which he was willing to take; but the authorities "could not imagine that so much latitude was left for them to decline from the prescribed form"; and his lordship sailed back to England, leaving in Virginia, in token of his intention to return, his servants and "his lady," who, by the way, was not the lawful wife of this conscientious and religious gentleman.

Returned to London, he at once set in motion the powerful influences at his command to secure a charter for a tract of land south of the James River, and when this was defeated by the energetic opposition of the friends of Virginia, he succeeded in securing a grant of land north and east of the Potomac, with a charter bestowing on him and his heirs "the most ample rights and privileges ever conferred by a sovereign of England."[55:1] The protest of Virginia that it was an invasion of the former grant to that colony was unavailing. The free-handed generosity with which the Stuarts were in the habit of giving away what did not belong to them rarely allowed itself to be embarrassed by the fear of giving the same thing twice over to different parties.

The first Lord Baltimore died three months before the charter of Maryland received the great seal, but his son Cecilius took up the business with energy and great liberality of investment. The cost of fitting out the first emigration was estimated at not less than forty thousand pounds. The company consisted of "three hundred laboring men, well provided in all things," headed by Leonard and George Calvert, brothers of the lord proprietor, "with very near twenty other gentlemen of very good fashion." Two earnest Jesuit priests were quietly added to the expedition as it passed the Isle of Wight, but in general it was a Protestant emigration under Catholic patronage. It was stipulated in the charter that all liege subjects of the English king might freely transport themselves and their families to Maryland. To discriminate against any religious body in England would have been for the proprietor to limit his hope of rapid colonization and revenue and to embroil himself with political enemies at home. His own and his father's intimate acquaintance with failure in the planting of Virginia and of Newfoundland had taught him what not to do in such enterprises. If the proprietor meant to succeed (and he did mean to) he was shut up without alternative to the policy of impartial non-interference with religious differences among his colonists, and the promotion of mutual forbearance among sects. Lord Baltimore may not have been a profound political philosopher nor a prophet of the coming era of religious liberty, but he was an adroit courtier, like his father before him, and he was a man of practical good sense engaged in an enormous land speculation in which his whole fortune was embarked, and he was not in the least disposed to allow his religious predilections to interfere with business. Nothing would have brought speedier ruin to his enterprise than to have it suspected, as his enemies were always ready to allege, that it was governed in the interest of the Roman Catholic Church. Such a suspicion he took the most effective means of averting. He kept his promises to his colonists in this matter in good faith, and had his reward in the notable prosperity of his colony.[57:1]

The two priests of the first Maryland company began their work with characteristic earnestness and diligence. Finding no immediate access to the Indians, they gave the more constant attention to their own countrymen, both Catholic and Protestant, and were soon able to give thanks that by God's blessing on their labors almost all the Protestants of that year's arrival had been converted, besides many others. In 1640 the first-fruits of their mission work among the savages were gathered in; the chief of an Indian village on the Potomac nearly opposite Mount Vernon, and his wife and child, were baptized with solemn pomp, in which the governor and secretary of the colony took part.

The first start of the Maryland colony was of a sort to give promise of feuds and border strifes with the neighbor colony of Virginia, and the promise was abundantly fulfilled. The conflict over boundary questions came to bloody collisions by land and sea. It is needless to say that religious differences were at once drawn into the dispute. The vigorous proselytism of the Jesuit fathers, the only Christian ministers in the colony, under the patronage of the lord proprietor was of course reported to London by the Virginians; and in December, 1641, the House of Commons, then on the brink of open rupture with the king, presented a remonstrance to Charles at Hampton Court, complaining that he had permitted "another state, molded within this state, independent in government, contrary in interest and affection, secretly corrupting the ignorant or negligent professors of religion, and clearly uniting themselves against such." Lord Baltimore, perceiving that his property rights were coming into jeopardy, wrote to the too zealous priests, warning them that they were under English law and were not to expect from him "any more or other privileges, exemptions, or immunities for their lands, persons, or goods than is allowed by his Majesty or officers to like persons in England." He annulled the grants of land made to the missionaries by certain Indian chiefs, which they affected to hold as the property of their order, and confirmed for his colony the law of mortmain. In his not unreasonable anxiety for the tenure of his estate, he went further still; he had the Jesuits removed from the charge of the missions, to be replaced by seculars, and only receded from this severe measure when the Jesuit order acceded to his terms. The pious and venerable Father White records in his journal that "occasion of suffering has not been wanting from those from whom rather it was proper to expect aid and protection, who, too intent upon their own affairs, have not feared to violate the immunities of the church."[59:1] But the zeal of the Calverts for religious liberty and equality was manifested not only by curbing the Jesuits, but by encouraging their most strenuous opponents. It was in the year 1643, when the strength of Puritanism both in England and in New England was proved, that the Calverts made overtures, although in vain, to secure an immigration from Massachusetts. A few years later the opportunity occurred of strengthening their own colony with an accession of Puritans, and at the same time of weakening Virginia. The sturdy and prosperous Puritan colony on the Nansemond River were driven by the churlish behavior of Governor Berkeley to seek a more congenial residence, and were induced to settle on the Severn at a place which they called Providence, but which was destined, under the name of Annapolis, to become the capital of the future State. It was manifestly not merely a coincidence that Lord Baltimore appointed a Protestant governor, William Stone, and commended to the Maryland Assembly, in 1649, the enacting of "an Act concerning Religion," drawn upon the lines of the Ordinance of Toleration adopted by the Puritan House of Commons at the height of its authority, in 1647.[59:2] How potent was the influence of this transplanted Nansemond church is largely shown in the eventful civil history of the colony. When, in 1655, the lord proprietor's governor was so imprudent as to set an armed force in the field, under the colors of Lord Baltimore, in opposition to the parliamentary commissioners, it was the planters of the Severn who marched under the flag of the commonwealth of England, and put them to rout, and executed some of their leaders for treason. When at last articles of agreement were signed between the commissioners and Lord Baltimore, one of the conditions exacted from his lordship was a pledge that he would never consent to the repeal of the Act of Toleration adopted in 1649 under the influence of the Puritan colony and its pastor, Thomas Harrison.

In the turbulence of the colony during and after the civil wars of England, there becomes more and more manifest a growing spirit of fanaticism, especially in the form of antipopery crusading. While Jacobite intrigues or wars with France were in progress it was easy for demagogues to cast upon the Catholics the suspicion of disloyalty and of complicity with the public enemy. The numerical unimportance of the Catholics of Maryland was insufficient to guard them from such suspicions; for it had soon become obvious that the colony of the Catholic lord was to be anything but a Catholic colony. The Jesuit mission had languished; the progress of settlement, and what there had been of religious life and teaching, had brought no strength to the Catholic cause. In 1676 a Church of England minister, John Yeo, writes to the Archbishop of Canterbury of the craving lack of ministers, excepting among the Catholics and the Quakers, "not doubting but his Grace may so prevail with Lord Baltimore that a maintenance for a Protestant ministry may be established." The Bishop of London, echoing this complaint, speaks of the "total want of ministers and divine worship, except among those of the Romish belief, who, 'tis conjectured, does not amount to one of a hundred of the people." To which his lordship replies that all sects are tolerated and protected, but that it would be impossible to induce the Assembly to consent to a law that shall oblige any sect to maintain other ministers than its own. The bishop's figures were doubtless at fault; but Lord Baltimore himself writes that the nonconformists outnumber the Catholics and those of the Church of England together about three to one, and that the churchmen are much more numerous than the Catholics.

After the Revolution of 1688 it is not strange that a like movement was set on foot in Maryland. The "beneficent despotism" of the Calverts, notwithstanding every concession on their part, was ended for the time by the efforts of an "Association for the Defense of the Protestant Religion," and Maryland became a royal colony. Under the new régime it was easier to inflict annoyances and disabilities on the petty minority of the Roman Catholics than to confer the privileges of an established church on the hardly more considerable minority of Episcopalians. The Church of England became in name the official church of the colony, but two parties so remotely unlike as the Catholics and the Quakers combined successfully to defeat more serious encroachments on religious liberty. The attempt to maintain the church of a small minority by taxes extorted by a foreign government from the whole people had the same effect in Maryland as in Ireland: it tended to make both church and government odious. The efforts of Dr. Thomas Bray, commissary of the Bishop of London, a man of true apostolic fervor, accomplished little in withstanding the downward tendency of the provincial establishment. The demoralized and undisciplined clergy resisted the attempt of the provincial government to abate the scandal of their lives, and the people resisted the attempt to introduce a bishop. The body thus set before the people as the official representative of the religion of Christ "was perhaps as contemptible an ecclesiastical organization as history can show," having "all the vices of the Virginian church, without one of its safeguards or redeeming qualities."[62:1] The most hopeful sign in the morning sky of the eighteenth century was to be found in the growth of the Society of Friends and the swelling of the current of the Scotch-Irish immigration. And yet we shall have proof that the life-work of Commissary Bray, although he went back discouraged from his labors in Maryland and although this colony took little direct benefit from his efforts in England, was destined to have great results in the advancement of the kingdom of Christ in America; for he was the founder of the Society for the Propagation of the Gospel in Foreign Parts.

The Carolinas, North and South, had been the scene of the earliest attempts at Protestant colonization in America. The Huguenot enterprise at Beaufort, on Port Royal harbor, was planted in 1562 under the auspices of Coligny, and came to a speedy and unhappy end. The costly and disastrous experiment of Sir Walter Raleigh was begun in 1584 on Roanoke Island, and lasted not many months. But the actual occupation of the region was late and slow. When, after the Restoration, Charles II. took up the idea of paying his political debts with free and easy cessions of American lands, Clarendon, Albemarle, and Shaftesbury were among the first and luckiest in the scramble. When the representatives of themselves and their partners arrived in Carolina in 1670, bringing with them that pompous and preposterous anachronism, the "Fundamental Constitutions," contrived by the combined wisdom of Shaftesbury and John Locke to impose a feudal government upon an immense domain of wilderness, they found the ground already occupied with a scanty and curiously mixed population, which had taken on a simple form of polity and was growing into a state. The region adjoining Virginia was peopled by Puritans from the Nansemond country, vexed with the paltry persecutions of Governor Berkeley, and later by fugitives from the bloody revenge which he delighted to inflict on those who had been involved in the righteous rebellion led by Nathaniel Bacon. These had been joined by insolvent debtors not a few. Adventurers from New England settled on the Cape Fear River for a lumber trade, and kept the various plantations in communication with the rest of the world by their coasting craft plying to Boston. Dissatisfied companies from Barbadoes seeking a less torrid climate next arrived. Thus the region was settled in the first instance at second hand from older colonies. To these came settlers direct from England, such emigrants as the proprietors could persuade to the undertaking, and such as were impelled by the evil state of England in the last days of the Stuarts, or drawn by the promise of religious liberty.

South Carolina, on the other hand, was settled direct from Europe, first by cargoes of emigrants shipped on speculation by the great real-estate "operators" who had at heart not only the creation of a gorgeous aristocracy in the West, but also the realization of fat dividends on their heavy ventures. Members of the dominant politico-religious party in England were attracted to a country in which they were still to be regarded before the law as of the "only true and orthodox" church; and religious dissenters gladly accepted the offer of toleration and freedom, even without the assurance of equality. One of the most notable contributions to the new colony was a company of dissenters from Somersetshire, led by Joseph Blake, brother to Cromwell's illustrious admiral. Among these were some of the earliest American Baptists; and there is clear evidence of connection between their arrival and the coming, in 1684, of a Baptist church from the Massachusetts Colony, under the pastorate of William Screven. This planting was destined to have an important influence both on the religious and on the civil history of the colony. Very early there came two ship-loads of Dutch Calvinists from New York, dissatisfied with the domineering of their English victors. But more important than the rest was that sudden outflow of French Huguenots, representing not only religious fidelity and devotion, but all those personal and social virtues that most strengthen the foundations of a state, which set westward upon the revocation of the Edict of Nantes in 1685. This, with the later influx of the Scotch-Irish, profoundly marked the character of South Carolina. The great names in her history are generally either French or Scotch.

It ought to have been plain to the proprietors, in their monstrous conceit of political wisdom, that communities so constituted should have been the last on which to impose the uniformity of an established church. John Locke did see this, but was overruled. The Church of England was established in name, but for long years had only this shadow of existence. We need not, however, infer from the absence of organized church and official clergy among the rude and turbulent pioneers of North Carolina that the kingdom of God was not among them, even from the beginning. But not until the year 1672 do we find manifestation of it such as history can recognize. In that year came William Edmundson, "the voice of one crying in the wilderness," bringing his testimony of the light that lighteth every man that cometh into the world. The honest man, who had not thought it reasonable in the Christians of Massachusetts to be offended at one's sitting in the steeple-house with his hat on, found it an evidence that "they had little or no religion" when the rough woodsmen of Carolina beguiled the silent moments of the Friends' devotions by smoking their pipes; and yet he declares that he found them "a tender people." Converts were won to the society, and a quarterly meeting was established. Within a few months followed George Fox, uttering his deep convictions in a voice of singular persuasiveness and power, that reached the hearts of both high and low. And he too declared that he had found the people "generally tender and open," and rejoiced to have made among them "a little entrance for truth." The church of Christ had been begun. As yet there had been neither baptism nor sacramental supper; these outward and visible signs were absent; but inward and spiritual grace was there, and the thing signified is greater than the sign. The influence diffused itself like leaven. Within a decade the society was extended through both the Carolinas and became the principal form of organized Christianity. It was reckoned in 1710 to include one seventh of the population of North Carolina.[65:1]

The attempt of a foreign proprietary government to establish by law the church of an inconsiderable and not preëminently respectable minority had little effect except to exasperate and alienate the settlers. Down to the end of the seventeenth century the official church in North Carolina gave no sign of life. In South Carolina almost twenty years passed before it was represented by a single clergyman. The first manifestation of church life seems to have been in the meetings on the banks of the Cooper and the Santee, in which the French refugees worshiped their fathers' God with the psalms of Marot and Beza.

But with the eighteenth century begins a better era for the English church in the Carolinas. The story of the founding and the work of the Society for the Propagation of the Gospel in Foreign Parts, taken in connection with its antecedents and its results, belongs to this history, not only as showing the influence of European Christianity upon America, but also as indicating the reaction of America upon Europe.

In an important sense the organization of religious societies which is characteristic of modern Christendom is of American origin. The labors of John Eliot among the Indians of New England stirred so deep an interest in the hearts of English Christians that in 1649 an ordinance was passed by the Long Parliament creating a corporation to be called "The President and Society for the Propagation of the Gospel in New England"; and a general collection made under Cromwell's direction produced nearly twelve thousand pounds, from the income of which missionaries were maintained among some of the Northern tribes of Indians. With the downfall of the Commonwealth the corporation became defunct; but through the influence of the saintly Richard Baxter, whose tender interest in the work of Eliot is witnessed by a touching passage in his writings, the charter was revived in 1662, with Robert Boyle for president and patron. It was largely through his generosity that Eliot was enabled to publish his Indian Bible. This society, "The New England Company," as it is called, is still extant—the oldest of Protestant missionary societies.[66:1]

It is to that Dr. Thomas Bray who returned in 1700 to England from his thankless and discouraging work as commissary in Maryland of the Bishop of London, that the Church of England owes a large debt of gratitude for having taken away the reproach of her barrenness. Already his zeal had laid the foundations on which was reared the Society for the Promotion of Christian Knowledge. In 1701 he had the satisfaction of attending the first meeting of the Society for the Propagation of the Gospel in Foreign Parts, which for nearly three quarters of a century, sometimes in the spirit of a narrow sectarianism, but not seldom in a more excellent way, devoted its main strength to missions in the American colonies. Its missionaries, men of a far different character from the miserable incumbents of parishes in Maryland and Virginia, were among the first preachers of the gospel in the Carolinas. Within the years 1702-40 there served under the commission of this society in North Carolina nine missionaries, in South Carolina thirty-five.[67:1]

But the zeal of these good men was sorely encumbered with the armor of Saul. Too much favorable legislation and patronizing from a foreign proprietary government, too arrogant a tone of superiority on the part of official friends, attempts to enforce conformity by imposing disabilities on other sects—these were among the chief occasions of the continual collision between the people and the colonial governments, which culminated in the struggle for independence. By the time that struggle began the established church in the Carolinas was ready to vanish away.

CHAPTER VII. THE DUTCH CALVINIST COLONY ON THE HUDSON AND THE SWEDISH LUTHERAN COLONY ON THE DELAWARE—THEY BOTH FALL UNDER THE SHADOW OF GREAT BRITAIN.

When the Englishman Henry Hudson, in the Dutch East India Company's ship, the "Half-moon," in September, 1609, sailed up "the River of Mountains" as far as the site of Albany, looking for the northwest passage to China, the English settlement at Jamestown was in the third year of its half-perishing existence. More than thirteen years were yet to pass before the Pilgrims from England by way of Holland should make their landing on Plymouth Rock. But we are not at liberty to assign so early a date to the Dutch settlement of New York, and still less to the church. There was a prompt reaching out, on the part of the immensely enterprising Dutch merchants, after the lucrative trade in peltries; there was a plying to and fro of trading-vessels, and there were trading-posts established on Manhattan Island and at the head of navigation on the Hudson, or North River, and on the South River, or Delaware. Not until the great Dutch West India Company had secured its monopoly of trade and perfected its organization, in 1623, was there a beginning of colonization. In that year a company of Walloons, or French-speaking Hollanders, was planted near Albany, and later arrivals were settled on the Delaware, on Long Island, and on Manhattan. At length, in 1626, came Peter Minuit with an ample commission from the all-powerful Company, who organized something like a system of civil government comprehending all the settlements. Evidences of prosperity and growing wealth began to multiply. But one is impressed with the merely secular and commercial character of the enterprise and with the tardy and feeble signs of religious life in the colony. In 1626, when the settlement of Manhattan had grown to a village of thirty houses and two hundred souls, there arrived two official "sick-visitors," who undertook some of the public duties of a pastor. On Sundays, in the loft over the horse-mill, they would read from the Scriptures and the creeds. And two years later, in 1628, the village, numbering now about two hundred and seventy souls, gave a grateful welcome to Jonas Michaelius, minister of the gospel. He rejoiced to gather no less than fifty communicants at the first celebration of the Lord's Supper, and to organize them into a church according to the Reformed discipline. The two elders were the governor and the Company's storekeeper, men of honest report who had served in like functions in churches of the fatherland. The records of this period are scanty; the very fact of this beginning of a church and the presence of a minister in the colony had faded out of history until restored by the recent discovery of a letter of the forgotten Michaelius.[69:1]

The sagacious men in control of the Dutch West India Company were quick to recognize that weakness in their enterprise which in the splendid colonial attempt of the French proved ultimately to be fatal. Their settlements were almost exclusively devoted to the lucrative trade with the Indians and were not taking root in the soil. With all its advantages, the Dutch colony could not compete with New England.[70:1] To meet this difficulty an expedient was adopted which was not long in beginning to plague the inventors. A vast tract of territory, with feudal rights and privileges, was offered to any man settling a colony of fifty persons. The disputes which soon arose between these powerful vassals and the sovereign Company had for one effect the recall of Peter Minuit from his position of governor. Never again was the unlucky colony to have so competent and worthy a head as this discarded elder of the church. Nevertheless the scheme was not altogether a failure.

In 1633 arrived a new pastor, Everard Bogardus, in the same ship with a schoolmaster—the first in the colony—and the new governor, Van Twiller. The governor was incompetent and corrupt, and the minister was faithful and plain-spoken; what could result but conflict? During Van Twiller's five years of mismanagement, nevertheless, the church emerged from the mill-loft and was installed in a barn-like meeting-house of wood. During the equally wretched administration of Kieft, the governor, listening to the reproaches of a guest, who quoted the example of New England, where the people were wont to build a fine church as soon as they had houses for themselves, was incited to build a stone church within the fort. There seems to have been little else that he did for the kingdom of heaven. Pastor Bogardus is entitled to the respect of later ages for the chronic quarrel that he kept up with the worthless representatives of the Company. At length his righteous rebuke of an atrociously wicked massacre of neighboring Indians perpetrated by Kieft brought matters to a head. The two antagonists sailed in the same ship, in 1647, to lay their dispute before the authorities in Holland, the Company and the classis. The case went to a higher court. The ship was cast away and both the parties were drowned.

Meanwhile the patroon Van Rensselaer, on his great manor near Albany, showed some sense of his duty to the souls of the people whom he had brought out into the wilderness. He built a church and put into the pastoral charge over his subjects one who, under his travestied name of Megapolensis, has obtained a good report as a faithful minister of Jesus Christ. It was he who saved Father Jogues, the Jesuit missionary, from imminent torture and death among the Mohawks, and befriended him, and saw him safely off for Europe. This is one honorable instance, out of not a few, of personal respect and kindness shown to members of the Roman clergy and the Jesuit society by men who held these organizations in the severest reprobation. To his Jesuit brother he was drawn by a peculiarly strong bond of fellowship, for the two were fellow-laborers in the gospel to the red men. For Domine Megapolensis is claimed[71:1] the high honor of being the first Protestant missionary to the Indians.

In 1647, to the joy of all the colonists, arrived a new governor, Peter Stuyvesant, not too late to save from utter ruin the colony that had suffered everything short of ruin from the incompetency and wickedness of Kieft. About the time that immigration into New England ceased with the triumph of the Puritan party in England, there began to be a distinct current of population setting toward the Hudson River colony. The West India Company had been among the first of the speculators in American lands to discover that a system of narrow monopoly is not the best nurse for a colony; too late to save itself from ultimate bankruptcy, it removed some of the barriers of trade, and at once population began to flow in from other colonies, Virginia and New England. Besides those who were attracted by the great business advantages of the Dutch colony, there came some from Massachusetts, driven thence by the policy of exclusiveness in religious opinion deliberately adopted there. Ordinances were set forth assuring to several such companies "liberty of conscience, according to the custom and manner of Holland." Growing prosperously in numbers, the colony grew in that cosmopolitan diversity of sects and races which went on increasing with its years. As early as 1644 Father Jogues was told by the governor that there were persons of eighteen different languages at Manhattan, including Calvinists, Catholics, English Puritans, Lutherans, Anabaptists (here called Mennonists), etc. No jealousy seems to have arisen over this multiplication of sects until, in 1652, the Dutch Lutherans, who had been attendants at the Dutch Reformed Church, presented a respectful petition that they might be permitted to have their own pastor and church. Denied by Governor Stuyvesant, the request was presented to the Company and to the States-General. The two Reformed pastors used the most strenuous endeavors through the classis of Amsterdam to defeat the petition, under the fear that the concession of this privilege would tend to the diminution of their congregation. This resistance was successfully maintained until at last the petitioners were able to obtain from the Roman Catholic Duke of York the religious freedom which Dutch Calvinism had failed to give them.

Started thus in the wrong direction, it was easy for the colonial government to go from bad to worse. At a time when the entire force of Dutch clergy in the colony numbered only four, they were most unapostolically zealous to prevent any good from being done by "unauthorized conventicles and the preaching of unqualified persons," and procured the passing of an ordinance forbidding these under penalty of fine and imprisonment. The mild remonstrances of the Company, which was eager to get settlers without nice inquiries as to their religious opinions, had little effect to restrain the enterprising orthodoxy of Peter Stuyvesant. The activity of the Quakers among the Long Island towns stirred him to new energy. Not only visiting missionaries, but quiet dwellers at home, were subjected to severe and ignominious punishments. The persecution was kept up until one of the banished Friends, John Bowne, reached Amsterdam and laid the case before the Company. This enlightened body promptly shortened the days of tribulation by a letter to the superserviceable Stuyvesant, conceived in a most commercial spirit. It suggested to him that it was doubtful whether further persecution was expedient, unless it was desired to check the growth of population, which at that stage of the enterprise ought rather to be encouraged. No man, they said, ought to be molested so long as he disturbed neither his neighbors nor the government. "This maxim has always been the guide of the magistrates of this city, and the consequence has been that from every land people have flocked to this asylum. Tread thus in their steps, and we doubt not you will be blessed."

The stewardship of the interests of the kingdom of Christ in the New Netherlands was about to be taken away from the Dutch West India Company and the classis of Amsterdam. It will hardly be claimed by any that the account of their stewardship was a glorious one. The supply of ministers of the gospel had been tardy, inconstant, and scanty. At the time when the Dutch ministers were most active in hindering the work of others, there were only four of themselves in a vast territory with a rapidly increasing population. The clearest sign of spiritual life in the first generation of the colony is to be found in the righteous quarrel of Domine Bogardus with the malignant Kieft, and the large Christian brotherly kindness, the laborious mission work among the Indians, and the long-sustained pastoral faithfulness of Domine Megapolensis. Doubtless there is a record in heaven of faithful living and serving of many true disciples among this people, whose names are unknown on earth; but in writing history it is only with earthly memorials that we have to do. The records of the Dutch régime present few indications of such religious activity on the part of the colonists as would show that they regarded religion otherwise than as something to be imported from Holland at the expense of the Company.

A studious and elegant writer, Mr. Douglas Campbell, has presented in two ample and interesting volumes[74:1] the evidence in favor of his thesis that the characteristic institutions established by the Puritans in New England were derived, directly or indirectly, not from England, but from Holland. One of the gravest answers to an argument which contains so much to command respect is found in the history of the New Netherlands. In the early records of no one of the American colonies is there less manifestation of the Puritan characteristics than in the records of the colony that was absolutely and exclusively under Dutch control and made up chiefly of Dutch settlers. Nineteen years from the beginning of the colony there was only one church in the whole extent of it; at the end of thirty years there were only two churches. After ten years of settlement the first schoolmaster arrived; and after thirty-six years a Latin school was begun, for want of which up to that time young men seeking a classical education had had to go to Boston for it. In no colony does there appear less of local self-government or of central representative government, less of civil liberty, or even of the aspiration for it. The contrast between the character of this colony and the heroic antecedents of the Dutch in Holland is astonishing and inexplicable. The sordid government of a trading corporation doubtless tended to depress the moral tone of the community, but this was an evil common to many of the colonies. Ordinances, frequently renewed, for the prevention of disorder and brawling on Sunday and for restricting the sale of strong drinks, show how prevalent and obstinate were these evils. In 1648 it is boldly asserted in the preamble to a new law that one fourth of the houses in New Amsterdam were devoted to the sale of strong drink. Not a hopeful beginning for a young commonwealth.

Before bidding a willing good-bye to the Dutch régime of the New Netherlands, it remains to tell the story of another colony, begun under happy auspices, but so short-lived that its rise and fall are a mere episode in the history of the Dutch colony.

As early as 1630, under the feudal concessions of the Dutch West India Company, extensive tracts had been taken on the South River, or Delaware, and, after purchase from the Indians, settled by a colony under the conduct of the best of all the Dutch leaders, De Vries. Quarrels with the Indians arose, and at the end of a twelvemonth the colony was extinguished in blood. The land seemed to be left free for other occupants.

Years before, the great Gustavus Adolphus had pondered and decided on an enterprise of colonization in America.[76:1] The exigencies of the Thirty Years' War delayed the execution of his plan, but after the fatal day of Lützen the project resumed by the fit successor of Gustavus in the government of Sweden, the Chancellor Oxenstiern. Peter Minuit, who had been rejected from his place as the first governor of New Amsterdam, tendered to the Swedes the aid of his experience and approved wisdom; and in the end of the year 1637, against the protest of Governor Kieft, the strong foundations of a Swedish Lutheran colony were laid on the banks of the Delaware. A new purchase was made of the Indians (who had as little scruple as the Stuart kings about disposing of the same land twice over to different parties), including the lands from the mouth of the bay to the falls near Trenton. A fort was built where now stands the city of Wilmington, and under the protection of its walls Christian worship was begun by the first pastor, Torkillus. Strong reinforcements arrived in 1643, with the energetic Governor Printz and that man of "unwearied zeal in always propagating the love of God," the Rev. John Campanius, who through faith has obtained a good report by his brief most laborious ministry both to his fellow-countrymen and to the Delaware Indians.

The governor fixed his residence at Tinicum, now almost included within the vast circumference of Philadelphia, and there, forty years before the arrival of William Penn, Campanius preached the gospel of peace in two languages, to the red men and to the white. The question of the Swedish title, raised at the outset by the protest of the Dutch governor, could not long be postponed. It was suddenly precipitated on the arrival of Governor Rising, in 1654, by his capture of Fort Casimir, which the Dutch had built for the practical assertion of their claim. It seems a somewhat grotesque act of piety on the part of the Swedes, when, having celebrated the festival of Trinity Sunday by whipping their fellow-Christians out of the fort, they commemorated the good work by naming it the Fort of the Holy Trinity. It was a fatal victory. The next year came Governor Stuyvesant with an overpowering force and demanded and received the surrender of the colony to the Dutch. Honorable terms of surrender were conceded; among them, against the protest, alas! of good Domine Megapolensis, was the stipulation of religious liberty for the Lutherans.

It was the end of the Swedish colony, but not at once of the church. The Swedish community of some seven hundred souls, cut off from reinforcement and support from the fatherland, cherished its language and traditions and the mold of doctrine in which it had been shaped; after more than forty years the reviving interest of the mother church was manifested by the sending out of missionaries to seek and succor the daughter long absent and neglected in the wilderness. Two venerable buildings, the Gloria Dei Church in the southern part of Philadelphia, and the Old Swedes' Church at Wilmington, remain as monuments of the honorable story. The Swedish language ceased to be spoken; the people became undistinguishably absorbed in the swiftly multiplying population about them.

It was a short-lived triumph in which the Dutch colony reduced the Swedish under its jurisdiction. It only prepared a larger domain for it to surrender, in its turn, to superior force. With perfidy worthy of the House of Stuart, the newly restored king of England, having granted to his brother, the Duke of York, territory already plighted to others and territory already occupied by a friendly power, stretching in all from the Connecticut to the Delaware, covered his designs with friendly demonstrations, and in a time of profound peace surprised the quiet town of New Amsterdam with a hostile fleet and land force and a peremptory demand for surrender. The only hindrance interposed was a few hours of vain and angry bluster from Stuyvesant. The indifference of the Dutch republic, which had from the beginning refused its colony any promise of protection, and the sordid despotism of the Company, and the arrogant contempt of popular rights manifested by its governors, seem to have left no spark of patriotic loyalty alive in the population. With inert indifference, if not even with satisfaction, the colony transferred its allegiance to the British crown, henceforth sovereign from Maine to the Carolinas. The rights of person and property, religious liberty, and freedom of trade were stipulated in the capitulation.

The British government was happy in the character of Colonel Nicolls, who came as commandant of the invading expedition and remained as governor. Not only faithful to the terms of the surrender, but considerate of the feelings and interests of the conquered province, he gave the people small reason to regret the change of government. The established Dutch church not only was not molested, but was continued in full possession of its exceptional privileges. And it continued to languish. At the time of the surrender the province contained "three cities, thirty villages, and ten thousand inhabitants,"[78:1] and for all these there were six ministers. The six soon dribbled away to three, and for ten years these three continued without reinforcement. This extreme feebleness of the clergy, the absence of any vigorous church life among the laity, and the debilitating notion that the power and the right to preach the gospel must be imported from Holland, put the Dutch church at such a disadvantage as to invite aggression. Later English governors showed no scruple in violating the spirit of the terms of surrender and using their official power and influence to force the establishment of the English church against the almost unanimous will of the people. Property was unjustly taken and legal rights infringed to this end, but the end was not attained. Colonel Morris, an earnest Anglican, warned his friends against the folly of taking by force the salaries of ministers chosen by the people and paying them over to "the ministers of the church." "It may be a means of subsisting those ministers, but they won't make many converts among a people who think themselves very much injured." The pious efforts of Governor Fletcher, the most zealous of these official propagandists, are even more severely characterized in a dispatch of his successor, the Earl of Bellomont: "The late governor, ... under the notion of a Church of England to be put in opposition to the Dutch and French churches established here, supported a few rascally English, who are a scandal to their nation and the Protestant religion."[79:1] Evidently such support would have for its main effect to make the pretended establishment odious to the people. Colonel Morris sharply points out the impolicy as well as the injustice of the course adopted, claiming that his church would have been in a much better position without this political aid, and citing the case of the Jerseys and Pennsylvania, where nothing of the kind had been attempted, and where, nevertheless, "there are four times the number of churchmen that there are in this province of New York; and they are so, most of them, upon principle, whereas nine parts in ten of ours will add no great credit to whatever church they are of."[80:1]

It need not be denied that government patronage, even when dispensed by the dirty hands of such scurvy nursing fathers as Fletcher and Lord Cornbury, may give strength of a certain sort to a religious organization. Whatever could be done in the way of endowment or of social preferment in behalf of the English church was done eagerly. But happily this church had a better resource than royal governors in the well-equipped and sustained, and generally well-chosen, army of missionaries of the Society for the Propagation of the Gospel. Not fewer than fifty-eight of them were placed by the society in this single province. And if among them there were those who seemed to "preach Christ of envy and strife," as if the great aim of the preacher of the gospel were to get a man out of one Christian sect into another, there were others who showed a more Pauline and more Christian conception of their work, taking their full share of the task of bringing the knowledge of Christ to the unevangelized, whether white, red, or black.[80:2]

The diversity of organization which was destined to characterize the church in the province of New York was increased by the inflow of population from New England. The settlement of Long Island was from the beginning Puritan English. The Hudson Valley began early to be occupied by New Englanders bringing with them their pastors. In 1696 Domine Selyns, the only Dutch pastor in New York City, in his annual report congratulates himself, "Our number is now full," meaning that there are four Dutch ministers in the whole province of New York, and adds: "In the country places here there are many English preachers, mostly from New England. They were ordained there, having been in a large measure supplied by the University of Cambridge [Mass.]." The same letter gives the names of the three eminent French pastors ministering to the communities of Huguenot refugees at New Rochelle and New York and elsewhere in the neighborhood. The Scotch-Irish Presbyterians, more important to the history of the opening century than any of the rest, were yet to enter.

The spectacle of the ancient Dutch church thus dwindling, and seemingly content to dwindle, to one of the least of the tribes, is not a cheerful one, nor one easy to understand. But out of this little and dilapidated Bethlehem was to come forth a leader. Domine Frelinghuysen, arriving in America in 1720, was to begin a work of training for the ministry, which would result, in 1784, in the establishment of the first American professorship of theology;[81:1] and by the fervor of his preaching he was to win the signal glory of bringing in the Great Awakening.

CHAPTER VIII. THE PLANTING OF THE CHURCH IN NEW ENGLAND—PILGRIM AND PURITAN.

The attitude of the Church of England Puritans toward the Separatists from that church was the attitude of the earnest, patient, hopeful reformer toiling for the removal of public abuses, toward the restless "come-outer" who quits the conflict in despair of succeeding, and, "without tarrying for any," sets up his little model of good order outside. Such defection seemed to them not only of the nature of a military desertion and a weakening of the right side, but also an implied assertion of superior righteousness which provoked invidious comparison and mutual irritation of feeling. The comparison must not be pressed too far if we cite in illustration the feeling of the great mass of earnest, practical antislavery men in the American conflict with slavery toward the faction of "come-outer" abolitionists, who, despairing of success within the church and the state, seceded from both, thenceforth predicting failure for every practical enterprise of reform on the part of their former workfellows, and at every defeat chuckling, "I told you so."

If we should compare the English Separatist of the seventeenth century with this American Separatist of the nineteenth, we should be in still greater danger of misleading. Certainly there were those among the Separatists from the Church of England who, in the violence of their alienation and the bitterness of their sufferings, did not refrain from sour and acrid censoriousness toward the men who were nearest them in religious conviction and pursuing like ends by another course. One does not read far in the history of New England without encountering reformers of this extreme type. But not such were the company of true worshipers who, at peril of liberty and life, were wont to assemble each Lord's day in a room of the old manor-house of Scrooby, of which William Brewster was lessee, for Christian fellowship and worship, and for instruction in Christian truth and duty from the saintly lips of John Robinson. The extreme radicals of their day, they seem to have been divinely preserved from the besetting sins of radicalism—its narrowness, its self-righteousness, its censoriousness and intolerance. Those who read the copious records of the early New England colonization are again and again surprised at finding that the impoverished little company of Separatists at Leyden and Plymouth, who were so sharply reprobated by their Puritan brethren of the Church of England for their schismatic attitude, their over-righteousness and exclusiveness, do really excel, in liberality and patient tolerance and catholic and comprehensive love toward all good men, those who sat in judgment on them. Something of this is due to the native nobleness of the men themselves, of whom the world was not worthy; something of it to their long discipline in the passive virtues under bitter persecution in their native land and in exile in Holland and in the wilderness; much of it certainly to the incomparably wise and Christ-like teaching of Robinson both at Scrooby and at Leyden, and afterward through the tender and faithful epistles with which he followed them across the sea; and all of it to the grace of God working in their hearts and glorified in their living and their dying.

It would be incompatible with the limits of this volume to recite in detail the story of the Pilgrims; it has been told more amply and with fuller repetition than almost any other chapter of human history, and is never to be told or heard without awakening that thrill with which the heartstrings respond to the sufferings and triumphs of Christ's blessed martyrs and confessors. But, more dispassionately studied with reference to its position and relations in ecclesiastical history, it cannot be understood unless the sharp and sometimes exasperated antagonism is kept in view that existed between the inconsiderable faction, as it was esteemed, of the Separatists, and the great and growing Puritan party at that time in disfavor with king and court and hierarchy, but soon to become the dominant party not only in the Church of England, but in the nation. It is not strange that the antagonism between the two parties should be lost sight of. The two are identified in their theological convictions, in their spiritual sympathies, and, for the most part, in their judgment on questions concerning the externals of the church; and presently their respective colonies, planted side by side, not without mutual doubts and suspicions, are to grow together, leaving no visible seam of juncture,

Like kindred drops commingling into one.[84:1]

To the Puritan reformer within the Church of England, the act of the Pilgrims at Scrooby in separating themselves from the general mass of English Christians, mingled though that mass might be with a multitude of unworthy was nothing less than the sin of schism. One effect of the act was to reflect odium upon the whole party of Puritans, and involve them in the suspicion of that sedition which was so unjustly, but with such fatal success, imputed to the Separatists. It was a hard and doubtful warfare that the Puritans were waging against spiritual wickedness in high places; the defection of the Separatists doubly weakened them in the conflict. It is not strange, however it may seem so, that the animosity of Puritan toward Separatist was sometimes acrimonious, nor that the public reproaches hurled at the unpopular little party should have provoked recriminations upon the assailants as being involved in the defilements and the plagues of Babylon, and should have driven the Separatists into a narrower exclusiveness of separation, cutting themselves off not only from communion with abuses and corruptions in the Church of England, but even from fellowship with good and holy men in the national church who did not find it a duty to secede.

Nothing of this bitterness and narrowness is found in Robinson. Strenuously as he maintained the right and duty of separation from the Establishment, he was, especially in his later years, no less earnest in condemning the "Separatists who carried their separation too far and had gone beyond the true landmarks in matters of Christian doctrine or of Christian fellowship."[85:1] His latest work, "found in his studie after his decease," was "A Treatise of the Lawfulness of Hearing of the Ministers in the Church of England."

The moderateness of Robinson's position, and the brotherly kindness of his temper, could not save him and his people from the prevailing odium that rested upon the Separatist. Many and grave were the sorrows through which the Pilgrim church had to pass in its way from the little hamlet of Scrooby to the bleak hill of Plymouth. They were in peril from the persecutor at home and in peril in the attempt to escape; in peril from greedy speculators and malignant politicians; in peril from the sea and from cold and from starvation; in peril from the savages and from false brethren privily sent among them to spy out their liberties; but an added bitterness to all their tribulations lay in this, that, for the course which they were constrained in conscience to pursue, they were subject to the reprobation of those whom they most highly honored as their brethren in the faith of Christ. Some of the most heartbreaking of their trials arose directly from the unwillingness of English Puritans to sustain, or even countenance, the Pilgrim colony.

In the year 1607, when the ships of the Virginia Company were about landing their freight of emigrants and supplies at Jamestown, the first and unsuccessful attempt of the Pilgrims was made to escape from their native land to Holland. Before the end of 1608 the greater part of them, in scattering parties, had effected the passage of the North Sea, and the church was reunited in a land of religious freedom. With what a blameless, diligent, and peaceful life they adorned the name of disciple through all the twelve years of their sojourn, how honored and beloved they were among the churches and in the University of Leyden, there are abundant testimonies. The twelve years of seclusion in an alien land among a people of strange language was not too long a discipline of preparation for that work for which the Head of the church had set them apart. This was the period of Robinson's activity as author. In erudite studies, in grave debate with gainsayers at home and with fellow-exiles in Holland, he was maturing in his own mind, and in the minds of the church, those large and liberal yet definite views of church organization and duty which were destined for coming ages so profoundly to influence the American church in all its orders and divisions. "He became a reformer of the Separation."[87:1]

We pass by the heroic and pathetic story of the consultations and correspondences, the negotiations and disappointments, the embarkation and voyage, and come to that memorable date, November 11 (= 21), 1620, when, arrived off the shore of Cape Cod, the little company, without charter or warrant of any kind from any government on earth, about to land on a savage continent in quest of a home, gathered in the cabin of the "Mayflower," and after a method quite in analogy with that in which, sixteen years before, they had constituted the church at Scrooby, entered into formal and solemn compact "in the presence of God and one of another, covenanting and combining themselves together into a civil body politic."

It is difficult, in reading the instrument then subscribed, to avoid the conviction that the theory of the origin of the powers of civil government in a social compact, which had long floated in literature before it came to be distinctly articulated in the "Contrat Social" of Jean Jacques Rousseau, was familiar to the minds of those by whom the paper was drawn. Thoughtful men at the present day universally recognize the fallacy of this plausible hypothesis, which once had such wide currency and so serious an influence on the course of political history in America. But whether or not they were affected by the theory, the practical good sense of the men and their deference to the teachings of the Bible secured them from the vicious and absurd consequences deducible from it. Not all the names of the colonists were subscribed to the compact,—a clear indication of the freedom of individual judgment in that company,—but it was never for a moment held that the dissentients were any the less bound by it. When worthless John Billington, who had somehow got "shuffled into their company," was sentenced for disrespect and disobedience to Captain Myles Standish "to have his neck and heels tied together," it does not seem to have occurred to him to plead that he had never entered into the social compact; nor yet when the same wretched man, ten years later, was by a jury convicted of willful murder, and sentenced to death and executed. Logically, under the social-compact theory, it would have been competent for those dissenting from this compact to enter into another, and set up a competing civil government on the same ground; but what would have been the practical value of this line of argument might have been learned from Mr. Thomas Morton, of Furnivall's Inn, after he had been haled out of his disorderly house at Merry Mount by Captain Standish, and convented before the authorities at Plymouth.

The social-compact theory as applied to the church, implying that the mutual duties of Christian disciples in society are derived solely from mutual stipulations, is quite as transparently fallacious as when it is applied to civil polity, and the consequences deducible from it are not less absurd. But it cannot be claimed for the Plymouth men, and still less for their spiritual successors, that they have wholly escaped the evil consequences of their theory in its practical applications. The notion that a church of Christ is a club, having no authority or limitations but what it derives from club rules agreed on among the members, would have been scouted by the Pilgrims; among those who now claim to sit in their seats there are some who would hesitate to admit it, and many who would frankly avow it with all its mischievous implications. Planted in the soil of Plymouth, it spread at once through New England, and has become widely rooted in distant and diverse regions of the American church.[89:1]

The church of Plymouth, though deprived of its pastor, continued to be rich in faith and in all spiritual gifts, and most of all in the excellent gift of charity. The history of it year after year is a beautiful illustration of brotherly kindness and mutual self-sacrifice among themselves and of forgiving patience toward enemies. But the colony, beginning in extreme feebleness and penury, never became either strong or rich. One hundred and two souls embarked in the "Mayflower," of whom nearly one half were dead before the end of four months. At the end of four years the number had increased to one hundred and eighty. At the end of ten years the settlement numbered three hundred persons.

It could not have been with joy wholly unalloyed with misgivings that this feeble folk learned of a powerful movement for planting a Puritan colony close in the neighborhood. The movement had begun in the heart of the national church, and represented everything that was best in that institution. The Rev. John White, rector of Dorchester, followed across the sea with pastoral solicitude the young men of his parish, who, in the business of the fisheries, were wont to make long stay on the New England coast, far from home and church. His thought was to establish a settlement that should be a sort of depot of supplies for the fishing fleets, and a temporary home attended with the comforts and safeguards of Christian influence. The project was a costly failure; but it was like the corn of wheat falling into the ground to die, and bringing forth much fruit. A gentleman of energy and dignity, John Endicott, pledged his personal service as leader of a new colony. In September, 1628, he landed with a pioneering party at Naumkeag, and having happily composed some differences that arose with the earlier comers, they named the place Salem, which is, by interpretation, "Peace." Already, with the newcomers and the old, the well-provided settlement numbered more than fifty persons, busy in preparation for further arrivals. Meanwhile vigorous work was doing in England. The organization to sustain the colony represented adequate capital and the highest quality of character and influence. A royal charter, drawn with sagacious care to secure every privilege the Puritan Company desired, was secured from the fatuity of the reigning Stuart, erecting in the wilderness such a free commonwealth as his poor little soul abhorred; and preparation was made for sending out, in the spring of 1629, a noble fleet of six vessels, carrying three hundred men and a hundred women and children, with ample equipment of provisions, tools and arms, and live stock. The Company had taken care that there should be "plentiful provision of godly ministers." Three approved clergymen of the Church of England—Higginson, Skelton, and Bright—had been chosen by the Company to attend the expedition, besides whom one Ralph Smith, a Separatist minister, had been permitted to take passage before the Company "understood of his difference in judgment in some things" from the other ministers. He was permitted to continue his journey, yet not without a caution to the governor that unless he were found "conformable to the government" he was not to be suffered to remain within the limits of its jurisdiction. An incident of this departure rests on the sole authority of Cotton Mather, and is best told in his own words:

"When they came to the Land's End, Mr. Higginson, calling up his children and other passengers unto the stern of the ship to take their last sight of England, said, 'We will not say, as the Separatists were wont to say at their leaving of England, Farewell, Babylon! farewell, Rome! but we will say, Farewell, dear England! farewell, the church of God in England, and all the Christian friends there! We do not go to New England as Separatists from the Church of England, though we cannot but separate from the corruptions in it; but we go to practice the positive part of church reformation and propagate the gospel in America.'"

The story ought to be true, for the intrinsic likeliness of it; and it is all the likelier for the fact that among the passengers, kindly and even fraternally treated, and yet the object of grave misgivings, was the honest Separatist minister, Ralph Smith.[91:1] The ideal of the new colony could hardly have been better expressed than in these possibly apocryphal words ascribed to Mr. Higginson. These were not fugitives seeking asylum from persecution. Still less were they planning an asylum for others. They were intent on the planting of a new commonwealth, in which the church of Christ, not according to the imperfect and perverted pattern of the English Establishment, but according to a fairer pattern, that had been showed them in their mounts of vision, should be both free and dominant. If this purpose of theirs was wrong; if they had no right to deny themselves the comforts and delights of their native land, and at vast cost of treasure to seclude themselves within a defined tract of wilderness, for the accomplishment of an enterprise which they conceived to be of the highest beneficence to mankind—then doubtless many of the measures which they took in pursuance of this purpose must fall under the same condemnation with the purpose itself. If there are minds so constituted as to perceive no moral difference between banishing a man from his native home, for opinion's sake, and declining, on account of difference of opinion, to admit a man to partnership in a difficult and hazardous enterprise organized on a distinctly exclusive basis, such minds will be constrained to condemn the Puritan colonists from the start and all along. Minds otherwise constituted will be able to discriminate between the righteous following of a justifiable policy and the lapses of the colonial governments from high and Christian motives and righteous courses. Whether the policy of rigorous exclusiveness, building up communities of picked material, homogeneous in race, language, and religion, is on the whole less wise for the founders of a new commonwealth than a sweepingly comprehensive policy, gathering in people mutually alien in speech and creed and habits, is a fairly open question for historical students. Much light might be thrown upon it by the comparative history of Massachusetts and Rhode Island, of New England and Pennsylvania. It is not a question that is answered at once by the mere statement of it.

We do not need to be told that to the little Separatist settlement at Plymouth, still in the first decade of its feeble existence, the founding, within a day's journey, of this powerful colony, on ecclesiastical principles distinctly antagonistic to their own, was a momentous, even a formidable fact. Critical, nay, vital questions emerged at once, which the subtlest churchcraft might have despaired of answering. They were answered, solved, harmonized, by the spirit of Christian love.

That great spiritual teacher, John Robinson, besides his more general exhortations to brotherly kindness and charity, had spoken, in the spirit of prophecy, some promises and assurances which came now to a divine fulfillment. Pondering "sundry weighty and solid reasons" in favor of removal from Holland, the pilgrims put on record that "their pastor would often say that many of those who both wrote and preached against them would practice as they did if they were in a place where they might have liberty and live conformably." One of the most affectionate of his disciples, Edward Winslow, wrote down some of the precious and memorable words which the pastor, who was to see their face no more, uttered through his tears as they were about to leave him. "'There will be no difference,' he said, 'between the unconformable ministers and you, when they come to the practice of the ordinances out of the kingdom.' And so he advised us to close with the godly party of the kingdom of England, and rather to study union than division, viz., how near we might possibly without sin close with them, rather than in the least measure to affect division or separation from them."

The solitude of the little starving hamlet by the sea was favorable to the springing and fructifying of this seed in the good and honest hearts into which it had been cast. Before the great fleet of colonists, with its three unconformable Church of England clergymen, had reached the port of Salem the good seed had been planted anew in other hearts not less honest and good. It fell on this wise. The pioneer party at Salem who came with Endicott, "arriving there in an uncultivated desert, many of them, for want of wholesome diet and convenient lodgings, were seized with the scurvy and other distempers, which shortened many of their days, and prevented many of the rest from performing any great matter of labor that year for advancing the work of the plantation." Whereupon the governor, hearing that at Plymouth lived a physician "that had some skill that way," wrote thither for help, and at once the beloved physician and deacon of the Plymouth church, Dr. Samuel Fuller, hastened to their relief. On what themes the discourse revolved between the Puritan governor just from England and the Separatist deacon already for so many years an exile, and whither it tended, is manifested in a letter written soon after by Governor Endicott, of Salem, to Governor Bradford, of Plymouth, under date May 11 (= 21), 1629. The letter marks an epoch in the history of American Christianity:

"To the worshipful and my right worthy friend, William Bradford, Esq., Governor of New Plymouth, these:

"Right worthy Sir: It is a thing not usual that servants to one Master and of the same household should be strangers. I assure you I desire it not; nay, to speak more plainly, I cannot be so to you. God's people are marked with one and the same mark, and sealed with one and the same seal, and have, for the main, one and the same heart, guided by one and the same Spirit of truth; and where this is there can be no discord—nay, here must needs be sweet harmony. The same request with you I make unto the Lord, that we may as Christian brethren be united by a heavenly and unfeigned love, bending all our hearts and forces in furthering a work beyond our strength, with reverence and fear fastening our eyes always on him that only is able to direct and prosper all our ways.

"I acknowledge myself much bound to you for your kind love and care in sending Mr. Fuller among us, and I rejoice much that I am by him satisfied touching your judgments of the outward form of God's worship.[94:1] It is, as far as I can yet gather, no other than is warranted by the evidence of truth, and the same which I have professed and maintained ever since the Lord in mercy revealed himself to me, being very far different from the common report that hath been spread of you touching that particular. But God's children must not look for less here below, and it is the great mercy of God that he strengthens them to go through with it.

"I shall not need at this time to be tedious unto you, for, God willing, I purpose to see your face shortly. In the meantime I humbly take my leave of you, committing you to the Lord's blessed protection, and rest

"Your assured loving friend and servant,

"John Endicott."

"The positive part of church reformation," which Higginson and his companions had come into the wilderness to practice, appeared in a new light when studied under the new conditions. The question of separation from the general fellowship of English Christians, which had lain heavily on their consciences, was no longer a question; instead of it arose the question of separation from their beloved and honored fellow-Christians at Plymouth. The Act of Uniformity and the tyrannous processes by which it was enforced no longer existed for them. They were free to build the house of God simply according to the teaching of the divine Word. What form will the structure take?

One of the first practical questions to emerge was the question by what authority their ministry was to be exercised. On one point they seem to have been quite clear. The episcopal ordination, which each of them had received in England, whatever validity it may have had in English law, gave them no authority in the church of God in Salem. Further, their appointment from the Company in London, although it was a regular commission from the constituted civil government of the colony, could confer no office in the spiritual house. A day of solemn fasting was held, by the governor's appointment, for the choice of pastor and teacher, and after prayer the two recognized candidates for the two offices, Skelton and Higginson, were called upon to give their views as to a divine call to the ministry. "They acknowledged there was a twofold calling: the one, an inward calling, when the Lord moved the heart of a man to take that calling upon him, and fitted him with gifts for the same; the second (the outward calling) was from the people, when a company of believers are joined together in covenant to walk together in all the ways of God." Thereupon the assembly proceeded to a written ballot, and its choice fell upon Mr. Skelton and Mr. Higginson. It remained for the ministers elect to be solemnly inducted into office, which was done with prayer and the laying on of hands in benediction.

But presently there were searchings of heart over the anterior question as to the constituency of the church. Were all the population of Salem to be reckoned as of the church of Salem? and if not, who should "discern between the righteous and the wicked"? The result of study of this question, in the light of the New Testament, was this—that it was "necessary for those who intended to be of the church solemnly to enter into a covenant engagement one with another, in the presence of God, to walk together before him according to his Word." Thirty persons were chosen to be the first members of the church, who in a set form of words made public vows of faithfulness to each other and to Christ. By the church thus constituted the pastor and teacher, already installed in office in the parish, were instituted as ministers of the church.[96:1]

Before the solemnities of that notable day were concluded, a belated vessel that had been eagerly awaited landed on the beach at Salem the "messengers of the church at Plymouth." They came into the assembly, Governor Bradford at the head, and in the name of the Pilgrim church declared their "approbation and concurrence," and greeted the new church, the first-born in America, with "the right hand of fellowship." A thoughtful and devoted student declares this day's proceedings to be "the beginning of a distinctively American church history."[97:1]

The immediate sequel of this transaction is characteristic and instructive. Two brothers, John and Samuel Browne, members of the council of the colony, took grave offense at this departure from the ways of the Church of England, and, joining to themselves others like-minded, set up separate worship according to the Book of Common Prayer. Being called to account before the governor for their schismatic procedure, they took an aggressive tone and declared that the ministers, "were Separatists, and would be Anabaptists." The two brothers were illogical. The ministers had not departed from the Nationalist and anti-Separatist principles enunciated by Higginson from the quarter-deck of the "Talbot." What they had just done was to lay the foundations of a national church for the commonwealth that was in building. And the two brothers, trying to draw off a part of the people into their schism-shop, were Separatists, although they were doubtless surprised to discover it. There was not the slightest hesitation on the governor's part as to the proper course to be pursued. "Finding those two brothers to be of high spirits, and their speeches and practices tending to mutiny and faction, the governor told them that New England was no place for such as they, and therefore he sent them both back for England at the return of the ships the same year."[98:1] Neither then nor afterward was there any trace of doubt in the minds of the New England settlers, in going three thousand miles away into the seclusion of the wilderness, of their indefeasible moral right to pick their own company. There was abundant opportunity for mistake and temptation to wrong-doing in the exercise of this right, but the right itself is so nearly self-evident as to need no argument.

While the civil and ecclesiastical foundations of the Salem community are thus being laid, there is preparing on the other side of the sea that great coup d'état which is to create, almost in a day, a practically independent American republic. Until this is accomplished the colonial organization is according to a common pattern, a settlement on a distant shore, equipped, sustained, and governed with authority all but sovereign by a commercial company at the metropolis, within the reach, and thus under the control, of the supreme power. Suppose, now, that the shareholders in the commercial company take their charter conferring all but sovereign authority, and transport themselves and it across the sea to the heart of the settlement, there to admit other planters, at their discretion, to the franchise of the Company, what then? This was the question pondered and decided in those dark days of English liberty, when the triumph of despotism, civil and spiritual, over the rights of Englishmen seemed almost achieved. The old officers of the Company resigned; their places were filled by Winthrop and Dudley and others, who had undertaken to emigrate; and that memorable season of 1630 not less than seventeen ships, carrying about one thousand passengers, sailed from English ports for Massachusetts Bay. It was the beginning of the great Puritan exodus. Attempts were made by the king and the archbishop to stay the flow of emigration, but with only transient success. "At the end of ten years from Winthrop's arrival about twenty-one thousand Englishmen, or four thousand families, including the few hundreds who were here before him, had come over in three hundred vessels, at a cost of two hundred thousand pounds sterling."[99:1] What could not be done by despotism was accomplished by the triumph of the people over the court. The meeting of the Long Parliament in 1640 made it safe for Puritans to stay in England; and the Puritans stayed. The current of migration was not only checked, but turned backward. It is reckoned that within four generations from that time more persons went to old England than originally came thence. The beginnings of this return were of high importance. Among the home-going companies were men who were destined to render eminent service in the reconstruction of English society, both in the state and in the army, and especially in the church. The example of the New England churches, voluminously set forth in response to written inquiries from England, had great influence in saving the mother country from suffering the imposition of a Presbyterian hierarchy that threatened to be as intolerant and as intolerable as the tyranny of Laud.

For the order of the New England churches crystallized rapidly into a systematic and definite church polity, far removed from mere Separatism even in the temperate form in which this had been illustrated by Robinson and the Pilgrim church. The successive companies of emigrants as they arrived, ship-load after ship-load, each with its minister or college of ministers, followed with almost monotonous exactness the method adopted in the organization of the church in Salem. A small company of the best Christians entered into mutual covenant as a church of Christ, and this number, growing by well-considered accessions, added to itself from time to time other believers on the evidence and confession of their faith in Christ. The ministers, all or nearly all of whom had been clergymen in the orders of the Church of England, were of one mind in declining to consider their episcopal ordination in England as conferring on them any spiritual authority in a church newly gathered in America. They found rather in the free choice of the brotherhood the sign of a divine call to spiritual functions in the church, and were inducted into office by the primitive form of the laying on of hands.

In many ways, but especially in the systematized relations of the churches with one another and in their common relations with the civil government, the settled Nationalism of the great Puritan migration was illustrated. With the least possible constraint on the individual or on the church, they were clear in their purpose that their young state should have its established church.

Through what rude experiences the system and the men were tested has been abundantly told and retold.[100:1] Roger Williams, learned, eloquent, sincere, generous, a man after their own heart, was a very malignant among Separatists, separating himself not only from the English church, but from all who would not separate from it, and from all who would not separate from these, and so on, until he could no longer, for conscience' sake, hold fellowship with his wife in family prayers. After long patience the colonial government deemed it necessary to signify to him that if his conscience would not suffer him to keep quiet, and refrain from stirring up sedition, and embroiling the colony with the English government, he would have to seek freedom for that sort of conscience outside of their jurisdiction; and they put him out accordingly, to the great advantage of both parties and without loss of mutual respect and love. A little later, a clever woman, Mrs. Ann Hutchinson, with a vast conceit of her superior holiness and with the ugly censoriousness which is a usual accompaniment of that grace, demonstrated her genius for mixing a theological controversy with personal jealousies and public anxieties, and involved the whole colony of the Bay in an acrimonious quarrel, such as to give an unpleasant tone of partisanship and ill temper to the proceedings in her case, whether ecclesiastical or civil. She seems clearly to have been a willful and persistent nuisance in the little community, and there were good reasons for wanting to be rid of her, and right ways to that end. They took the wrong way and tried her for heresy. In like manner, when the Quakers came among them,—not of the mild, meek, inoffensive modern variety to which we are accustomed, but of the fierce, aggressive early type,—instead of proceeding against them for their overt offenses against the state, disorderly behavior, public indecency, contempt of court, sedition, they proceeded against them distinctly as Quakers, thus putting themselves in the wrong and conceding to their adversaries that crown of martyrdom for which their souls were hankering and to which they were not fully entitled.

Of course, in maintaining the principle of Nationalism, the New England Puritans did not decline the implications and corollaries of that principle. It was only to a prophetic genius like the Separatist Roger Williams that it was revealed that civil government had no concern to enforce "the laws of the first table." But the historical student might be puzzled to name any other church establishment under which less of molestation was suffered by dissenters, or more of actual encouragement given to rival sects, than under the New England theocracies. The Nationalist principle was exclusive; the men who held it in New England (subject though they were to the temptations of sectarian emulation and fanatic zeal) were large-minded and generous men.

The general uniformity of church organization among the Puritan plantations is the more remarkable in view of the notable independence and originality of the leading men, who represented tendencies of opinion as widely diverging as the quasi-Presbyterianism of John Eliot and the doctrinaire democracy of John Wise. These variations of ecclesiastico-political theory had much to do with the speedy diffusion of the immigrant population. For larger freedom in building his ideal New Jerusalem, the statesmanlike pastor, Thomas Hooker, led forth his flock a second time into the great and terrible wilderness, and with his associates devised what has been declared to be "the first example in history of a written constitution—a distinct organic law constituting a government and defining its powers."[102:1] The like motive determined the choice company under John Davenport and Theophilus Eaton to refuse all inducements and importunities to remain in Massachusetts, choosing rather to build on no other man's foundations at New Haven.[102:2] At the end of a hundred years from the settlement of Boston the shores and river valleys of Massachusetts and Connecticut were planted with towns, each self-governing as a pure democracy, each with its church and educated minister and its system of common schools. The two colleges at Cambridge and New Haven were busy with their appointed work of training young men to the service of God "in church or civil state." And this great and prosperous and intelligent population was, with inconsiderable exceptions, the unmingled progeny of the four thousand English families who, under stress of the tyranny of Charles Stuart and the persecution of William Laud, had crossed the sea in the twelve years from 1628 to 1640.

The traditions of the fathers of New England had been piously cherished down to this third and fourth generation. The model of an ideal state that had been set up had, meanwhile, been more or less deformed, especially in Massachusetts, by the interference of England; the dominance of the established churches had been slightly infringed by the growth here and there of dissenting churches, Baptist, Episcopalian, and Quaker; but the framework both of church and of state was wonderfully little decayed or impaired. The same simplicity in the outward order of worship was maintained; the same form of high Calvinistic theology continued to be cherished as a norm of sound preaching and as a vehicle of instruction to children. All things continued as they had been; and yet it would have been a most superficial observer who had failed to detect signs of approaching change. The disproportions of the Calvinistic system, exaggerated in the popular acceptation, as in the favorite "Day of Doom" of Michael Wigglesworth, forced the effort after practical readjustments. The magnifying of divine sovereignty in the saving of men, to the obscuring of human responsibility, inevitably mitigated the church's reprobation of respectable people who could testify of no experience of conversion, and yet did not wish to relinquish for themselves or their families their relation to the church. Out of the conflict between two aspects of theological truth, and the conflict between the Nationalist and the Separatist conceptions of the church, and especially out of the mistaken policy of restricting the civil franchise to church-members, came forth that device of the "Half-way Covenant" which provided for a hereditary quasi-membership in the church for worthy people whose lives were without scandal, and who, not having been subjects of an experience of conscious conversion, were felt to be not altogether to blame for the fact. From the same causes came forth, and widely prevailed, the tenet of "Stoddardeanism," so called as originating in the pastoral work, and, it is said, in the personal experience, of Solomon Stoddard, the saintly minister of Northampton from 1669 till 1729, when he was succeeded by his colleague and grandson, Jonathan Edwards. It is the view that the Lord's Supper is instituted as a means of regeneration as well as of sanctification, and that those who are consciously "in a natural condition" ought not to be repelled, but rather encouraged to come to it. From the same causes, by natural sequence, came that so-called Arminianism[104:1] which, instead of urging the immediate necessity and duty of conversion, was content with commending a "diligent use of means," which might be the hopeful antecedent of that divine grace.

These divergences from the straight lines of the primeval New England Calvinism had already begun to be manifest during the lifetime of some of the founders. Of not less grave import was the deflection from the lofty moral standard of the fathers. A great New Englander, Horace Bushnell, maintaining his thesis that great migrations are followed by a tendency to barbarism, has cited in proof this part of New England history.[105:1] As early as the second generation, the evil tendency seemed so formidable as to lead to the calling, by the General Court of Massachusetts, of the "Reforming Synod" of 1679. No one can say that the heroic age of New England was past. History has no nobler record to show, of courage and fortitude in both men and women, than that of New England in the Indian wars. But the terrors of those days of tribulation, the breaking up of communities, the decimation of the population, the long absences of the young men on the bloody business of the soldier, were not favorable for maturing the fruits of the Spirit. Withal, the intrigues of British politicians, the threatened or actual molestations of the civil governments of the colonies, and the corrupting influences proceeding from every center of viceregal authority, abetted the tendency to demoralization. By the end of the first third of the eighteenth century, New England, politically, ecclesiastically, theologically, and morally, had come into a state of unstable equilibrium. An overturn is impending.

The set and sturdy resolution of the founders of the four colonies of the New England confederacy that the first planting of their territory should be on rigorously exclusive principles, with a homogeneous and mutually congenial population, under a firm discipline both civil and ecclesiastical, finds an experimental justification in the history of the neighbor colony of Rhode Island. No commonwealth can boast a nobler and purer name for its founder than the name of Roger Williams. Rhode Island, founded in generous reaction from the exclusiveness of Massachusetts, embodied the principle of "soul-liberty" in its earliest acts. The announcement that under its jurisdiction no man was to be molested by the civil power for his religious belief was a broad invitation to all who were uncomfortable under the neighboring theocracies.[106:1] And the invitation was freely accepted. The companions of Williams were reinforced by the friends of Mrs. Hutchinson, some of them men of substance and weight of character. The increasing number of persons inclined to Baptist views found in Rhode Island a free and congenial atmosphere. Williams himself was not long in coming to the Baptist position and passing beyond it. The Quakers found Rhode Island a safe asylum from persecution, whether Puritan or Dutch. More disorderly and mischievous characters, withal, quartered themselves, unwelcome guests, on the young commonwealth, a thorn in its side and a reproach to its principles. It became clear to Williams before his death that the declaration of individual rights and independence is not of itself a sufficient foundation for a state. The heterogeneous population failed to settle into any stable polity. After two generations the tyranny of Andros, so odious elsewhere in New England, was actually welcome as putting an end to the liberty that had been hardly better than anarchy.

The results of the manner of the first planting on the growth of the church in Rhode Island were of a like sort. There is no room for question that the material of a true church was there, in the person of faithful and consecrated disciples of Christ, and therefore there must have been gathering together in common worship and mutual edification. But the sense of individual rights and responsibilities seems to have overshadowed the love for the whole brotherhood of disciples. The condition of the church illustrated the Separatism of Williams reduced to the absurd. There was feeble organization of Christians in knots and coteries. But sixty years passed before the building of the first house of worship in Providence, and at the end of almost a century "there had not existed in the whole colony more than eight or ten churches of any denomination, and these were mostly in a very feeble and precarious state."[107:1]

Meanwhile the inadequate compensations of a state of schism began to show themselves. In the absence of any organized fellowship of the whole there grew up, more than elsewhere, a mutual tolerance and even love among the petty sects, the lesson of which was learned where it was most needed. The churches of "the standing order" in Massachusetts not only admired but imitated "the peace and love which societies of different modes of worship entertained toward each other in Rhode Island." In 1718, not forty years from the time when Baptist churches ceased to be religio illicita in Massachusetts, three foremost pastors of Boston assisted in the ordination of a minister to the Baptist church, at which Cotton Mather preached the sermon, entitled "Good Men United." It contained a frank confession of repentance for the persecutions of which the Boston churches had been guilty.[107:2]

There is a double lesson to be learned from the history of these neighbor colonies: first, that a rigorously exclusive selection of men like-minded is the best seed for the first planting of a commonwealth in the wilderness; secondly, that the exclusiveness that is justified in the infancy of such a community cannot wisely, nor even righteously, nor even possibly, be maintained in its adolescence and maturity. The church-state of Massachusetts and New Haven was overthrown at the end of the first generation by external interference. If it had continued a few years longer it must have fallen of itself; but it lasted long enough to be the mold in which the civilization of the young States should set and harden.

CHAPTER IX. THE MIDDLE COLONIES: THE JERSEYS, DELAWARE, AND PENNSYLVANIA—THE QUAKER COLONIZATION—GEORGIA.

The bargainings and conveyancings, the confirmations and reclamations, the setting up and overturning, which, after the conquest of the New Netherlands, had the effect to detach the peninsula of New Jersey from the jurisdiction of New York, and to divide it for a time into two governments, belong to political history; but they had, of course, an important influence on the planting of the church in that territory. One result of them was a wide diversity of materials in the early growth of the church.

Toward the end of the Dutch occupation, one lonely congregation had been planted in that region which, at a later time, when the Dutch church in America had awaked from its lethargy, was to become known as "the garden of the Dutch church."[109:1]

After the extinction of the high theocracy of the New Haven Colony by the merger of it in Connecticut, a whole church and town, headed by the pastor, having secured such guaranty of their political liberty as the unstable government of New Jersey was able to give, left the homes endeared to them by thirty years of toil and thrift, and lifting the ark of the covenant by the staves, set themselves down beside the Passaic, calling their plantation the New-Ark, and reinstituted their fundamental principle of restricting the franchise to members of the church. Thus "with one heart they resolved to carry on their spiritual and town affairs according to godly government." The Puritan migration, of which this was the nucleus, had an influence on the legislation and the later history of New Jersey out of all proportion to its numbers.

Twenty years later the ferocious persecution of the Scottish Covenanters, which was incited by the fears or the bloody vindictiveness of James II. after the futile insurrection of Monmouth, furnished a motive for emigration to the best people in North Britain, which was quickly seized and exploited by the operators in Jersey lands. Assurances of religious liberty were freely given; men of influence were encouraged to bring over large companies; and in 1686 the brother of the martyred Duke of Argyle was made governor of East Jersey. The considerable settlements of Scotchmen found congenial neighbors in the New Englanders of Newark. A system of free schools, early established by a law of the commonwealth, is naturally referred to their common influence.

Meanwhile a series of events of the highest consequence to the future of the American church had been in progress in the western half of the province. Passing from hand to hand, the ownership and lordship of West Jersey had become vested in a land company dominated by Quakers. For the first time in the brief history of that sect, it was charged with the responsibility of the organization and conduct of government. Hitherto it had been publicly known by the fierce and defiant and often outrageous protests of its representatives against existing governments and dignities both in state and in church, such as exposed them to the natural and reasonable suspicion of being wild and mischievous anarchists. The opportunities and temptations that come to those in power would be a test of the quality of the sect more severe than trial by the cart-tail and the gibbet.

The Quakers bore the test nobly. Never did a commercial company show itself so little mercenary; never was a sovereign more magnanimous and unselfish. With the opening of the province to settlement, the proprietors set forth a statement of their purposes: "We lay a foundation for after ages to understand their liberty as men and Christians, that they may not be brought into bondage but by their own consent; for we put the power in the people." This was followed by a code of "Concessions and Agreements" in forty-four articles, which were at once a constitution of government and a binding compact with such as should enter themselves as colonists on these terms. They left little to be desired in securities for personal, political, and religious liberty.[111:1]

At once population began to flow amain. In 1677 two hundred and thirty Quakers came in one ship and founded the town of Burlington. By 1681 there had come fourteen hundred. Weekly, monthly, quarterly meetings were established; houses of worship were built; and in August, 1681, the Quaker hierarchy (if it may so be called without offense) was completed by the establishment of the Burlington Yearly Meeting. The same year the corporation, encouraged by its rapid success, increased its numbers and its capital, bought out the proprietors of East Jersey, and appointed as governor over the whole province the eminent Quaker theologian, Robert Barclay. The Quaker régime continued, not always smoothly, till 1688, when it was extinguished by James II. at the end of his perfidious campaigns against American liberties. This enterprise of the Quaker purchase and settlement of New Jersey brings upon the stage of American history the great apostle of Christian colonization, William Penn. He came into relation to the New Jersey business as arbiter of some differences that arose between the two Friends who had bought West Jersey in partnership. He continued in connection with it when the Quaker combination had extended itself by purchase over the whole Jersey peninsula, and he was a trusted counselor of the corporation, and the representative of its interests at court. Thus there grew more and more distinct before his peculiarly adventurous and enterprising mind the vision of the immense possibilities, political, religious, and commercial, of American colonization. With admirable business shrewdness combined with courtly tact, he canceled an otherwise hopeless debt from the crown in consideration of the concession to him of a domain of imperial wealth and dimensions, with practically unlimited rights of jurisdiction. At once he put into exercise the advantages and opportunities which were united in him so as never before in the promoter of a like enterprise, and achieved a success speedy and splendid beyond all precedent.

The providential preparations for this great enterprise—"the Holy Experiment," as Penn delighted to call it—had been visibly in progress in England for not more than the third part of a century. It was not the less divine for being wholly logical and natural, that, just when the Puritan Reformation culminated in the victory of the Commonwealth, the Quaker Reformation should suddenly break forth. Puritanism was the last expression of that appeal from the church to the Scriptures, from existing traditions of Christianity to its authentic original documents, which is the essence of Protestantism. In Puritanism, reverence for the Scriptures is exaggerated to the point of superstition. The doctrine that God of old had spoken by holy men was supplemented by the pretension that God had long ago ceased so to speak and never would so speak again. The claim that the Scriptures contain a sufficient guide to moral duty and religious truth was exorbitantly stretched to include the last details of church organization and worship, and the minute direction of political and other secular affairs. In many a case the Scriptures thus applied did highly ennoble the polity and legislation of the Puritans.[113:1] In other cases, not a few, the Scriptures, perverted from their true purpose and wrested by a vicious and conceited exegesis, were brought into collision with the law written on the heart. The Bible was used to contradict the moral sense. It was high time for the Quaker protest, and it was inevitable that this protest should be extravagant and violent.

In their bold reassertion of the doctrine of the Holy Spirit, that his light "lighteth every man who cometh into the world," it is not strange that the first Quakers should sometimes have lost sight of those principles the enunciation of which gives such a character of sober sanity to the apostolic teachings on this subject—that a divine influence on the mind does not discharge one from the duty of self-control, but that "the spirits of the prophets are subject to the prophets"; that the divine inworking does not suspend nor supersede man's volition and activity, but that it behooves man to "work, because God worketh in him to will and to work." The lapse from these characteristically Christian principles into the enthusiastic, fanatic, or heathen conception of inspiration has been a perpetually recurring incident in the history of the church in all ages, and especially in times of deep and earnest spiritual feeling. But in the case of the Quaker revival it was attended most conspicuously by its evil consequences. Half-crazy or more than half-crazy adventurers and hysterical women, taking up fantastical missions in the name of the Lord, and never so happy as when they felt called of God to some peculiarly outrageous course of behavior, associated themselves with sincere and conscientious reformers, adding to the unpopularity of the new opinions the odium justly due to their own misdemeanors. But the prophet whose life and preaching had begun the Quaker Reformation was not found wanting in the gifts which the case required. Like other great religious founders, George Fox combined with profound religious conviction a high degree of tact and common sense and the faculty of organization. While the gospel of "the Light that lighteth every man" was speeding with wonderful swiftness to the ends of the earth, there was growing in the hands of the founder the framework of a discipline by which the elements of disorder should be controlled.[114:1] The result was a firmly articulated organization compacted by common faith and zeal and mutual love, and by the external pressure of fierce persecution extending throughout the British empire on both sides of the ocean.

Entering into continental Europe, the Quaker Reformation found itself anticipated in the progress of religious history. The protests of the Anabaptists against what they deemed the shortcomings of the Lutheran Reformation had been attended with far wilder extravagances than those of the early Quakers, and had been repressed with ruthless severity. But the political and militant Anabaptists were succeeded by communities of mild and inoffensive non-resistants, governing themselves by a narrow and rigorous discipline, and differing from the order of Quakers mainly at this point, that whereas the Quakers rejected all sacraments, these insisted strenuously on their own views of Baptism and the Supper, and added to them the ordinance of the Washing of Feet. These communities were to be found throughout Protestant Europe, from the Alps to the North Sea, but were best known in Holland and Lower Germany, where they were called Mennonites, from the priest, Menno Simons, who, a hundred years before George Fox, had enunciated the same principles of duty founded on the strict interpretation of the Sermon on the Mount.

The combination of circumstances to promote the "Holy Experiment" of William Penn is something prodigious. How he could be a petted favorite at the shameful court of the last two Stuarts, while his brethren throughout the realm were languishing under persecution, is a fact not in itself honorable, but capable of being honorably explained; and both the persecution and the court favor helped on his enterprise. The time was opportune; the period of tragical uncertainty in colonization was past; emigration had come to be a richly promising enterprise. For leader of the enterprise what endowment was lacking in the elegantly accomplished young courtier, holding as his own the richest domain that could be carved out of a continent, who was at the same time brother, in unaffected humility and unbounded generosity, in a great fraternity bound together by principles of ascetic self-denial and devotion to the kingdom of God?

Penn's address inviting colonists to his new domain announced the outlines of his scheme. His great powers of jurisdiction were held by him only to be transferred to the future inhabitants in a free and righteous government. "I purpose," said he, conscious of the magnanimity of the intention, "for the matters of liberty, I purpose that which is extraordinary—to leave myself and successors no power of doing mischief, that the will of one man may not hinder the good of a whole country;" and added, in language which might have fallen from his intimate friend, Algernon Sidney, but was fully expressive of his own views, "It is the great end of government to support power in reverence with the people, and to secure the people from the abuse of power; for liberty without obedience is confusion, and obedience without liberty is slavery."[116:1] With assurances of universal civil and religious liberty in conformity with these principles, he offered land at forty shillings for a hundred acres, subject to a small quit-rent.

Through the correspondence of the Friends' meetings, these proposals could be brought to the attention of many thousands of people, sifted and culled by persecution, the best stuff for a colony in all the United Kingdom. The response was immediate. Within a year three ship-loads of emigrants went out. The next year Penn himself went with a company of a hundred, and stayed long enough to see the government organized by the free act of the colonists on the principles which he had set forth, and in that brief sojourn of two years to witness the beginnings of a splendid prosperity. His city of Philadelphia consisted in August, 1683, of three or four little cottages. Two years afterward it contained about six hundred houses, and the schoolmaster and the printing-press had begun their work.[117:1] The growth went on accelerating. In one year seven thousand settlers are said to have arrived; before the end of the century the colonists numbered more than twenty thousand, and Philadelphia had become a thriving town.[117:2]

But Great Britain, although the chief source of population, was not the only source. It had been part of the providential equipment of Penn for his great work to endow him with the gift of tongues and bring him into intimate relations with the many congregations of the broken and persecuted sects kindred to his own on the continent of Europe. The summer and autumn of 1678, four years before his coming to Pennsylvania, had been spent by him, in company with George Fox, Robert Barclay, and other eminent Friends, in a mission tour through Holland (where he preached in his mother's own language) and Germany. The fruit of this preaching and of previous missions appeared in an unexpected form. One of the first important accessions to the colony was the company of Mennonites led by Pastorius, the "Pennsylvania Pilgrim," who founded Germantown, now a beautiful suburb of Philadelphia. Group after group of picturesque devotees that had been driven into seclusion and eccentricity by long and cruel persecution—the Tunkers, the Schwenkfelders, the Amish—kept coming and bringing with them their traditions, their customs, their sacred books, their timid and pathetic disposition to hide by themselves, sometimes in quasi-monastic communities like that at Ephrata, sometimes in actual hermitage, as in the ravines of the Wissahickon. But the most important contribution of this kind came from the suffering villages of the Rhenish Palatinate ravaged with fire and sword by the French armies in 1688. So numerous were the fugitives from the Palatinate that the name of Palatine came to be applied in general to German refugees, from whatever region. This migration of the German sects (to be distinguished from the later migration from the established Lutheran and Reformed churches) furnished the material for that curious "Pennsylvania Dutch" population which for more than two centuries has lain encysted, so to speak, in the body politic and ecclesiastic of Pennsylvania, speaking a barbarous jargon of its own, and refusing to assimilate with the surrounding people.

It was the rough estimate of Dr. Franklin that colonial Pennsylvania was made up of one third Quakers, one third Germans, and one third miscellaneous. The largest item under this last head was the Welsh, most of them Quakers, who had been invited by Penn with the promise of a separate tract of forty thousand acres in which to maintain their own language, government, and institutions. Happily, the natural and patriotic longing of these immigrants for a New Wales on this side the sea was not to be realized. The "Welsh Barony" became soon a mere geographical tradition, and the whole strength of this fervid and religious people enriched the commonwealth.[118:1]

Several notable beginnings of church history belong to the later part of the period under consideration.

An interesting line of divergence from the current teachings of the Friends was led, toward the end of the seventeenth century, by George Keith, for thirty years a recognized preacher of the Society. One is impressed, in a superficial glance at the story, with the reasonableness and wisdom of some of Keith's positions, and with the intellectual vigor of the man. But the discussion grew into an acrimonious controversy, and the controversy deepened into a schism, which culminated in the disowning of Keith by the Friends in America, and afterward by the London Yearly Meeting, to which he had appealed. Dropped thus by his old friends, he was taken up by the English Episcopalians and ordained by the Bishop of London, and in 1702 returned to America as the first missionary of the newly organized Society for the Propagation of the Gospel in Foreign Parts. An active missionary campaign was begun and sustained by the large resources of the Venerable Society until the outbreak of the War of Independence. The movement had great advantages for success. It was next of kin to the expiring Swedish Lutheran Church in the three counties that became afterward the State of Delaware, and heir to its venerable edifices and its good will; it was the official and court church of the royal governors, and after the degenerate sons of William Penn abandoned the simple worship, as well as the clean living, in which their father delighted, it was the church promoted by the proprietary interest; withal it proved itself, both then and afterward, to hold a deposit of truth and of usages of worship peculiarly adapted to supplement the defects of the Quaker system. It is not easy to explain the ill success of the enterprise. In Philadelphia it took strong root, and the building, in 1727, of Christ Church, which survives to this day, a monument of architectural beauty as well as historical interest, marks an important epoch in the progress of Christianity in America. But in the rural districts the work languished. Parishes, seemingly well equipped, fell into a "deplorable condition"; churches were closed and parishes dwindled away. About the year 1724 Governor Keith reported to the Bishop of London that outside the city there were "twelve or thirteen little edifices, at times supplied by one or other of the poor missionaries sent from the society." Nearly all that had been gained by the Episcopal Church in Pennsylvania, where the "Venerable Society" had maintained at times forty-seven missionaries and twenty-four central stations, was wiped out by the Revolutionary War.[120:1]

Another great beginning that comes within the field of vision in the first four decades of the eighteenth century is the planting of the great national churches of Germany. We have observed the migration of the minor sects of Germany—so complete, in some cases, that the entire sect was transplanted, leaving no representative in the fatherland. In the mixed multitude of refugees from the Palatinate and other ravaged provinces were many belonging both to the Lutheran and to the Reformed churches, as well as some Catholics. But they were scattered as sheep having no shepherd. The German Lutheran and Reformed immigration was destined to attain by and by to enormous proportions; but so late was the considerable expansion of it, and so tardy and inefficient the attention given to this diaspora by the mother churches, that the classical organization of the Reformed Church dates only from 1747, and that of the Lutheran Church from 1760.[121:1] The beautiful career of the Moravians began in Pennsylvania so late as 1734. In general it may be said that the German-American church was affected only indirectly by the Great Awakening.

But the greatest in its consequences, both religious and political, of the great beginnings in the early part of the eighteenth century, was the first flow of the swelling tide of the Scotch-Irish immigration. Already, in 1669, an English Presbyterian, Matthew Hill, persuaded to the work by Richard Baxter, was ministering to "many of the Reformed religion" in Maryland; and in 1683 an appeal from them to the Irish presbytery of Laggan had brought over to their aid that sturdy and fearless man of God, Francis Makemie, whose successful defense in 1707, when unlawfully imprisoned in New York by that unsavory defender of the Anglican faith, Lord Cornbury, gave assurance of religious liberty to his communion throughout the colonies. In 1705 he was moderator of the first presbytery in America, numbering six ministers. At the end of twelve years the number of ministers, including accessions from New England, had grown to seventeen. But it was not until 1718 that this migration began in earnest. As early as 1725 James Logan, the Scotch-Irish-Quaker governor of Pennsylvania, speaking in the spirit of prophecy, declares that "it looks as if Ireland were to send all her inhabitants hither; if they continue to come they will make themselves proprietors of the province." It was a broad-spread, rich alluvium superimposed upon earlier strata of immigration, out of which was to spring the sturdy growth of American Presbyterianism, as well as of other Christian organizations. But by 1730 it was only the turbid and feculent flood that was visible to most observers; the healthful and fruitful growth was yet to come.[122:1]

The colony of Georgia makes its appearance among the thirteen British colonies in America, in 1733, as one born out of due time. But no colony of all the thirteen had a more distinctly Christian origin than this. The foundations of other American commonwealths had been laid in faith and hope, but the ruling motive of the founding of Georgia was charity, and that is the greatest of these three. The spirit which dominated in the measures taken for the beginning of the enterprise was embodied in one of the most interesting personages of the dreary eighteenth century—General James Oglethorpe. His eventful life covered the greater part of the eighteenth century, but in some of the leading traits of his character and incidents of his career he was rather a man of the nineteenth. At the age of twenty-one he was already a veteran of the army of Prince Eugene, having served with honorable distinction on the staff of that great commander. Returning to England, in 1722 he entered Parliament, and soon attained what in that age was the almost solitary distinction of a social reformer. He procured the appointment of a special committee to investigate the condition of the debtors' prisons; and the shocking revelations that ensued led to a beginning of reformation of the cruel and barbarous laws of England concerning imprisonment for debt. But being of the higher type of reformers, he was not content with such negative work. He cherished and elaborated a scheme that should open a new career for those whose ill success in life had subjected them to the pains and the ignominy due to criminals. It was primarily for such as these that he projected the colony of Georgia. But to a mind like his the victims of injustice in every land were objects of practical sympathy. His colony should be an asylum for sufferers from religious persecution from whatever quarter. The enterprise was organized avowedly as a work of charity. The territory was vested in trustees, who should receive no pay or emolument for their services. Oglethorpe himself gave his unpaid labor as military and civil head of the colony, declining to receive in return so much as a settler's allotment of land. An appropriation of ten thousand pounds was made by Parliament for the promotion of the work—the only government subsidy ever granted to an American colony. With eager and unselfish hopes of a noble service to be rendered to humanity, the generous soldier embarked with a picked company of one hundred and twenty emigrants, and on the 12th of February, 1733, landed at the foot of the bluff on which now stands the city of Savannah. The attractions of the genial climate and fertile soil, the liberal terms of invitation, and the splendid schemes of profitable industry were diligently advertised, and came to the knowledge of that noble young enthusiast, Zinzendorf, count and Moravian bishop, whose estate of Herrnhut in Lusatia had become an asylum for persecuted Christians; and missionary colonists of that Moravian church of which every member was a missionary, and companies of the exiled Salzburgers, the cruelty of whose sufferings aroused the universal indignation of Protestant Europe, were mingled with the unfortunates from English prisons in successive ship-loads of emigrants. One such ship's company, among the earliest to be added to the new colony, included some mighty factors in the future church history of America and of the world. In February, 1736, a company of three hundred colonists, with Oglethorpe at their head, landed at Savannah. Among them was a reinforcement of twenty colonists for the Moravian settlement, with Bishop David Nitschmann, and young Charles Wesley, secretary to the governor, and his elder brother, John, now thirty-three years old, eager for the work of evangelizing the heathen Indians—an intensely narrow, ascetic, High-church ritualist and sacramentarian. The voyage was a memorable one in history. Amid the terrors of a perilous storm, Wesley, so liable to be lifted up with the pride that apes humility, was humbled as he contrasted the agitations of his own people with the cheerful faith and composure of his German shipmates; and soon after the landing he was touched with the primitive simplicity and beauty of the ordination service with which a pastor was set over the Moravian settlement by Bishop Nitschmann. During the twenty-two months of his service in Georgia, through the ascetic toils and privations which he inflicted on himself and tried to inflict on others, he seems as one whom the law has taken severely in hand to lead him to Christ. It was after his return from America, among the Moravians, first at London and afterward on a visit to Herrnhut, that he was "taught the way of the Lord more perfectly."[125:1]

The three shipmates, the Wesleys and Bishop Nitschmann, did not remain long together. Nitschmann soon returned to Germany to lead a new colony of his brethren to Pennsylvania; Charles Wesley remained for four months at Frederica, and then recrossed the ocean, weary of the hardness of the people's hearts; and, except for the painful and humiliating discipline which was preparing him to "take the whole world to be his parish," it had been well for John Wesley if he had returned with his brother. Never did a really great and good man act more like a fool than he did in his Georgia mission. The priestly arrogance with which he attempted to enforce his crotchets of churchmanship on a mixed community in the edge of the wilderness culminated at last in his hurling the thunderbolts of excommunication at a girl who had jilted him, followed by his slipping away from the colony between two days, with an indictment for defamation on record against him, and his returning to London to resign to the Society for the Propagation of the Gospel his commission as missionary. Just as he was landing, the ship was setting sail which bore to his deserted field his old Oxford friend and associate in "the Methodist Club," George Whitefield, then just beginning the career of meteoric splendor which for thirty-two years dazzled the observers of both hemispheres. He landed in Savannah in May, 1738. This was the first of Whitefield's work in America. But it was not the beginning of the Great Awakening. For many years there had been waiting and longing as of them that watch for the morning. At Raritan and New Brunswick, in New Jersey, and elsewhere, there had been prelusive gleams of dawn. And at Northampton, in December, 1734, Jonathan Edwards had seen the sudden daybreak and rejoiced with exceeding great joy.

CHAPTER X. THE AMERICAN CHURCH ON THE EVE OF THE GREAT AWAKENING—A GENERAL VIEW.

By the end of one hundred years from the settlement of Massachusetts important changes had come upon the chain of colonies along the Atlantic seaboard in America. In the older colonies the people had been born on the soil at two or three generations' remove from the original colonists, or belonged to a later stratum of migration superimposed upon the first. The exhausting toil and privations of the pioneer had been succeeded by a good measure of thrift and comfort. There were yet bloody campaigns to be fought out against the ferocity and craft of savage enemies wielded by the strategy of Christian neighbors; but the severest stress of the Indian wars was passed. In different degrees and according to curiously diverse types, the institutions of a Christian civilization were becoming settled.

In the course of this hundred years the political organization of these various colonies had been drawn into an approach to uniformity. In every one of them, excepting Connecticut and Rhode Island, the royal or proprietary government was represented by a governor and his staff, appointed from England, and furnishing a point of contact which was in every case and all the time a point of friction and irritation between the colony and the mother country. The reckless laxity of the early Stuart charters, which permitted the creation of practically independent democratic republics with churches free from the English hierarchy, was succeeded, under the House of Orange, by something that looked like a statesmanlike care for the prerogatives of the crown and the privileges of the English church. Throughout the colonies, at every viceregal residence, it was understood that this church, even where it was not established by law, was the favored official and court church. But inasmuch as the royal governors were officially odious to the people, and at the same time in many cases men of despicable personal character, their influence did little more than create a little "sect of the Herodians" within the range of their patronage. But though it gave no real advantage to the preferred church, it was effective (as in Massachusetts) in breaking down the exclusive pretensions of other organizations.

The Massachusetts theocracy, so called, fell with the revocation of the charter by James II. It had stood for nearly fifty years—long enough to accomplish the main end of that Nationalist principle which the Puritans, notwithstanding their fraternizing with the Pilgrim Separatists, had never let go. The organization of the church throughout New England, excepting Rhode Island, had gone forward in even step with the advance of population. Two rules had with these colonists the force of axioms: first, that it was the duty of every town, as a Christian community, to sustain the town church; secondly, that it was the duty of every citizen of the town to contribute to this end according to his ability. The breaking up of the town church by schisms and the shirking of individual duty on the ground of dissent were alike discountenanced, sometimes by severely intolerant measures. The ultimate collision of these principles with the sturdy individualism that had been accepted from the Separatists of Plymouth was inevitable. It came when the "standing order" encountered the Baptist and the Quaker conscience. It came again when the missionaries of the English established church, with singular unconsciousness of the humor of the situation, pleaded the sacred right of dissenting and the essential injustice of compelling dissenters to support the parish church.[129:1] The protest may have been illogical, but it was made effective by "arguments of weight," backed by all the force of the British government. The exclusiveness of the New England theocracies, already relaxed in its application to other sects, was thenceforth at an end. The severity of church establishment in New England was so far mitigated as at last to put an actual premium on dissent. Holding still that every citizen is bound to aid in maintaining the institutions of public worship, it relieved any one of his assessment for the support of the parish church upon his filing a certificate that he was contributing to the support of another congregation, thus providing that any disaffection to the church of the town must be organized and active. It was the very euthanasia of establishment. But the state-church and church-state did not cease to be until they had accomplished that for New England which has never been accomplished elsewhere in America—the dividing of the settled regions into definite parishes, each with its church and its learned minister. The democratic autonomy of each church was jealously guarded, and yet they were all knit together by terms of loose confederation into a vital system. The impracticable notion of a threefold ministry in each church, consisting of pastor, teacher, and ruling elder, failed long before the first generation had passed; but, with this exception, it may justly be said that the noble ideal of the Puritan fathers of New England of a Christian state in the New World, "wherein dwelleth righteousness," was, at the end of a hundred years from their planting, realized with a completeness not common to such prophetic dreams.

So solid and vital, at the point of time which we have assumed (1730), seemed the cohesion of the "standing order" in New England, that only two inconsiderable defections are visible to the historian.

The tendency toward Baptist principles early disclosed itself among the colonists. The example of Roger Williams was followed by less notable instances; the shameful intolerance with which some of these were treated shows how formidable this tendency seemed to those in authority. But a more startling defection appeared about the year 1650, when President Dunster of Harvard College, a man most honorable and lovable, signified his adoption of the Baptist tenets. The treatment of him was ungenerous, and for a time the petty persecutions that followed served rather to discredit the clergy than really to hinder the spread of Baptist principles. In the year 1718 the Baptist church of Boston received fraternal recognition from the foremost representatives of the Congregational clergy of Boston, with a public confession of the wrong that they had done.[130:1] It is surprising to find, after all this agitation and sowing of "the seed of the church," that in all New England outside of Rhode Island there are in 1730 only six Baptist churches, including (an honorable item) two Indian churches on the islands of Martha's Vineyard and Nantucket.[131:1]

The other departure from the "standing order" was at this date hardly more extensive. The early planting of Episcopalian churches in Maine and New Hampshire, with generous patronage and endowment, had languished and died. In 1679 there was no Episcopal minister in all New England. In 1702 were begun the energetic and richly supported missions of the "S. P. G." At the end of twenty-eight years there were in Rhode Island four Episcopalian churches; in Massachusetts, three, two of them in the city of Boston; in Connecticut, three.[131:2] But in the last-named colony an incident had occurred, having apparently no intimate connection with the "Venerable Society's" missions, but charged with weighty, and on the whole beneficent, consequences for the future of the kingdom of Christ in America. The incident was strikingly parallel to that of seventy years before, when the president of Harvard College announced his acceptance of Baptist principles. The day after the Yale commencement in September, 1722, a modest and respectful paper was presented to the trustees of the college, signed by Rector Timothy Cutler and Tutor Brown (who constituted the entire faculty of the college) and by five pastors of good standing in the Connecticut churches. Two other pastors of note were named as assenting to the paper, although not subscribing it. It seemed a formidable proportion of the Connecticut clergy. The purport of the paper was to signify that the signers were doubtful of the validity, or persuaded of the invalidity, of presbyterial as distinguished from episcopal ordination. The matter was considered with the gravity which it merited, and a month later, at the time of the meeting of the colonial legislature, was made the subject of a public discussion, presided over with great dignity and amenity by Governor Gurdon Saltonstall, formerly pastor of the church in New London. The result was that, of the seven pastors assenting to the paper of the two college men, only two adhered to them; but one of these two was that able and excellent Samuel Johnson, whose later career as president of King's College in New York, as well as the career of his no less distinguished son, is an ornament to American history both of church and state.

This secession, small in number, but weighty in character, was of course a painful shock to the hitherto unbroken unity of the church and clergy of Connecticut. But it was not quite like a thunderbolt from a clear sky. It had been immediately preceded by not a little conference and correspondence with Connecticut pastors on the one hand, and on the other hand with representatives of the powerful and wealthy Propagation Society, on the question of support to be received from England for those who should secede. Its prior antecedents reached farther back into history. The Baptist convictions of the president of Harvard in 1650 were not more clearly in line with the individualism of the Plymouth Separatists than the scruples of the rector of Yale in 1722 were in line with the Nationalism of Higginson and Winthrop. This sentiment, especially strong in Connecticut, had given rise to much study as to the best form of a colonial church constitution; and the results of this had recently been embodied (in 1708) in the mildly classical system of the Saybrook Platform. The filial love of the Puritan colonists toward the mother church of England was by no means extinct in the third generation. Alongside of the inevitable repugnance felt and manifested toward the arrogance, insolence, and violence with which the claims of the Episcopal Church were commended by royal governors and their attachés and by some of the imported missionaries, there is ample evidence of kindly and fraternal feeling, far beyond what might have been expected, on the part of the New England clergy toward the representatives of the Church of England. The first missionaries of the "Venerable Society," Keith and Talbot, arriving in New England in 1702, met with welcome from some of the ministers, who "both hospitably entertained us in their houses and requested us to preach in their congregations, which accordingly we did, and received great thanks both from the ministers and people."[133:1] One of these hospitable pastors was the Rev. Gurdon Saltonstall, of New London, who twenty years later, as governor of the colony, presided at the debate which followed upon the demission of Rector Cutler. The immediate results of what had been expected to lead off a large defection from the colonial clergy were numerically insignificant; but very far from insignificant was the fact that in Connecticut a sincere and spontaneous movement toward the Episcopal Church had arisen among men honored and beloved, whose ecclesiastical views were not tainted with self-seeking or servility or with an unpatriotic shame for their colonial home and sympathy with its political enemies. Elsewhere in New England, and largely in Connecticut also, the Episcopal Church in its beginnings was handicapped with a dead-weight of supercilious and odious Toryism. The example of a man like Johnson showed that one might become an Episcopalian without ceasing to be a patriotic American and without holding himself aloof from the fellowship of good men. The conference in Yale College library, September 13, 1722, rather than the planting of a system of exotic missions, marks the true epoch from which to date the progress of a genuinely American Episcopal Church.[134:1]

Crossing the recently settled boundary line into New York, not yet risen to rank with the foremost colonies, we find in 1730 a deepening of the early character, which had marked that colony, of wide diversity among the Christian people in point of race, language, doctrinal opinion, and ecclesiastical connection.

The ancient Dutch church, rallying from its almost asphyxia, had begun not only to receive new life, but, under the fervid spiritual influence of Domine Frelinghuysen, to "have it more abundantly" and to become a means of quickening to other communions. It was bearing fruit, but its fruit had not seed within itself after its kind. It continued to suffer, in common with some other imported church systems, from depending on a transatlantic hierarchy for the succession of its ministry. The supply of imported ministers continued to be miserably inadequate to the need. In the first four decades of the century the number of its congregations more than doubled, rising to a total of sixty-five in New York and New Jersey; and for these sixty-five congregations there were nineteen ministers, almost all of them from Europe. This body of churches, so inadequately manned, was still further limited in its activities by the continually contracting barrier of the Dutch language.

The English church, enjoying "the prestige of royal favor and princely munificence," suffered also the drawbacks incidental to these advantages—the odium attending the unjust and despotic measures resorted to for its advancement, the vile character of royal officials, who condoned their private vices by a more ostentatious zeal for their official church, and the well-founded popular suspicion of its pervading disloyalty to the interests and the liberties of the colonies in their antagonism to the encroachments of the British government. It was represented by one congregation in the city of New York, and perhaps a dozen others throughout the colony.[135:1] It is to the honor of the ministers of this church that it succeeded in so good a measure in triumphing over its "advantages." The early pastors of Trinity Church adorned their doctrine and their confession, and one such example as that of the Rev. Thoroughgood Moor did much to redeem the character of the church from the disgrace cast upon it by the lives of its patrons. This faithful missionary had the signal honor of being imprisoned by the dirty but zealous Lord Cornbury (own cousin to her Majesty the Queen, and afterward Earl of Clarendon), of whom he had said, what everybody knew, that he "deserved to be excommunicated"; and he had further offended by refusing the communion to the lieutenant-governor, "upon the account of some debauch and abominable swearing."[135:2] There was surely some vigorous spiritual vitality in a religious body which could survive the patronizing of a succession of such creatures as Cornbury and his crew of extortioners and profligates.

A third element in the early Christianity of New York was the Presbyterians. These were represented, at the opening of the eighteenth century, by that forerunner of the Scotch-Irish immigration, Francis Makemie. The arrest and imprisonment of Makemie in 1706, under the authority of Lord Cornbury, for the offense of preaching the gospel without a license from the government, his sturdy defense and his acquittal, make an epoch in the history of religious liberty in America, and a perceptible step in the direction of American political liberty and independence.

The immense volume and strength of the Scotch-Irish immigration had hardly begun to be perceptible in New York as early as 1730. The total strength of the Presbyterian Church in 1705 was organized in Philadelphia into a solitary presbytery containing six ministers. In 1717, the number having grown to seventeen, the one presbytery was divided into four, which constituted a synod; and one of the four was the presbytery of New York and New Jersey. But it was observed, at least it might have been observed, that the growing Presbyterianism of this northernmost region was recruited mainly from old England and from New England—a fact on which were to depend important consequences in later ecclesiastical history.

The chief increment of the presbytery of New York and New Jersey was in three parts, each of them planted from New England. The churches founded from New Haven Colony in the neighborhood of Newark and Elizabethtown, and the churches founded by Connecticut settlers on Long Island when this was included in the jurisdiction of Connecticut, easily and without serious objection conformed their organization to the Presbyterian order. The first wave of the perennial westward migration of the New Englanders, as it flowed over the hills from the valley of the Housatonic into the valley of the Hudson, was observed by Domine Selyns, away back in 1696, to be attended by many preachers educated at Harvard College.[137:1] But the churches which they founded grew into the type, not of Cambridge nor of Saybrook, but of Westminster.

The facility with which the New England Christians, moving westward or southwestward from their cold northeastern corner of the country, have commonly consented to forego their cherished usages and traditions of church order and accept those in use in their new homes, and especially their readiness in conforming to the Presbyterian polity, has been a subject of undue lamentation and regret to many who have lacked the faculty of recognizing in it one of the highest honors of the New England church. But whether approved or condemned, a fact so unusual in church history, and especially in the history of the American church, is entitled to some study. 1. It is to be explained in part, but not altogether, by the high motive of a willingness to sacrifice personal preferences, habits, and convictions of judgment, on matters not of primary importance, to the greater general good of the community. 2. The Presbyterian polity is the logical expression of that Nationalist principle which was cherished by many of the Puritan fathers, which contended at the birth of New England with the mere Independency of the Pilgrims, and which found an imperfect embodiment in the platforms of Cambridge and Saybrook. The New England fathers in general, before their views suffered a sea-change in the course of their migrations, were Episcopalians and Presbyterians rather than Congregationalists; and if, in the course of this history, we shall find many in their later generations conforming to a mitigated form of the Westminster polity, or to a liberalized and Americanized Episcopal Church, instead of finding this to be a degeneration, we shall do well to ask whether it is not rather a reversion to type. 3. Those who grow up in a solidly united Christian community are in a fair way to be trained in the simplicity of the gospel, and not in any specialties of controversy with contending or competing sects. Members of the parish churches of New England going west had an advantage above most others, in that they could go simply as representatives of the church of Christ, and not of a sect of the church, or of one side of some controversy in which they had never had occasion to interest themselves. 4. The principle of congregational independency, not so much inculcated as acted on in New England, carries with it the corollary that a congregation may be Presbyterian or Episcopalian or Methodist, if it judges best, without thereby giving the individual Christian any justification for secession or schism. 5. The change, in the westward movement of Christian civilization, from the congregational order to the classical, coincides with the change in the frame of civil polity from town government to county government. In the beginning the civil state in New England was framed after the model of the church.[138:1] It is in accordance with the common course of church history that when the people were transported from the midst of pure democracies to the midst of representative republics their church institutions should take on the character of the environment.

The other factors of the religious life of New York require only brief mention.

There were considerable Quaker communities, especially on western Long Island, in Flushing and its neighborhood. But before the year 1730 the fervid and violent and wonderfully brief early enthusiasm of this Society had long been waning, and the Society, winning no accessions and suffering frequent losses in its membership, was lapsing into that "middle age of Quakerism"[139:1] in which it made itself felt in the life of the people through its almost passive, but yet effective, protests against popular wrongs.

Inconsiderable in number, but of the noblest quality, was the immigration of French Huguenots, which just before and just after the revocation of the Edict of Nantes brought to New York and its neighborhood a half-dozen congregations, accompanied by pastors whose learning, piety, and devotion to the work of Christ were worthy of that school of martyrdom in which they had been trained. They were not numerous enough, nor compactly enough settled, to maintain their own language in use, and soon became merged, some in the Dutch church and some in the English. Some of their leading pastors accepted salaries from the Propagation Society, tendered to them on condition of their accepting the ordination and conforming to the ritual of the English church. The French Reformed Church does not appear organically in the later history of the colony, but the history of the State and of the nation is never largely written without commemorating, by the record of family names made illustrious in every department of honorable activity, the rich contribution made to the American church and nation by the cruel bigotry and the political fatuity of Louis XIV.[139:2]

The German element in the religious life of New York, at the period under consideration, was of even less historical importance. The political philanthropy of Queen Anne's government, with a distinct understanding between the right hand and the left, took active measure to promote the migration of Protestant refugees from all parts of Germany to the English colonies in America. In the year 1709 a great company of these unhappy exiles, commonly called "poor Palatines" from the desolated region whence many of them had been driven out, were dropped, helpless and friendless, in the wilderness of Schoharie County, and found themselves there practically in a state of slavery through their ignorance of the country and its language. There were few to care for their souls. The Society for the Propagation of the Gospel was promptly in the field, with its diligent missionaries and its ignoble policy of doing the work of Christ and humanity with a shrewd eye to the main chance of making proselytes to its party.[140:1] With a tardiness which it is difficult not to speak of as characteristic, after the lapse of twenty-one years the classis of Amsterdam recognized its responsibility for this multitude of wandering sheep; and at last, in 1793, the German Reformed Church had so far emancipated itself from its bondage to the old-country hierarchy as to assume, almost a century too late, the cure of these poor souls. But this migration added little to the religious life of the New York Colony, except a new element of diversity to a people already sufficiently heterogeneous. The greater part of these few thousands gladly found their way to the more hospitable colony of Pennsylvania, leaving traces of themselves in family names scattered here and there, and in certain local names, like that of Palatine Bridge.

The general impression left on the mind by this survey of the Christian people of New York in 1730 is of a mass of almost hopelessly incongruous materials, out of which the brooding Spirit of God shall by and by bring forth the unity of a new creation.

The population of the two Jerseys continued to bear the character impressed on it by the original colonization. West Jersey was predominantly Quaker; East Jersey showed in its institutions of church and school the marks made upon it by the mingling of Scotch and Yankee. But there was one point at which influences had centered which were to make New Jersey the seed-plot of a new growth of church life for the continent.

The intolerable tyranny of Lord Cornbury in New York, at the beginning of the century, had driven many of the Dutch Christians of that colony across the Hudson. The languishing vine throve by transplanting. In the congenial neighborhood of the Calvinists of Scotland and New England the cluster of churches in the region of New Brunswick came to be known as "the garden of the Dutch church." To this region, bearing a name destined to great honor in American church history, came from Holland, in 1720, Domine Theodore J. Frelinghuysen. The fervor and earnestness of his preaching, unwonted in that age, wakened a religious feeling in his own congregation, which overflowed the limits of a single parish and became as one of the streams that make glad the city of God.

In the year 1718 there arrived at the port of Philadelphia an Irishman, William Tennent, with his four sons, the eldest a boy of fifteen. He was not a Scotch-Irishman, but an English-Irishman—a clergyman of the established Protestant Episcopal Church of Ireland. He lost no time in connecting himself with the Presbyterian synod of Philadelphia, and after a few years of pastoral service in the colony of New York became pastor of the Presbyterian church at Neshaminy, in Pennsylvania, twenty miles north of Philadelphia. Here his zeal for Christian education moved him to begin a school, which, called from the humble building in which it was held, became famous in American Presbyterian history as the Log College. Here were educated many men who became eminent in the ministry of the gospel, and among them the four boys who had come with their father from Ireland. Gilbert, the eldest and most distinguished of them, came in 1727, from his temporary position as tutor in the Log College, to be pastor to the Presbyterian church in New Brunswick, where Frelinghuysen, in the face of opposition from his own brethren in the ministry, had for seven years pursued his deeply spiritual and fruitful work as pastor to the Dutch church. Whatever debate there may be over the question of an official and tactual succession in the church, the existence of a vital and spiritual succession, binding "the generations each to each," need not be disputed by any. Sometimes, as here, the succession is distinctly traceable. Gilbert Tennent was own son in the ministry to Theodore Frelinghuysen as truly as Timothy to Paul, but he became spiritual father to a great multitude.

In the year 1730 the total population of Pennsylvania was estimated by Governor Gordon at forty-nine thousand. In the less than fifty years since the colony was settled it had outstripped all the older colonies, and Philadelphia, its chief town, continued to be by far the most important port for the landing of immigrants. The original Quaker influence was still dominant in the colony, but the very large majority of the population was German; and presently the Quakers were to find their political supremacy departing, and were to acquiesce in the change by abdicating political preferment.[143:1] The religious influence of the Society of Friends continued to be potent and in many respects most salutary. But the exceptional growth and prosperity of the colony was attended with a vast "unearned increment" of wealth to the first settlers, and the maxim, "Religio peperit divitias, et mater devorata est a prole,"[143:2] received one of the most striking illustrations in all history. So speedily the Society had entered on its Middle Age;[143:3] the most violent of protests against formalism had begun to congeal into a precise and sometimes frivolous system of formalities. But the lasting impress made on the legislation of the colony by Penn and his contemporaries is a monument of their wise and Christian statesmanship. Up to their time the most humane penal codes in Christendom were those of New England, founded on the Mosaic law. But even in these, and still more in the application of them, there were traces of that widely prevalent feeling that punishment is society's bitter and malignant revenge on the criminal. The penal code and the prison discipline of Pennsylvania became an object of admiring study for social reformers the world over, and marked a long stage in the advancement of the kingdom of God. The city of Philadelphia early took the lead of American towns, not only in size, but in its public charities and its cultivation of humane arts.

Notwithstanding these eminent honors, there is much in the later history of the great commonwealth in which Quakerism held dominion for the greater part of a century to reflect doubt on the fitness of that form of Christianity for conducting the affairs, either civil or religious, of a great community.

There is nothing in the personal duty of non-resistance of evil, as inculcated in the New Testament, that conflicts with the functions of the civil governor—even the function of bearing the sword as God's minister. Rather, each of these is the complement and counterpart of the other. Among the early colonial governors no man wielded the sword of the ruler more effectively than the Quaker Archdale in the Carolinas. It is when this law of personal duty is assumed as the principle of public government that the order of society is inverted, and the function of the magistrate is inevitably taken up by the individual, and the old wilderness law of blood-revenge is reinstituted. The legislation of William Penn involved no abdication of the power of the sword by the civil governor. The enactment, however sparing, of capital laws conceded by implication every point that is claimed by Christian moralists in justification of war. But it is hardly to be doubted that the tendency of Quaker politics so to conduct civil government as that it shall "resist not evil" is responsible for some of the strange paradoxes in the later history of Pennsylvania. The commonwealth was founded in good faith on principles of mutual good will with the Indians and tender regard for Indian rights, of religious liberty and interconfessional amity, and of a permanent peace policy. Its history has been characterized, beyond that of other States, by foul play toward the Indians and protracted Indian wars, by acrimonious and sometimes bloody sectarian conflicts, by obstinate insurrections against public order,[144:1] and by cruel and exterminating war upon honest settlers, founded on a mere open question of title to territory.[144:2]

The failure of Quakerism is even more conspicuous considered as a church discipline. There is a charm as of apostolic simplicity and beauty in its unassuming hierarchy of weekly, monthly, quarterly, and yearly meetings, corresponding by epistles and by the visits of traveling evangelists, which realizes the type of the primitive church presented in "The Teaching of the Twelve Apostles." But it was never able to outgrow, in the large and free field to which it was transplanted, the defects incident to its origin in a protest and a schism. It never learned to commend itself to men as a church for all Christians, and never ceased to be, even in its own consciousness, a coterie of specialists. Penn, to be sure, in his youthful overzeal, had claimed exclusive and universal rights for Quakerism as "the alone good way of life and salvation," all religions, faiths, and worships besides being "in the darkness of apostasy."[145:1] But after the abatement of that wonderful first fervor which within a lifetime carried "its line into all the earth, and its words to the ends of the world," it was impossible to hold it to this pitch. Claiming no divine right to all men's allegiance, it felt no duty of opening the door to all men's access. It was free to exclude from the meeting on arbitrary and even on frivolous grounds. As zeal decayed, the energies of the Society were mainly shown in protesting and excluding and expelling. God's husbandry does not prosper when his servants are over-earnest in rooting up tares. The course of the Society of Friends in the eighteenth century was suicidal. It held a noble opportunity of acting as pastor to a great commonwealth. It missed this great opportunity, for which it was perhaps constitutionally disqualified, and devoted itself to edifying its own members and guarding its own purity. So it was that, saving its soul, it lost it. The vineyard must be taken away from it.

And there were no other husbandmen to take the vineyard. The petty German sects, representing so large a part of the population, were isolated by their language and habits. The Lutherans and the Reformed, trained in established churches to the methods and responsibilities of parish work, were not yet represented by any organization. The Scotch-Irish Presbyterian immigration was pouring in at Philadelphia like a flood, sometimes whole parishes at once, each bringing its own pastor; and it left large traces of itself in the eastern counties of Pennsylvania, while it rushed to the western frontier and poured itself like a freshet southwesterly through the valleys of the Blue Ridge and the Alleghanies. But the Presbyterian churches of eastern Pennsylvania, even as reinforced from England and New England, were neither many nor strong; the Baptists were feebler yet, although both these bodies were giving signs of the strength they were both about to develop.[147:1] The Episcopalians had one strong and rapidly growing church in Philadelphia, and a few languishing missions in country towns sustained by gifts from England. There were as yet no Methodists.

Crossing the boundary line from Pennsylvania into Maryland—the line destined to become famous in political history as Mason and Dixon's—we come to the four Southern colonies, Maryland, Virginia, and the two Carolinas. Georgia in 1730 has not yet begun to be. All these have strongly marked characteristics in common, which determine in advance the character of their religious history. They are not peculiar in being slave colonies; there is no colony North or South in which slaves are not held under sanction of law. Georgia, in its early years, is to have the solitary honor of being an antislavery and prohibitionist colony. But the four earlier Southern colonies are unlike their Northern neighbors in this, that the institution of slavery dominates their whole social life. The unit of the social organism is not the town, for there are no towns; it is the plantation. In a population thus dispersed over vast tracts of territory, schools and churches are maintained with difficulty, or not maintained at all. Systems of primary and secondary schools are impracticable, and, for want of these, institutions of higher education either languish or are never begun. A consequent tendency, which, happily, there were many influences to resist, was for this townless population to settle down into the condition of those who, in distinction from the early Christians, came to be called pagani, or "men of the hamlets," and Heiden, or "men of the heath."

Another common characteristic of the four Southern colonies is that upon them all was imposed by foreign power a church establishment not acceptable to the people. In the Carolinas the attempted establishment of the English church was an absolute failure. It was a church (with slight exceptions) without parishes, without services, without clergy, without people, but with certain pretensions in law which were hindrances in the way of other Christian work, and which tended to make itself generally odious. In the two older colonies the Established Church was worse than a failure. It had endowments, parsonages, glebes, salaries raised by public tax, and therefore it had a clergy—and such a clergy! Transferring to America the most shameful faults of the English Establishment, it gave the sacred offices of the Christian ministry by "patronage" into the hands of debauched and corrupt adventurers, whose character in general was below the not very lofty standard of the people whom they pretended to serve in the name of Jesus Christ. Both in Virginia and in Maryland the infliction of this rabble of simonists as a burden upon the public treasury was a nuisance under which the people grew more and more restive from year to year. There was no spiritual discipline to which this prêtraille was amenable.[148:1] It was the constant effort of good citizens, in the legislature and in the vestries, if not to starve out the vermin, at least to hold them in some sort of subjection to the power of the purse. The struggle was one of the antecedents of the War of Independence, and the vestries of the Virginia parishes, with their combined ecclesiastical and civil functions, became a training-school for some of the statesmen of the Revolution.

In the general dereliction of churchly care for the people of the Southern colonies, on the part of those who professed the main responsibility for it, the duty was undertaken, in the face of legal hindrances, by earnest Christians of various names, whom the established clergy vainly affected to despise. The Baptists and the Presbyterians, soon to be so powerfully prevalent throughout the South, were represented by a few scattered congregations. But the church of the people of the South at this period seems to have been the Quaker meeting, and the ministry the occasional missionary who, bearing credentials from some yearly meeting, followed in the pioneer footsteps of George Fox, and went from one circle of Friends to another, through those vast expanses of thinly settled territory, to revive and confirm and edify. The early fervors of the Society were soon spent. Its work was strangely unstable. The proved defects of it as a working system were grave. The criticism of George Keith seems justified by the event—its candle needed a candlestick. But no man can truly write the history of the church of Christ in the United States without giving honor to the body which for so long a time and over so vast an area bore the name and testimony of Jesus almost alone; and no man can read the journeys and labors of John Woolman, mystic and ascetic saint, without recognizing that he and others like-minded were nothing less than true apostles of the Lord Jesus.

One impression made by this general survey of the colonies is that of the absence of any sign of unity among the various Christian bodies in occupation. One corner of the great domain, New England, was thickly planted with homogeneous churches in mutual fellowship. One order of Christians, the Quakers, had at least a framework of organization conterminous with the country. In general there were only scattered members of a Christian community, awaiting the inbreathing of some quickening spiritual influence that should bring bone to its bone and erect the whole into a living church.

Another and very gratifying impression from the story thus far is the general fidelity of the Christian colonists in the work of the gospel among the heathen Indians. There was none of the colonies that did not make profession of a zealous purpose for the Christianizing of the savages; and it is only just to say, in the face of much unjust and evil talk, that there was none that did not give proof of its sincerity. In Virginia, the Puritans Whitaker and Thomas Dale; in Maryland, the earliest companies of Jesuit missionaries; Campanius among the Swedish Lutherans; Megapolensis among the Dutchmen, and the Jesuit martyr Jogues in the forests of New York; in New England, not only John Eliot and Roger Williams and the Mayhews, but many a village pastor like Fitch of Norwich and Pierson of Branford, were distinguished in the first generation by their devotion to this duty.[150:1] The succession of faithful missionaries has never failed from that day to this. The large expectations of the churches are indicated by the erection of one of the earliest buildings at Harvard College for the use of Indian students. At William and Mary College not less than seventy Indian students at one time are said to have been gathered for an advanced education. It was no fault of the colonial churches that these earnest and persistent efforts yielded small results. "We discover a strange uniformity of feature in the successive failures.... Always, just when the project seemed most hopeful, an indiscriminate massacre of missionaries and converts together swept the enterprise out of existence. The experience of all was the same."[151:1]

It will be a matter of growing interest, as we proceed, to trace the relation of the American church to negro slavery.

It is a curious fact, not without some later analogies, that the introduction into the New World of this "direful spring of woes unnumbered" was promoted, in the first instance, by the good Las Casas, as the hopeful preventive of a worse evil. Touched by the spectacle of whole tribes and nations of the Indians perishing under the cruel servitude imposed upon them by the Spanish, it seemed to him a less wrong to transfer the infliction of this injustice to shoulders more able to bear it. But "man's inhumanity to man" needed no pretext of philanthropy. From the landing of the Dutch ship at Jamestown in 1619, with her small invoice of fourteen negroes, the dismal trade went on increasing, in spite of humane protest and attempted prohibition. The legislature of Massachusetts, which was the representative of the church, set forth what it conceived to be the biblical ethics on the subject. Recognizing that "lawful captives taken in just wars" may be held in bondage, it declared among its earliest public acts, in 1641, that, with this exception, no involuntary bond-slavery, villeinage, or captivity should ever be in the colony; and in 1646 it took measures for returning to Africa negroes who had been kidnapped by a slaver. It is not strange that reflection on the golden rule should soon raise doubts whether the precedents of the Book of Joshua had equal authority with the law of Christ. In 1675 John Eliot, from the midst of his work among the Indians, warned the governor against the sale of Indians taken in war, on the ground that "the selling of souls is dangerous merchandise," and "with a bleeding and burning passion" remonstrated against "the abject condition of the enslaved Africans." In 1700 that typical Puritan, Judge Samuel Sewall, published his pamphlet on "The Selling of Joseph," claiming for the negroes the rights of brethren, and predicting that there would be "no progress in gospeling" until slavery should be abolished. Those were serious days of antislavery agitation, when Cotton Mather, in his "Essays to Do Good," spoke of the injustice of slavery in terms such that his little book had to be expurgated by the American Tract Society to accommodate it to the degenerate conscience of a later day, and when the town of Boston in 1701 took measures "to put a period to negroes being slaves." Such endeavors after universal justice and freedom, on the part of the Christians of New England, thwarted by the insatiable greed of British traders and politicians, were not to cease until, with the first enlargement of independence, they should bring forth judgment to victory.

The voice of New England was echoed from Pennsylvania. The Mennonites of Germantown, in 1688, framed in quaint and touching language their petition for the abolition of slavery, and the Quaker yearly meetings responded one to another with unanimous protest. But the mischief grew and grew. In the Northern colonies the growth was stunted by the climate. Elsewhere the institution, beginning with the domestic service of a few bondmen attached to their masters' families, took on a new type of malignity as it expanded. In proportion as the servile population increases to such numbers as to be formidable, laws of increasing severity are directed to restraining or repressing it. The first symptoms of insurrection are followed by horrors of bloody vengeance, and "from that time forth the slave laws have but one quality— that of ferocity engendered by fear."[153:1] It was not from the willful inhumanity of the Southern colonies, but from their terrors, that those slave codes came forth which for nearly two centuries were the shame of America and the scandal of Christendom. It is a comfort to the heart of humanity to reflect that the people were better than their laws; it was only at the recurring periods of fear of insurrection that they were worse. In ordinary times human sympathy and Christian principle softened the rigors of the situation. The first practical fruits of the revival of religion in the Southern colonies were seen in efforts of Christian kindness toward the souls and bodies of the slaves.

CHAPTER XI. THE GREAT AWAKENING

It was not wholly dark in American Christendom before the dawn of the Great Awakening. The censoriousness which was the besetting sin of the evangelists in that great religious movement, the rhetorical temptation to glorify the revival by intensifying the contrast with the antecedent condition, and the exaggerated revivalism ever since so prevalent in the American church,—the tendency to consider religion as consisting mainly in scenes and periods of special fervor, and the intervals between as so much void space and waste time,—all these have combined to deepen the dark tints in which the former state is set before us in history.

The power of godliness was manifest in the earlier days by many infallible signs, not excluding those "times of refreshing" in which the simultaneous earnestness of many souls compels the general attention. Even in Northampton, where the doctrine of the venerable Stoddard as to the conditions of communion has been thought to be the low-water mark of church vitality, not less than five such "harvest seasons" were within recent memory. It was to this parish in a country town on the frontier of civilization, but the most important in Massachusetts outside of Boston, that there came, in the year 1727, to serve as colleague to his aged grandfather, Pastor Stoddard, a young man whose wonderful intellectual and spiritual gifts had from his childhood awakened the pious hopes of all who had known him, and who was destined in his future career to be recognized as the most illustrious of the saints and doctors of the American church. The authentic facts of the boyhood of Jonathan Edwards read like the myths that adorn the legendary Lives of the Saints. As an undergraduate of Yale College, before the age of seventeen, his reflections on the mysteries of God, and the universe, and the human mind, were such as even yet command the attention and respect of students of philosophy. He remained at New Haven two years after graduation, for the further study of theology, and then spent eight months in charge of the newly organized Presbyterian church in New York.[156:1] After this he spent two years as tutor at Yale,—"one of the pillar tutors, and the glory of the college,"—at the critical period after the defection of Rector Cutler to the Church of England.[156:2] From this position he was called in 1726, at the age of twenty-three, to the church at Northampton. There he was ordained February 15, 1727, and thither a few months later he brought his "espousèd saint," Sarah Pierpont, consummate flower of Puritan womanhood, thenceforth the companion not only of his pastoral cares and sorrows, but of his seraphic contemplations of divine things.

The intensely earnest sermons, the holy life, and the loving prayers of one of the greatest preachers in the history of the church were not long in bearing abundant fruit. In a time of spiritual and moral depression, when the world, the flesh, and the devil seemed to be gaining against the gospel, sometime in the year 1733 signs began to be visible of yielding to the power of God's Word. The frivolous or wanton frolics of the youth began to be exchanged for meetings for religious conference. The pastor was encouraged to renewed tenderness and solemnity in his preaching. His themes were justification by faith, the awfulness of God's justice, the excellency of Christ, the duty of pressing into the kingdom of God. Presently a young woman, a leader in the village gayeties, became "serious, giving evidence," even to the severe judgment of Edwards, "of a heart truly broken and sanctified." A general seriousness began to spread over the whole town. Hardly a single person, old or young, but felt concerned about eternal things. According to Edwards's "Narrative":

"The work of God, as it was carried on, and the number of true saints multiplied, soon made a glorious alteration in the town, so that in the spring and summer, anno 1735, the town seemed to be full of the presence of God. It was never so full of love, nor so full of joy, and yet so full of distress, as it was then. There were remarkable tokens of God's presence in almost every house. It was a time of joy in families on the account of salvation's being brought unto them; parents rejoicing over their children as being new-born, and husbands over their wives, and wives over their husbands. The goings of God were then seen in his sanctuary. God's day was a delight, and his tabernacles were amiable. Our public assemblies were then beautiful; the congregation was alive in God's service, every one intent on the public worship, every hearer eager to drink in the words of the minister as they came from his mouth; the assembly in general were from time to time in tears while the Word was preached, some weeping with sorrow and distress, others with joy and love, others with pity and concern for the souls of their neighbors. Our public praises were then greatly enlivened; God was then served in our psalmody in some measure in the beauty of holiness."

The crucial test of the divineness of the work was given when the people presented themselves before the Lord with a solemn act of thanksgiving for his great goodness and his gracious presence in the town of Northampton, with publicly recorded vows to renounce their evil ways and put away their abominations from before his eyes. They solemnly promise thenceforth, in all dealings with their neighbor, to be governed by the rules of honesty, justice, and uprightness; not to overreach or defraud him, nor anywise to injure him, whether willfully or through want of care; to regard not only their own interest, but his; particularly, to be faithful in the payment of just debts; in the case of past wrongs against any, never to rest till they have made full reparation; to refrain from evil speaking, and from everything that feeds a spirit of bitterness; to do nothing in a spirit of revenge; not to be led by private or partisan interest into any course hurtful to the interests of Christ's kingdom; particularly, in public affairs, not to allow ambition or partisanship to lead them counter to the interest of true religion. Those who are young promise to allow themselves in no diversions that would hinder a devout spirit, and to avoid everything that tends to lasciviousness, and which will not be approved by the infinitely pure and holy eye of God. Finally, they consecrate themselves watchfully to perform the relative duties of parents and children, husbands and wives, brothers and sisters, masters, mistresses, and servants.

So great a work as this could not be hid. The whole region of the Connecticut Valley, in Massachusetts and Connecticut, and neighboring regions felt the influence of it. The fame of it went abroad. A letter of Edwards's in reply to inquiries from his friend, Dr. Colman, of Boston, was forwarded to Dr. Watts and Dr. Guise, of London, and by them published under the title of "Narrative of Surprising Conversions." A copy of the little book was carried in his pocket for wayside reading on a walk from London to Oxford by John Wesley, in the year 1738. Not yet in the course of his work had he "seen it on this fashion," and he writes in his journal: "Surely this is the Lord's doing, and it is marvelous in our eyes."

Both in this narrative and in a later work on "The Distinguishing Marks of a Work of the Spirit of God," one cannot but admire the divine gift of a calm wisdom with which Edwards had been endowed as if for this exigency. He is never dazzled by the incidents of the work, nor distracted by them from the essence of it. His argument for the divineness of the work is not founded on the unusual or extraordinary character of it, nor on the impressive bodily effects sometimes attending it, such as tears, groans, outcries, convulsions, or faintings, nor on visions or ecstasies or "impressions." What he claims is that the work may be divine, notwithstanding the presence of these incidents.[159:1] It was doubtless owing to the firm and judicious guidance of such a pastor that the intense religious fervor of this first awakening at Northampton was marked by so much of sobriety and order. In later years, in other regions, and under the influence of preachers not of greater earnestness, but of less wisdom and discretion, there were habitual scenes of extravagant and senseless enthusiasm, which make the closing pages of this chapter of church history painfully instructive.

It is not difficult to understand how one of the first places at a distance to feel the kindling example of Northampton should be the neighborhood of Newark. To this region, planted, as we have seen, with so strong a stock from New England, from old England, and from Scotland, came, in 1708, a youth of twenty years, Jonathan Dickinson, a native of the historic little town of Hatfield, next neighbor to Northampton. He was pastor at Elizabeth, but his influence and activity extended through all that part of New Jersey, and he became easily the leader of the rapidly growing communion of Presbyterian churches in that province, and the opponent, in the interest of Christian liberty and sincerity, of rigid terms of subscription, demanded by men of little faith. There is a great career before him; but that which concerns the present topic is his account of what took place "sometime in August, 1739 (the summer before Mr. Whitefield came first into these parts), when there was a remarkable revival at Newark.... This revival of religion was chiefly observable among the younger people, till the following March, when the whole town in general was brought under an uncommon concern about their eternal interests, and the congregation appeared universally affected under some sermons that were then preached to them."

Like scenes of spiritual quickening were witnessed that same season in other parts of New Jersey; but special interest attaches to the report from New Londonderry, Penn., where a

Scotch-Irish community received as its pastor, in the spring of 1740, Samuel Blair, a native of Ireland, trained in the Log College of William Tennent. He describes the people, at his first knowledge of them, as sunk in a religious torpor, ignorance, and indifference. The first sign of vitality was observed in March, 1740, during the pastor's absence, when, under an alarming sermon from a neighbor minister:

"There was a visible appearance of much soul-concern among the hearers; so that some burst out with an audible noise into bitter crying, a thing not known in these parts before.... The first sermon I preached after my return to them was from Matthew vi. 33: 'Seek ye first the kingdom of God, and his righteousness.' After opening up and explaining the parts of the text, when in the improvement I came to press the injunction in the text upon the unconverted and ungodly, and offered this as one reason among others why they should now first of all seek the kingdom and righteousness of God, viz., that they had neglected too long to do so already, this consideration seemed to come and cut like a sword upon several in the congregation; so that while I was speaking upon it they could no longer contain, but burst out in the most bitter mourning. I desired them as much as possible to restrain themselves from making any noise that would hinder themselves or others from hearing what was spoken; and often afterward I had occasion to repeat the same counsel. I still advised people to endeavor to moderate and bound their passions, but not so as to resist and stifle their convictions. The number of the awakened increased very fast. Frequently under sermons there were some newly convicted and brought into deep distress of soul about their perishing estate. Our Sabbath assemblies soon became vastly large, many people from almost all parts around inclining very much to come where there was such appearance of the divine power and presence. I think there was scarcely a sermon or lecture preached here through that whole summer but there were manifest evidences of impressions on the hearers, and many times the impressions were very great and general. Several would be overcome and fainting; others deeply sobbing, hardly able to contain; others crying in a most dolorous manner; many others more silently weeping, and a solemn concern appearing in the countenances of many others. And sometimes the soul-exercises of some (though comparatively but very few) would so far affect their bodies as to occasion some strange, unusual bodily motions. I had opportunities of speaking particularly with a great many of those who afforded such outward tokens of inward soul-concern in the time of public worship and hearing of the Word. Indeed, many came to me of themselves, in their distress, for private instruction and counsel; and I found, so far as I can remember, that with by far the greater part their apparent concern in public was not just a transient qualm of conscience or merely a floating commotion of the affections, but a rational, fixed conviction of their dangerous, perishing estate....

"In some time many of the convinced and distressed afforded very hopeful, satisfying evidence that the Lord had brought them to true closure with Jesus Christ, and that their distresses and fears had been in a great measure removed in a right gospel way, by believing in the Son of God. Several of them had very remarkable and sweet deliverances this way. It was very agreeable to hear their accounts how that when they were in the deepest perplexity and darkness, distress and difficulty, seeking God as poor, condemned, hell-deserving sinners, the scene of recovering grace through a Redeemer has been opened to their understandings with a surprising beauty and glory, so that they were enabled to believe in Christ with joy unspeakable and full of glory."[162:1]

The experience of Gilbert Tennent at New Brunswick had no connection with the first awakening at Northampton, but had important relations with later events. He was the eldest of the four sons whom William Tennent, the Episcopalian minister from Ireland, had brought with him to America and educated at his Log College. In 1727 he became pastor of a church at New Brunswick, where he was much impressed with what he saw of the results of the work of the Rev. Theodore Frelinghuysen, who for seven years had been pastor of a neighboring Dutch church. The example and fraternal counsel of this good man made him sensible of the fruitlessness of his own work, and moved him to more earnest prayers and labors. Having been brought low with sickness, he prayed to God to grant him one half-year more in which to "endeavor to promote his kingdom with all my might at all adventures." Being raised up from sickness, he devoted himself to earnest personal labors with individuals and to renewed faithfulness in the pulpit, "which method was sealed by the Holy Spirit in the conviction and conversion of a considerable number of persons, at various times and in different places, in that part of the country, as appeared by their acquaintance with experimental religion and good conversation." This bit of pastoral history, in which is nothing startling or prodigious, was at least five years previous to the "Surprising Conversions" at Northampton. There must have been generally throughout the country a preparedness for the Great Awakening.

It was in that year (1735) in which the town of Northampton was all ablaze with the glory of its first revival under Edwards that George Whitefield, first among the members of Wesley's "Holy Club" at Oxford, attained to that "sense of the divine love" from which he was wont to date his conversion. In May, 1738, when the last reflections from the Northampton revival had faded out from all around the horizon, the young clergyman, whose first efforts as a preacher in pulpits of the Church of England had astonished all hearers by the power of his eloquence, arrived at Savannah, urged by the importunity of the Wesleys to take up the work in Georgia in which they had so conspicuously failed. He entered eagerly into the sanguine schemes for the advantage of the young colony, and especially into the scheme for building and endowing an orphan-house in just that corner of the earth where there was less need of such an institution than anywhere else. After three months' stay he started on his return to England to seek priest's orders for himself, and funds for the orphans that might be expected sometime in Georgia. He was successful in both his errands. He was ordained; he collected more than one thousand pounds for the orphan-house; and being detained in the kingdom by an embargo, he began that course of evangelistic preaching which continued on either side of the ocean until his death, and which is without a parallel in church history. His incomparable eloquence thronged the parish churches, until the churches were closed against him, and the Bishop of London warned the people against him in a pastoral letter. Then he went out into the open fields, in the service, as he said, of him "who had a mountain for his pulpit, and the heavens for his sounding-board, and who, when his gospel was refused by the Jews, sent his servants into the highways and hedges." Multitudes of every rank thronged him; but especially the heathenized and embruted colliers near Bristol listened to the unknown gospel, and their awakened feelings were revealed to the preacher by his observing the white gutters made by the tears that ran down their grimy faces. At last the embargo was raised, and committing his work to Wesley, whom he had drawn into field-preaching, he sailed in August, 1739, for Philadelphia, on his way to Georgia. His fame had gone before him, and the desire to hear him was universal. The churches would not contain the throngs. It was long remembered how, on those summer evenings, he would take his stand in the balcony of the old court-house in Market Street, and how every syllable from his wonderful voice would be heard aboard the river-craft moored at the foot of the street, four hundred feet away.

At New York the Episcopal church was closed against him, but the pastor of the Presbyterian church, Mr. Pemberton, from Boston, made him welcome, and the fields were free to him and his hearers. On the way to New York and back, the tireless man preached at every town. At New Brunswick he saw and heard with profound admiration Gilbert Tennent, thenceforth his friend and yokefellow.

Seeing the solemn eagerness of the people everywhere to hear him, he determined to make the journey to Savannah by land, and again he turned the long journey into a campaign of preaching. Arriving at Savannah in January, 1740, he laid the foundation of his orphan-house, "Bethesda," and in March was again on his way northward on a tour of preaching and solicitation of funds. Touching at Charleston, where the bishop's commissary, Dr. Garden, was at open controversy with him, he preached five times and received seventy pounds for his charitable work. Landing at New Castle on a Sunday morning, he preached morning and evening. Monday morning he preached at Wilmington to a vast assemblage. Tuesday evening he preached on Society Hill, in Philadelphia, "to about eight thousand," and at the same place Wednesday morning and evening. Then once more he made the tour to New York and back, preaching at every halting-place. A contemporary newspaper contains the following item: "New Castle, May 15th. This evening Mr. Whitefield went on board his sloop here in order to sail for Georgia. On Sunday he preached twice in Philadelphia, and in the evening, when he preached his farewell sermon, it is supposed he had twenty thousand hearers. On Monday he preached at Darby and Chester; on Tuesday at Wilmington and Whiteclay Creek; on Wednesday, twice at Nottingham; on Thursday at Fog's Manor and New Castle. The congregations were much increased since his being here last. The presence of God was much seen in the assemblies, especially at Nottingham and Fog's Manor, where the people were under such deep soul-distress that their cries almost drowned his voice. He has collected in this and the neighboring provinces about four hundred and fifty pounds sterling for his orphans in Georgia."

Into the feeble but rapidly growing presbyteries and the one synod of the American Presbyterian Church the revival had brought, not peace, but a sword. The collision was inevitable between the fervor and unrestrained zeal of the evangelists and the sense of order and decorum, and of the importance of organization and method, into which men are trained in the ministry of an established church. No man, even at this day, can read the "standards" of the Presbyterian Church without seeing that they have had to be strained to admit those "revival methods" which ever since the days of Whitefield have prevailed in that body. The conflict that arose was not unlike that which from the beginning of New England history had subsisted between Separatist and Nationalist. In the Presbyterian conflict, as so often in religious controversies, disciplinary and doctrinal questions were complicated with a difference of race. The "Old Side" was the Scotch and Irish party; the "New Side" was the New England party, to which many of the old-country ministers adhered. For successive years the mutual opposition had shown itself in the synod; and in 1740, at the synod meeting at Philadelphia, soon after the departure of Whitefield, the real gravamen of the controversy appeared, in the implied and even express impeachment of the spiritual character of the Old Side ministers. The impeachment had been implied in the coming of the evangelists uninvited into other men's parishes, as if these were mission ground. And now it was expressed in papers read before the synod by Blair and Gilbert Tennent. The action of the synod went so far toward sustaining the men of the New Side as to repeal the rule restraining ministers from preaching outside of their own parishes, and as to put on record a thanksgiving for the work of God in the land. Through all the days of the synod's meeting, daily throngs on Society Hill were addressed by the Tennents and other "hot gospelers" of the revival, and churches and private houses were resounding with revival hymns and exhortations. Already the preaching and printing of Gilbert Tennent's "Nottingham Sermon" had made further fellowship between the two parties for the time impossible. The sermon flagrantly illustrated the worst characteristic of the revivalists— their censoriousness. It was a violent invective on "The Danger of an Unconverted Ministry," which so favorable a critic as Dr. Alexander has characterized as "one of the most severely abusive sermons which was ever penned." The answer to it came in a form that might have been expected. At the opening of the synod of 1741 a solemn protestation was presented containing an indictment in seven grave counts against the men of the New Side, and declaring them to "have at present no right to sit and vote as members of this synod, and that if they should sit and vote, the doings of the synod would be of no force or obligation." The protestation was adopted by the synod by a bare majority of a small attendance. The presbytery of New Brunswick found itself exscinded by this short and easy process of discipline; the presbytery of New York joined with it in organizing a new synod, and the schism was complete.

It is needless further to follow in detail the amazing career of Whitefield, "posting o'er land and ocean without rest," and attended at every movement by such storms of religious agitation as have been already described. In August, 1740, he made his first visit to New England. He met with a cordial welcome. At Boston all pulpits were opened to him, and churches were thronged with eager and excited hearers.[168:1] He preached on the common in the open air, and the crowds were doubled. All the surrounding towns, and the coast eastward to Maine, and the interior as far as Northampton, and the Connecticut towns along the road to New York, were wonderfully aroused by the preaching, which, according to the testimony of two nations and all grades of society, must have been of unequaled power over the feelings. Not only the clergy, including the few Church of England missionaries, but the colleges and the magistrates delighted to honor him. Belcher, the royal governor at Boston, fairly slobbered over him, with tears and embraces and kisses; and the devout Governor Talcott, at New Haven, gave God thanks, after listening to the great preacher, "for such refreshings on the way to our rest." So he was sped on his way back to the South.

Relieved thus of the glamor of his presence, the New England people began, some of them, to recognize in what an earthen vessel their treasure had been borne. Already, in his earlier youth, when his vast powers had been suddenly revealed to him and to the world, he had had wise counsel from such men as Watts and Doddridge against some of his perils. Watts warned him against his superstition of trusting to "impressions" assumed to be divine; and Doddridge pronounced him "an honest man, but weak, and a little intoxicated with popularity."[169:1] But no human strength could stand against the adulation that everywhere attended him. His vain conceit was continually betraying him into indiscretions, which he was ever quick to expiate by humble acknowledgment. At Northampton he was deeply impressed with the beauty of holiness in Edwards and his wife; and he listened with deference to the cautions of that wise counselor against his faith in "impressions" and against his censorious judgments of other men as "unconverted"; but it seemed to the pastor that his guest "liked him not so well for opposing these things."

The faults of Whitefield were intensified to a hateful degree in some of his associates and followers. Leaving Boston, he sent, to succeed to his work, Gilbert Tennent, then glowing with the heat of his noted Nottingham sermon on "An Unconverted Ministry." At once men's minds began to be divided. On the one hand, so wise and sober a critic as Thomas Prince, listening with severe attention, gave his strong and unreserved approval to the preaching and demeanor of Tennent.[169:2] At the other extreme, we have such testimony as this from Dr. Timothy Cutler, the former rector of Yale College, now the Episcopalian minister of Boston:

"It would be an endless attempt to describe that scene of confusion and disturbance occasioned by him [Whitefield]: the division of families, neighborhoods, and towns, the contrariety of husbands and wives, the undutifulness of children and servants, the quarrels among teachers, the disorders of the night, the intermission of labor and business, the neglect of husbandry and of gathering the harvest.... In many conventicles and places of rendezvous there has been checkered work indeed, several preaching and several exhorting and praying at the same time, the rest crying or laughing, yelping, sprawling, fainting, and this revel maintained in some places many days and nights together without intermission; and then there were the blessed outpourings of the Spirit!... After him came one Tennent, a monster! impudent and noisy, and told them they were all damn'd, damn'd, damn'd; this charmed them, and in the most dreadful winter I ever saw people wallowed in the snow night and day for the benefit of his beastly brayings, and many ended their days under these fatigues. Both of them carried more money out of these parts than the poor could be thankful for."[170:1]

This is in a tone of bitter sectarian railing. But, after all, the main allegations in it are sustained by the ample evidence produced by Dr. Charles Chauncy, pastor of the First Church in Boston, in his serious and weighty volume of "Seasonable Thoughts on the State of Religion in New England," published in 1743, as he sincerely says, "to serve the interests of Christ's kingdom," and "faithfully pointing out the things of a bad and dangerous tendency in the late and present religious appearance in the land." Dr. Chauncy was doubtless included in the sweeping denunciation of the Christian ministry in general as "unconverted," "Pharisees," "hypocrites." And yet it does not appear in historical evidence that Chauncy was not every whit as good a

Christian as Tennent or Whitefield.

The excesses of the revival went on from bad to worse. They culminated, at last, in the frenzy of poor James Davenport, great-grandson of the venerable founder of New Haven, who, under the control of "impressions" and "impulses" and texts of Scripture "borne in upon his mind," abandoned his Long Island parish, a true allotrio-episcopos, to thrust himself uninvited into the parishes of other ministers, denouncing the pastor as "unconverted" and adjuring the people to desert both pastor and church. Like some other self-appointed itinerants and exhorters of the time, he seemed bent upon schism, as if this were the great end of preaching. Being invited to New London to assist in organizing a Separatist church, he "published the messages which he said he received from the Spirit in dreams and otherwise, importing the great necessity of mortification and contempt of the world; and made them believe that they must put away from them everything that they delighted in, to avoid the heinous sin of idolatry—that wigs, cloaks and breeches, hoods, gowns, rings, jewels, and necklaces, must be all brought together into one heap into his chamber, that they might by his solemn decree be committed to the flames." On the Sabbath afternoon the pile was publicly burned amid songs and shouts. In the pile were many favorite books of devotion, including works of Flavel, Beveridge, Henry, and like venerated names, and the sentence was announced with a loud voice, "that the smoke of the torments of such of the authors of the above-said books as died in the same belief as when they set them out was now ascending in hell, in like manner as they saw the smoke of these books arise."[171:1] The public fever and delirium was passing its crisis. A little more than a year from this time, Davenport, who had been treated by his brethren with much forbearance and had twice been released from public process as non compos mentis, recovered his reason at the same time with his bodily health, and published an unreserved and affectionate acknowledgment of the wrong that he had done under the influence of a spirit of delusion which he had mistaken for the Spirit of truth. Those who had gone furthest with him in his excesses returned to a more sober and brotherly mind, and soon no visible trace remained of the wild storm of enthusiasm that had swept over New England, except a few languishing schisms in country towns of Connecticut.

As in the middle colonies, the revival had brought division in New England. But, after the New England fashion, it was division merely into ways of thinking, not into sects. Central in the agitated scene is the calm figure of Edwards, uniting the faith and zeal of an apostle with the acuteness of a philosopher, and applying the exquisite powers of his intellect to discriminate between a divine work and its human or Satanic admixtures, and between true and spurious religious affections. He won the blessing of the peacemaker. When half a generation had passed there had not ceased, indeed, to be differences of opinion, but there was none left to defend the wild extravagances which the very authors of them lamented, and there was none to deny, in face of the rich and enduring fruits of the revival, that the power of God had been present in it. In the twenty years ending in 1760 the number of the New England churches had been increased by one hundred and fifty.[172:1]

In the middle colonies there had been like progress. The Presbyterian ministry had increased from forty-five to more than a hundred; and the increase had been wholly on the "New Side." An early move of the conservative party, to require a degree from a British or a New England college as a condition of license to preach, was promptly recognized as intended to exclude the fervid students from the Log College. It was met by the organization of Princeton College, whose influence, more New Englandish than New England, directed by a succession of illustrious Yale graduates in full sympathy with the advanced theology of the revival, was counted on to withstand the more cautious orthodoxy of Yale. In this and other ways the Presbyterian schism fell out to the furtherance of the gospel.

In Virginia the quickening was as when the wind breathed in the valley of dry bones. The story of Samuel Morris and his unconscious mission, although authentic fact, belongs with the very romance of evangelism.[173:1] Whitefield and "One-eyed Robinson," and at last Samuel Davies, came to his aid. The deadly exclusiveness of the inert Virginia establishment was broken up, and the gospel had free course. The Presbyterian Church, which had at first been looked on as an exotic sect that might be tolerated out on the western frontier, after a brief struggle with the Act of Uniformity maintained its right to live and struck vigorous root in the soil. The effect of the Awakening was felt in the establishment itself. Devereux Jarratt, a convert of the revival, went to England for ordination, and returned to labor for the resuscitation of the Episcopal Church in his native State. "To him, and such as he, the first workings of the renewed energy of the church in Virginia are to be traced."[173:2]

An even more important result of the Awakening was the swift and wide extension of Baptist principles and churches. This was altogether logical. The revival had come, not so much in the spirit and power of Elijah, turning to each other the hearts of fathers and of children, as in the spirit of Ezekiel, the preacher of individual responsibility and duty. The temper of the revival was wholly congenial with the strong individualism of the Baptist churches. The Separatist churches formed in New England by the withdrawal of revival enthusiasts from the parish churches in many instances became Baptist. Cases of individual conversion to Baptist views were frequent, and the earnestness with which the new opinion was held approved itself not only by debating and proselyting, but by strenuous and useful evangelizing. Especially at the South, from Virginia to Georgia, the new preachers, entering into the labors of the annoyed and persecuted pioneers of their communion, won multitudes of converts to the Christian faith, from the neglected populations, both black and white, and gave to the Baptist churches a lasting preëminence in numbers among the churches of the South.

Throughout the country the effect of this vigorous propagation of rival sects openly, in the face of whatever there was of church establishment, settled this point: that the law of American States, by whomsoever administered, must sooner or later be the law of liberty and equality among the various religious communions. In the southern colonies, the empty shell of a church establishment had crumbled on contact with the serious earnestness of the young congregations gathered by the Presbyterian and Baptist evangelists. In New England, where establishment was in the form of an attempt by the people of the commonwealth to confirm the people of each town in the maintenance of common worship according to their conscience and judgment, the "standing order" had solid strength; but when it was attempted by public authority to curb the liberty of a considerable minority conscientiously intent on secession, the reins were ready to break. It soon came to be recognized that the only preëminence the parish churches could permanently hold was that of being "servants of all."

With equal and unlimited liberty, was to follow, as a prevailing characteristic of American Christianity, a large diversity of organization. Not only that men disagreeing in their convictions of truth would be enrolled in different bodies, but that men holding the same views, in the same statement of them, would feel free to go apart from one another, and stay apart. There was not even to be any one generally predominating organization from which minor ones should be reckoned as dissenting. One after another the organizations which should be tempted by some period of exceptional growth and prosperity to pretend to a hegemony among the churches—Catholic, Episcopalian, Presbyterian, Baptist, Methodist— would meet with some set-back as inexorable as "the law of nature that prevents the trees from growing up into the sky."

By a curious paradox, the same spiritual agitation which deepened the divisions of the American church aroused in the colonies the consciousness of a national religious unity. We have already seen that in the period before the Awakening the sole organ of fellowship reaching through the whole chain of the British colonies was the correspondence of the Quaker meetings and missionaries. In the glow of the revival the continent awoke to the consciousness of a common spiritual life. Ranging the continent literally from Georgia to Maine, with all his weaknesses and indiscretions, and with his incomparable eloquence, welcomed by every sect, yet refusing an exclusive allegiance to any, Whitefield exercised a true apostolate, bearing daily the care of all the churches, and becoming a messenger of mutual fellowship not only between the ends of the continent, but between the Christians of two hemispheres. Remote churches exchanged offices of service. Tennent came from New Jersey to labor in New England; Dickinson and Burr and Edwards were the gift of the northern colonies to the college at Princeton. The quickened sense of a common religious life and duty and destiny was no small part of the preparation for the birth of the future nation.

Whether for good or for evil, the few years from 1740 to 1750 were destined to impress upon the American church in its various orders, for a hundred years to come, the character of Methodism.[176:1]

In New England, the idea, into which the first pastors had been trained by their experience as parish ministers in the English established church, of the parochial church holding correlative rights and duties toward the community in all its families, succumbed at last, after a hundred years of more or less conscious antagonism, to the incompatible principle, adopted from the Separatists of Plymouth, of the church formed according to elective affinity by the "social compact" of persons of the age of discretion who could give account to themselves and to one another of the conscious act and experience of conversion. This view, subject to important mitigations or aggravations in actual administration, held almost unquestioned dominance in the New England churches until boldly challenged by Horace Bushnell, in his "epoch-making" volume on "Christian Nurture" (1846), as a departure from the orthodoxy of the fathers.

In the Presbyterian Church, revivalism as a principle of church life had to contend with rules distinctly articulated in its constitutional documents. So exclusively does the Westminster institute contemplate the church as an established parish that its "Directory for Worship" contains no provision for so abnormal an incident as the baptism of an adult, and all baptized children growing up and not being of scandalous life are to be welcomed to the Lord's Supper. It proves the immense power of the Awakening, that this rigid and powerful organization, of a people tenacious of its traditions to the point of obstinacy, should have swung so completely free at this point, not only of its long-settled usages, but of the distinct letter of its standards.

The Episcopal Church of the colonies was almost forced into an attitude of opposition to the revival. The unspeakable folly of the English bishops in denouncing and silencing the most effective preachers in the national church had betrayed Whitefield into his most easily besetting sin, that of censorious judgment, and his sweeping counter-denunciations of the Episcopalian clergy in general as unconverted closed to him many hearts and pulpits that at first had been hospitably open to him. Being human, they came into open antagonism to him and to the revival. From the protest against extravagance and disorder, it was a short and perilously easy step to the rejection of religious fervor and earnestness. The influence of the mother church of that dreary period and the influence of the official rings around every royal governor were all too potent in the same direction. The Propagation Society's missionaries boasted, with reason, of large accessions of proselytes alienated from other churches by their distaste for the methods of the revival. The effect on the Episcopal Church itself was in some respects unhappy. It "lowered a spiritual temperature already too low,"[177:1] and weakened the moral influence of the church, and the value of its testimony to important principles which there were few besides efficiently to represent—the duty of the church not to disown or shut out those of little faith, and the church's duty toward its children. Never in the history of the church have the Lord's husbandmen shown a fiercer zeal for rooting up tares, regardless of damage to the wheat, than was shown by the preachers of the Awakening. Never was there a wider application of the reproach against those who, instead of preaching to men that they should be converted and become as little children, preach to children that they must be converted and become like grown folks.[178:1] The attitude of the Episcopal Church at that period was not altogether admirable; but it is nothing to its dishonor that it bore the reproach of being a friend of publicans and sinners, and offered itself as a refugium peccatorum, thus holding many in some sort of relation to the kingdom of Christ who would otherwise have lapsed into sheer infidelity.

In all this the Episcopal Church was affected by the Awakening only by way of reaction. But it owes a debt to the direct influence of the Awakening which it has not always been careful to acknowledge. We have already seen that the requickening of the asphyxiated church of Virginia was part of the great revival, and this character remains impressed on that church to this day. The best of those traits by which the American Episcopal Church is distinguished from the Church of England, as, for instance, the greater purity of the ministry and of the membership, are family traits of the revival churches; the most venerated of its early bishops, White and Griswold, bore the same family likeness; and the "Evangelical party," for a time so influential in its counsels, was a tardy and mild afterglow from the setting of the Great Awakening.[179:1]

An incident of the revival, failing which it would have lacked an essential token of the presence of the Spirit of Christ, was the kindling of zeal for communicating the gospel to the ignorant, the neglected, and the heathen. Among the first-fruits of Whitefield's preaching at the South was a practical movement among the planters for the instruction of their slaves— devotees, most of them, of the most abject fetich-worship of their native continent. Of the evangelists and pastors most active in the revival, there were few, either North or South, whose letters or journals do not report the drawing into the churches of large numbers of negroes and Indians, whose daily lives witnessed to the sincerity of their profession of repentance and Christian faith. The Indian population of the southeastern corner of Connecticut with such accord received the gospel at the hands of the evangelists that heathenism seemed extinct among them.[179:2]

Among the first trophies of the revival at Norwich was a Mohegan boy named Samson Occum. Wheelock, pastor at Lebanon, one of the most ardent of the revival preachers, took him into his family as a student. This was the beginning of that school for the training of Indian preachers which, endowed in part with funds gathered by Occum in England, grew at last into Dartmouth College. The choicest spiritual gifts at the disposal of the church were freely spent on the missions. Whitefield visited the school and the field, and sped Kirkland on his way to the Oneidas. Edwards, leaving Northampton in sorrow of heart, gave his incomparable powers to the work of the gospel among the Stockbridge Indians until summoned thence to the presidency of Princeton College. When Brainerd fainted under his burden, it was William Tennent who went out into the wilderness to carry on the work of harvest. But the great gift of the American church to the cause of missions was the gift of David Brainerd himself. His life was the typical missionary's life—the scattering of precious seed with tears, the heart-sickness of hope deferred, at last the rejoicing of the harvest-home. His early death enrolled him in the canon of the saints of modern Christendom. The story of his life and death, written by Jonathan Edwards out of that fatherly love with which he had tended the young man's latest days and hours, may not have been an unmixed blessing to the church. The long-protracted introspections, the cherished forebodings and misgivings, as if doubt was to be cultivated as a Christian virtue, may not have been an altogether wholesome example for general imitation. But think what the story of that short life has wrought! To how many hearts it has been an inspiration to self-sacrifice and devotion to the service of God in the service of man, we cannot know. Along one line its influence can be partly traced. The "Life of David Brainerd" made Henry Martyn a missionary to the heathen. As spiritual father to Henry Martyn, Brainerd may be reckoned, in no unimportant sense, to be the father of modern missions to the heathen.

CHAPTER XII. CLOSE OF THE COLONIAL ERA—THE GERMAN CHURCHES—THE BEGINNINGS OF THE METHODIST CHURCH.

The quickening of religious feeling, the deepening of religious conviction, the clearing and defining of theological opinions, that were incidental to the Great Awakening, were a preparation for more than thirty years of intense political and warlike agitation. The churches suffered from the long distraction of the public mind, and at the end of it were faint and exhausted. But for the infusion of a "more abundant life" which they had received, it would seem that they could hardly have survived the stress of that stormy and revolutionary period.

The religious life of this period was manifested in part in the growth of the New England theology. The great leader of this school of theological inquiry, the elder Edwards, was born at the opening of the eighteenth century. The oldest and most eminent of his disciples and successors, Bellamy and Hopkins, were born respectively in 1719 and 1721, and entered into the work of the Awakening in the flush of their earliest manhood. A long dynasty of acute and strenuous argumentators has continued, through successive generations to the present day, this distinctly American school of theological thought. This is not the place for tracing the intricate history of their discussions,[182:1] but the story of the Awakening could not be told without some mention of this its attendant and sequel.

Not less notable than the new theology of the revival was the new psalmody. In general it may be said that every flood-tide of spiritual emotion in the church leaves its high-water mark in the form of "new songs to the Lord" that remain after the tide of feeling has assuaged. In this instance the new songs were not produced by the revival, but only adopted by it. It is not easy for us at this day to conceive the effect that must have been produced in the Christian communities of America by the advent of Isaac Watts's marvelous poetic work, "The Psalms of David Imitated in the Language of the New Testament." Important religious results have more than once followed in the church on the publication of religious poems—notably, in our own century, on the publication of "The Christian Year." But no other instance of the kind is comparable with the publication in America of Watts's Psalms. When we remember how scanty were the resources of religious poetry in American homes in the early eighteenth century, and especially how rude and even grotesque the rhymes that served in the various churches as a vehicle of worship, it seems that the coming of those melodious stanzas, in which the meaning of one poet is largely interpreted by the sympathetic insight of another poet, and the fervid devotion of the Old Testament is informed with the life and transfigured in the language of the New, must have been like a glow of sunlight breaking in upon a gray and cloudy day. Few pages of biography can be found more vividly illustrative of the times and the men than the page in which Samuel Hopkins recites the story of the sufferings of his own somber and ponderous mind under the rebuke of his college friend David Brainerd. He walked his solitary room in tears, and (he says) "took up Watts's version of the Psalms, and opened it at the Fifty-first Psalm, and read the first, second, and third parts in long meter with strong affections, and made it all my own language, and thought it was the language of my heart to God." There was more than the experience of a great and simple soul, there was the germ of a future system of theology, in the penitential confession which the young student "made his own language," and in the exquisite lines which, under the figure of a frightened bird, became the utterance of his first tremulous and faltering faith:

Lord, should thy judgment grow severe,
I am condemned, but thou art clear.
Should sudden vengeance seize my breath,
I must pronounce thee just in death;
And if my soul were sent to hell,
Thy righteous law approves it well.
Yet save a trembling sinner, Lord,
Whose hope, still hovering round thy word,
Would light on some sweet promise there,
Some sure support against despair.

The introduction of the new psalmody was not accomplished all at once, nor without a struggle. But we gravely mistake if we look upon the controversy that resulted in the adoption of Watts's Psalms as a mere conflict between enlightened good taste and stubborn conservatism. The action proposed was revolutionary. It involved the surrender of a long-settled principle of Puritanism. At the present day the objection to the use of "human composures" in public worship is unintelligible, except to Scotchmen. In the later Puritan age such use was reckoned an infringement on the entire and exclusive authority and sufficiency of the Scriptures, and a constructive violation of the second commandment. By the adoption of the new psalmody the Puritan and Presbyterian churches, perhaps not consciously, but none the less actually, yielded the major premiss of the only argument by which liturgical worship was condemned on principle. Thereafter the question of the use of liturgical forms became a mere question of expediency. It is remarkable that the logical consequences of this important step have been so tardy and hesitating.

It was not in the common course of church history that the period under consideration should be a period of vigorous internal activity and development in the old settled churches of America. The deep, often excessive, excitements of the Awakening had not only ceased, but had been succeeded by intense agitations of another sort. Two successive "French and Indian" wars kept the long frontier, at a time when there was little besides frontier to the British colonies, in continual peril of fire and scalping-knife.[184:1] The astonishingly sudden and complete extinction of the French politico-religious empire in Canada and the West made possible, and at no remote time inevitable, the separation of the British colonies from the mother country and the contentions and debates that led into the Revolutionary War began at once.

Another consequence of the prostrating of the French power in America has been less noticed by historians, but the course of this narrative will not be followed far without its becoming manifest as not less momentous in its bearing on the future history of the church. The extinction of the French-Catholic power in America made possible the later plantation and large and free development of the Catholic Church in the territory of the United States. After that event the Catholic resident or citizen was no longer subject to the suspicion of being a sympathizer with a hostile neighboring power, and the Jesuit missionary was no longer liable to be regarded as a political intriguer and a conspirator with savage assassins against the lives of innocent settlers and their families. If there are those who, reading the earlier pages of this volume, have mourned over the disappointment and annihilation of two magnificent schemes of Catholic domination on the North American continent as being among the painful mysteries of divine providence, they may find compensation for these catastrophes in later advances of Catholicism, which without these antecedents would seem to have been hardly possible.

Although the spiritual development of the awakened American churches, after the Awakening until the independence of the States was established and acknowledged, was limited by these great hindrances, this period was one of momentous influences from abroad upon American Christianity.

The Scotch-Irish immigration kept gathering volume and force. The great stream of immigrants entering at the port of Philadelphia and flowing westward and southwestward was joined by a tributary stream entering at Charleston. Not only the numbers of this people, occupying in force the hill-country from Pennsylvania to Georgia, but still more its extraordinary qualities and the discipline of its history, made it a factor of prime importance in the events of the times just before and just after the achievement of the national independence. For generations it had been schooled to the apprehension and acceptance of an elaborately articulated system of theology and church order as of divine authority. Its prejudices and animosities were quite as potent as its principles. Its fixed hereditary aversion to the English government and the English church was the natural fruit of long memories and traditions of outrages inflicted by both these; its influence was now about to be powerfully manifested in the overthrow of the English power and its feeble church establishments in the colonies. At the opening of the War of Independence the Presbyterian Church, reunited since the schism of 1741, numbered one hundred and seventy ministers in seventeen presbyteries; but its weight of influence was out of all proportion to its numbers, and this entire force, not altogether at unity with itself on ecclesiastical questions, was united as one man in the maintenance of American rights.

The great German immigration begins to flow in earnest in this period. Three successive tides of migration have set from Germany to America. The first was the movement of the petty sects under the invitation and patronage of William Penn, quartering themselves in the eastern parts of Pennsylvania. The second was the transportation of "the Palatines," expatriated by stress of persecution and war, not from the Rhenish Palatinate only, but from the archduchy of Salzburg and from other parts of Germany and Switzerland, gathered up and removed to America, some of them directly, some by way of England, as an act of political charity by Queen Anne's government, with the idea of strengthening the colonies by planting Protestant settlers for a safeguard against Spanish or French aggressions. The third tide continues flowing, with variable volume, to this day. It is the voluntary flow of companies of individual emigrants seeking to better the fortunes of themselves or their families. But this voluntary migration has been unhealthily and sometimes dishonestly stimulated, from the beginning of it, by the selfish interests of those concerned in the business of transportation or in the sale of land. It seems to have been mainly the greed of shipping merchants, at first, that spread abroad in the German states florid announcements of the charms and riches of America, decoying multitudes of ignorant persons to risk everything on these representations, and to mortgage themselves into a term of slavery until they should have paid the cost of their passage by their labor. This class of bondmen, called "redemptioners," made no inconsiderable part of the population of the middle colonies; and it seems to have been a worthy part. The trade of "trepanning" the unfortunates and transporting them and selling their term of service was not by several degrees as bad as the African slave-trade; but it was of the same sort, and the deadly horrors of its "middle passage" were hardly less.

In one way and another the German immigration had grown by the middle of the eighteenth century to great dimensions. In the year 1749 twelve thousand Germans landed at the port of Philadelphia. In general they were as sheep having no shepherd. Their deplorable religious condition was owing less to poverty than to diversity of sects.[188:1] In many places the number of sects rendered concerted action impossible, and the people remained destitute of religious instruction.

The famine of the word was sorely felt. In 1733 three great Lutheran congregations in Pennsylvania, numbering five hundred families each, sent messengers with an imploring petition to their coreligionists at London and Halle, representing their "state of the greatest destitution." "Our own means" (they say) "are utterly insufficient to effect the necessary relief, unless God in his mercy may send us help from abroad. It is truly lamentable to think of the large numbers of the rising generation who know not their right hand from their left; and, unless help be promptly afforded, the danger is great that, in consequence of the great lack of churches and schools, the most of them will be led into the ways of destructive error."

This urgent appeal bore fruit like the apples of Sodom. It resulted in a painful and pitiable correspondence with the chiefs of the mother church, these haggling for months and years over stipulations of salary, and refusing to send a minister until the salary should be pledged in cash; and their correspondents pleading their poverty and need.[188:2] The few and feeble churches of the Reformed confession were equally needy and ill befriended.

It seems to us, as we read the story after the lapse of a hundred and fifty years, as if the man expressly designed and equipped by the providence of God for this exigency in the progress of his kingdom had arrived when Zinzendorf, the Moravian, made his appearance at Philadelphia, December 10, 1741. The American church, in all its history, can point to no fairer representative of the charity that "seeketh not her own" than this Saxon nobleman, who, for the true love that he bore to Christ and all Christ's brethren, was willing to give up his home, his ancestral estates, his fortune, his title of nobility, his patrician family name, his office of bishop in the ancient Moravian church, and even (last infirmity of zealous spirits) his interest in promoting specially that order of consecrated men and women in the church catholic which he had done and sacrificed so much to save from extinction, and to which his "cares and toils were given." He hastened first up the Lehigh Valley to spend Christmas at Bethlehem, where the foundations had already been laid on which have been built up the half-monastic institutions of charity and education and missions which have done and are still doing so much to bless the world in both its hemispheres. It was in commemoration of this Christmas visit of Bishop Zinzendorf that the mother house of the Moravian communities in America received its name of Bethlehem. Returning to Philadelphia, he took this city as the base of his unselfish and unpartisan labors in behalf of the great and multiplying population from his fatherland, which through its sectarian divisions had become so helpless and spiritually needy. Already for twenty years there had been a few scattering churches of the Reformed confession, and for half that time a few Lutheran congregations had been gathered or had gathered themselves. But both the sects had been overcome by the paralysis resulting from habitual dependence on paternal governments, and the two were borne asunder, while every right motive was urging to coöperation and fellowship, by the almost spent momentum of old controversies. In Philadelphia two starveling congregations representing the two competing sects occupied the same rude meeting-place each by itself on alternate Sundays. The Lutherans made shift without a pastor, for the only Lutheran minister in Pennsylvania lived at Lancaster, sixty miles away.

To the scattered, distracted, and demoralized flocks of his German fellow-Christians in the middle colonies came Zinzendorf, knowing Jesus Christ crucified, knowing no man according to the flesh; and at once "the neglected congregations were made to feel the thrill of a strong religious life." "Aglow with zeal for Christ, throwing all emphasis in his teaching upon the one doctrine of redemption through the blood shed on Calvary, all the social advantages and influence and wealth which his position gave him were made subservient to the work of preaching Christ, and him crucified, to the rich and the poor, the learned and the ignorant."[190:1] The Lutherans of Philadelphia heard him gladly and entreated him to preach to them regularly; to which he consented, but not until he had assured himself that this would be acceptable to the pastor of the Reformed congregation. But his mission was to the sheep scattered abroad, of whom he reckoned (an extravagant overestimate) not less than one hundred thousand of the Lutheran party in Pennsylvania alone. Others, as he soon found, had been feeling, like himself, the hurt of the daughter of Zion. A series of conferences was held from month to month, in which men of the various German sects took counsel together over the dissensions of their people, and over the question how the ruinous effects of these dissensions could be avoided. The plan was, not to attempt a merger of the sects, nor to alienate men from their habitual affiliations, but to draw together in coöperation and common worship the German Christians, of whatever sect, in a fellowship to be called, in imitation of a Pauline phrase (Eph. ii. 22), "the Congregation of God in the Spirit." The plan seemed so right and reasonable and promising of beneficent results as to win general approval. It was in a fair way to draw together the whole miserably divided German population.[191:1]

At once the "drum ecclesiastic" beat to arms. In view of the impending danger that their scattered fellow-countrymen might come into mutual fellowship on the basis of their common faith in Christ, the Lutheran leaders at Halle, who for years had been dawdling and haggling over the imploring entreaties of the shepherdless Lutheran populations in America, promptly reconsidered their non possumus, and found and sent a man admirably qualified for the desired work, Henry Melchior Mühlenberg, a man of eminent ability and judgment, of faith, devotion, and untiring diligence, not illiberal, but a conscientious sectarian. An earnest preacher of the gospel, he was also earnest that the gospel should be preached according to the Lutheran formularies, to congregations organized according to the Lutheran discipline. The easier and less worthy part of the appointed task was soon achieved. The danger that the religious factions that had divided Germany might be laid aside in the New World was effectually dispelled. Six years later the governor of Pennsylvania was still able to write, "The Germans imported with them all the religious whimsies of their country, and, I believe, have subdivided since their arrival here;" and he estimates their number at three fifths of the population of the province. The more arduous and noble work of organizing and compacting the Lutherans into their separate congregations, and combining these by synodical assemblies, was prosecuted with wisdom and energy, and at last, in spite of hindrances and discouragements, with beneficent success. The American Lutheran Church of to-day is the monument of the labors of Mühlenberg.

The brief remainder of Zinzendorf's work in America may be briefly told. There is no doubt that, like many another eager and hopeful reformer, he overestimated the strength and solidity of the support that was given to his generous and beneficent plans. At the time of Mühlenberg's arrival Zinzendorf was the elected and installed pastor of the Lutheran congregation in Philadelphia. The conflict could not be a long one between the man who claimed everything for his commission and his sect and the man who was resolved to insist on nothing for himself. Notwithstanding the strong love for him among the people, Zinzendorf was easily displaced from his official station. When dispute arose about the use of the empty carpenter's shop that stood them instead of a church, he waived his own claims and at his own cost built a new house of worship. But it was no part of his work to stay and persist in maintaining a division. He retired from the field, leaving it in charge of Mühlenberg, "being satisfied if only Christ were preached," and returned to Europe, having achieved a truly honorable and most Christian failure, more to be esteemed in the sight of God than many a splendid success.

But his brief sojourn in America was not without visible fruit. He left behind him the Moravian church fully organized under the episcopate of Bishop David Nitschmann, with communities or congregations begun at nine different centers, and schools established in four places. An extensive itinerancy had been set in operation under careful supervision, and, most characteristic of all, a great beginning had been made of those missions to the heathen Indians, in which the devoted and successful labors of this little society of Christians have put to shame the whole American church besides. Not all of this is to be ascribed to the activity of Zinzendorf; but in all of it he was a sharer, and his share was a heroic one. The two years' visit of Count Zinzendorf to America forms a beautiful and quite singular episode in our church history. Returning to his ancestral estates splendidly impoverished by his free-handed beneficence, he passed many of the later years of his life at Herrnhut, that radiating center from which the light of the gospel was borne by the multitude of humble missionaries to every continent under the whole heaven. The news that came to him from the "economies" that he had planted in the forests of Pennsylvania was such as to fill his generous soul with joy. In the communities of Nazareth and Bethlehem was renewed the pentecostal consecration when no man called anything his own. The prosperous farms and varied industries, in which no towns in Pennsylvania could equal them, were carried on, not for private interest, but for the church. After three years the community work was not only self-supporting, but sustained about fifty missionaries in the field, and was preparing to send aid to the missions of the mother church in Germany. The Moravian settlements multiplied at distant points, north and south. The educational establishments grew strong and famous. But especially the Indian missions spread far and wide. The story of these missions is one of the fairest and most radiant pages in the history of the American church, and one of the bloodiest. Zinzendorf, dying at London in May, 1756, was spared, we may hope, the heartbreaking news of the massacre at Gnadenhütten the year before. But from that time on, through the French wars, the Revolutionary War, the War of 1812, and down to the infamy of Georgia and the United States in 1837, the innocent and Christlike Moravian missions have been exposed from every side to the malignity of savage men both white and red. No order of missionaries or missionary converts can show a nobler roll of martyrs than the Moravians.[194:1]

The work of Mühlenberg for the Lutherans stimulated the Reformed churches in Europe to a like work for their own scattered and pastorless sheep. In both cases the fear that the work of the gospel might not be done seemed a less effective incitement to activity than the fear that it might be done by others. It was the Reformed Church of Holland, rather than those of Germany, miserably broken down and discouraged by ravaging wars, that assumed the main responsibility for this task. As early as 1728 the Dutch synods had earnestly responded to the appeal of their impoverished brethren on the Rhine in behalf of the sheep scattered abroad.

And in 1743, acting through the classis of Amsterdam, they had made such progress toward beginning the preliminary arrangements of the work as to send to the Presbyterian synod of Philadelphia a proposal to combine into one the Presbyterian, or Scotch Reformed, the Dutch Reformed, and the German Reformed churches in America. It had already been proved impossible to draw together in common activity and worship the different sects of the same German race and language; the effort to unite in one organization peoples of different language, but of substantially the same doctrine and polity, was equally futile. It seemed as if minute sectarian division and subdivision was to be forced upon American Christianity as a law of its church life.

Diplomacies ended, the synods of Holland took up their work with real munificence. Large funds were raised, sufficient to make every German Reformed missionary in America a stipendiary of the classis of Amsterdam; and if these subsidies were encumbered with severe conditions of subordination to a foreign directory, and if they begot an enfeebling sense of dependence, these were necessary incidents of the difficult situation—res dura et novitas regni. The most important service which the synods of Holland rendered to their American beneficiaries was to find a man who should do for them just the work which Mühlenberg was already doing with great energy for the Lutherans. The man was Michael Schlatter. If in any respect he was inferior to Mühlenberg, it was not in respect to diligent devotion to the business on which he had been sent. It is much to the credit of both of them that, in organizing and promoting their two sharply competing sects, they never failed of fraternal personal relations. They worked together with one heart to keep their people apart from each other. The Christian instinct, in a community of German Christians, to gather in one congregation for common worship was solemnly discouraged by the two apostles and the synods which they organized. How could the two parties walk together when one prayed Vater unser, and the other unser Vater? But the beauty of Christian unity was illustrated in such incidents as this: Mr. Schlatter and some of the Reformed Christians, being present at a Lutheran church on a communion Sunday, listened to the preaching of the Lutheran pastor, after which the Reformed minister made a communion address, and then the congregation was dismissed, and the Reformed went off to a school-house to receive the Lord's Supper.[196:1] Truly it was fragrant like the ointment on the beard of Aaron!

Such was the diligence of Schlatter that the synod or cœtus of the Reformed Church was instituted in 1747, a year from his arrival. The Lutheran synod dates from 1748, although Mühlenberg was on the ground four years earlier than Schlatter. Thus the great work of dividing the German population of America into two major sects was conscientiously and effectually performed. Seventy years later, with large expenditure of persuasion, authority, and money, it was found possible to heal in some measure in the old country the very schism which good men had been at such pains to perpetuate in the new.

High honor is due to the prophetic wisdom of these two leaders of German-American Christianity, in that they clearly recognized in advance that the English was destined to be the dominant language of North America. Their strenuous though unsuccessful effort to promote a system of public schools in Pennsylvania was defeated through their own ill judgment and the ignorant prejudices of the immigrant people played upon by politicians. But the mere attempt entitles them to lasting gratitude. It is not unlikely that their divisive work of church organization may have contributed indirectly to defeat the aspirations of their fellow-Germans after the perpetuation of a Germany in America. The combination of the mass of the German population in one solid church organization would have been a formidable support to such aspirations. The splitting of this mass in half, necessitating petty local schisms with all their debilitating and demoralizing consequences, may have helped secure the country from a serious political and social danger.

So, then, the German church in America at the close of the colonial era exists, outside of the petty primeval sects, in three main divisions: the Lutheran, the Reformed, and the Moravian. There is free opportunity for Christians of this language to sort themselves according to their elective affinities. That American ideal of edifying harmony is well attained, according to which men of partial or one-sided views of truth shall be associated exclusively in church relations with others of like precious defects. Mühlenberg seems to have been sensible of the nature of the division he was making in the body of Christ, when, after severing successfully between the strict Lutherans in a certain congregation and those of Moravian sympathies, he finds it "hard to decide on which side of the controversy the greater justice lay. The greater part of those on the Lutheran side, he feared, was composed of unconverted men," while the Moravian party seemed open to the reproach of enthusiasm. So he concluded that each sort of Christians would be better off without the other. Time proved his diagnosis to be better than his treatment. In the course of a generation the Lutheran body, carefully weeded of pietistic admixtures, sank perilously deep in cold rationalism, and the Moravian church was quite carried away for a time on a flood of sentimentalism. What might have been the course of this part of church history if Mühlenberg and Schlatter had shared more deeply with Zinzendorf in the spirit of apostolic and catholic Christianity, and if all three had conspired to draw together into one the various temperaments and tendencies of the German Americans in the unity of the Spirit with the bond of peace, may seem like an idle historical conjecture, but the question is not without practical interest to-day. Perhaps the Moravians would have been the better for being ballasted with the weighty theologies and the conservative temper of the state churches; it is very certain that these would have gained by the infusion of something of that warmth of Christian love and zeal that pervaded to a wonderful degree the whole Moravian fellowship. But the hand and the foot were quite agreed that they had no need of each other or of the heart.[198:1]

By far the most momentous event of American church history in the closing period of the colonial era was the planting of the Methodist Episcopal Church. The Wesleyan revival was strangely tardy in reaching this country, with which it had so many points of connection. It was in America, in 1737, that John Wesley passed through the discipline of a humiliating experience, by which his mind had been opened, and that he had been brought into acquaintance with the Moravians, by whom he was to be taught the way of the Lord more perfectly. It was John Wesley who sent Whitefield to America, from whom, on his first return to England, in 1738, he learned the practice of field-preaching. It was from America that Edwards's "Narrative of Surprising Conversions" had come to Wesley, which, being read by him on the walk from London to Oxford, opened to his mind unknown possibilities of the swift advancement of the kingdom of God. The beginning of the Wesleyan societies in England followed in close connection upon the first Awakening in America. It went on with growing momentum in England and Ireland for quarter of a century, until, in 1765, it numbered thirty-nine circuits served by ninety-two itinerant preachers; and its work was mainly among the classes from which the emigration to the colonies was drawn. It is not easy to explain how it came to pass that through all these twenty-five years Wesleyan Methodism gave no sound or sign of life on that continent on which it was destined (if one may speak of predestination in this connection) to grow to its most magnificent proportions.

At last, in 1766, in a little group of Methodist families that had found one another out among the recent comers in New York, Philip Embury, who in his native Ireland long before had been a recognized local preacher, was induced by the persuasions and reproaches of a pious woman to take his not inconsiderable talent from the napkin in which he had kept it hidden for six years, and preach in his own house to as many as could be brought in to listen to him. The few that were there formed themselves into a "class" and promised to attend at future meetings.

A more untoward time for the setting on foot of a religious enterprise could hardly have been chosen. It was a time of prevailing languor in the churches, in the reaction from the Great Awakening; it was also a time of intense political agitation. The year before the Stamp Act had been passed, and the whole chain of colonies, from New Hampshire to Georgia, had been stirred up to resist the execution of it. This year the Stamp Act had been repealed, but in such terms as to imply a new menace and redouble the agitation. From this time forward to the outbreak of war in 1775, and from that year on till the conclusion of peace in 1783, the land was never at rest from turmoil. Through it all the Methodist societies grew and multiplied. In 1767 Embury's house had overflowed, and a sail-loft was hired for the growing congregation. In 1768 a lot on John Street was secured and a meeting-house was built. The work had spread to Philadelphia, and, self-planted in Maryland under the preaching of Robert Strawbridge, was propagating itself rapidly in that peculiarly congenial soil. In 1769, in response to earnest entreaties from America, two of Wesley's itinerant preachers, Boardman and Pilmoor, arrived with his commission to organize an American itinerancy; and two years later, in 1771, arrived Francis Asbury, who, by virtue of his preëminent qualifications for organization, administration, and command, soon became practically the director of the American work, a function to which, in 1772, he was officially appointed by commission from Wesley.

Very great is the debt that American Christianity owes to Francis Asbury. It may reasonably be doubted whether any one man, from the founding of the church in America until now, has achieved so much in the visible and traceable results of his work. It is very certain that Wesley himself, with his despotic temper and his High-church and Tory principles, could not have carried the Methodist movement in the New World onward through the perils of its infancy on the way to so eminent a success as that which was prepared by his vicegerent. Fully possessed of the principles of that autocratic discipline ordained by Wesley, he knew how to use it as not abusing it, being aware that such a discipline can continue to subsist, in the long run, only by studying the temper of the subjects of it, and making sure of obedience to orders by making sure that the orders are agreeable, on the whole, to the subjects. More than one polity theoretically aristocratic or monarchic in the atmosphere of our republic has grown into a practically popular government, simply through tact and good judgment in the administration of it, without changing a syllable of its constitution. Very early in the history of the Methodist Church it is easy to recognize the aptitude with which Asbury naturalizes himself in the new climate. Nominally he holds an absolute autocracy over the young organization. Whatever the subject at issue, "on hearing every preacher for and against, the right of determination was to rest with him."[201:1] Questions of the utmost difficulty and of vital importance arose in the first years of the American itinerancy. They could not have been decided so wisely for the country and the universal church if Asbury, seeming to govern the ministry and membership of the Society, had not studied to be governed by them. In spite of the sturdy dictum of Wesley, "We are not republicans, and do not intend to be," the salutary and necessary change had already begun which was to accommodate his institutes in practice, and eventually in form, to the habits and requirements of a free people.

The center of gravity of the Methodist Society, beginning at New York, moved rapidly southward. Boston had been the metropolis of the Congregationalist churches; New York, of the Episcopalians; Philadelphia, of the Quakers and the Presbyterians; and Baltimore, latest and southernmost of the large colonial cities, became, for a time, the headquarters of Methodism. Accessions to the Society in that region were more in number and stronger in wealth and social influence than in more northern communities. It was at Baltimore that Asbury fixed his residence—so far as a Methodist bishop, ranging the country with incessant and untiring diligence, could be said to have a fixed residence.

The record of the successive annual conferences of the Methodists gives a gauge of their increase. At the first, in 1773, at Philadelphia, there were reported 1160 members and 10 preachers, not one of these a native of America.

At the second annual conference, in Philadelphia, there were reported 2073 members and 17 preachers.

The third annual conference sat at Philadelphia in 1775, simultaneously with the Continental Congress. It was the beginning of the war. There were reported 3148 members. Some of the foremost preachers had gone back to England, unable to carry on their work without being compelled to compromise their royalist principles. The preachers reporting were 19. Of the membership nearly 2500 were south of Philadelphia—about eighty per cent.

At the fourth annual conference, at Baltimore, in 1776, were reported 4921 members and 24 preachers.

At the fifth annual conference, in Harford County, Maryland, were reported 6968 members and 36 preachers. This was in the thick of the war. More of the leading preachers, sympathizing with the royal cause, were going home to England. The Methodists as a body were subject to not unreasonable suspicion of being disaffected to the cause of independence. Their preachers were principally Englishmen with British sympathies. The whole order was dominated and its property controlled by an offensively outspoken Tory of the Dr. Johnson type.[202:1] It was natural enough that in their public work they should be liable to annoyance, mob violence, and military arrest. Even Asbury, a man of proved American sympathies, found it necessary to retire for a time from public activity.

In these circumstances, it is no wonder that at the conference of 1778, at Leesburg, Va., at which five circuits in the most disturbed regions were unrepresented, there was a decline in numbers. The members were fewer by 873; the preachers fewer by 7.

But it is really wonderful that the next year (1779) were reported extensive revivals in all parts not directly affected by the war, and an increase of 2482 members and 49 preachers. The distribution of the membership was very remarkable. At this time, and for many years after, there was no organized Methodism in New England. New York, being occupied by the invading army, sent no report. Of the total reported membership of 8577, 140 are credited to New Jersey, 179 to Pennsylvania, 795 to Delaware, and 900 to Maryland. Nearly all the remainder, about eighty per cent. of the whole, was included in Virginia and North Carolina. With the exception of 319 persons, the entire reported membership of the Methodist societies lived south of Mason and Dixon's line. The fact throws an honorable light on some incidents of the early history of this great order of preachers.

In the sixteen years from the meeting in Philip Embury's house to the end of the War of Independence the membership of the Methodist societies grew to about 12,000, served by about 70 itinerant preachers. It was a very vital and active membership, including a large number of "local preachers" and exhorters. The societies and classes were effectively organized and officered for aggressive work; and they were planted, for the most part, in the regions most destitute of Christian institutions.

Parallel with the course of the gospel, we trace in every period the course of those antichristian influences with which the gospel is in conflict. The system of slavery must continue, through many sorrowful years, to be in view from the line of our studies. We shall know it by the unceasing protest made against it in the name of the Lord. The arguments of John Woolman and Anthony Benezet were sustained by the yearly meetings of the Friends. At Newport, the chief center of the African slave-trade, the two Congregational pastors, Samuel Hopkins, the theologian, and the erudite Ezra Stiles, afterward president of Yale College, mutually opposed in theology and contrasted at every point of natural character, were at one in boldly opposing the business by which their parishioners had been enriched.[204:1] The deepening of the conflict for political liberty pointed the application of the golden rule in the case of the slaves. The antislavery literature of the period includes a printed sermon that had been preached by the distinguished Dr. Levi Hart "to the corporation of freemen" of his native town of Farmington, Conn., at their autumnal town-meeting in 1774; and the poem on "Slavery," published in 1775 by that fine character, Aaron Cleveland,[204:2] of Norwich, hatter, poet, legislator, and minister of the gospel. Among the Presbyterians of New Jersey, the father of Dr. Ashbel Green took the extreme ground which was taken by Dr. Hopkins's church in 1784, that no person holding a slave should be permitted to remain in the communion of the church.[204:3] In 1774 the first society in the world for the abolition of slavery was organized among the Friends in Pennsylvania, to be followed by others, making a continuous series of abolition societies from New England to Maryland and Virginia. But the great antislavery society of the period in question was the Methodist Society. Laboring through the War of Independence mainly in the Southern States, it publicly declared, in the conference of 1780, "that slavery is contrary to the laws of God, man, and nature, and hurtful to society; contrary to the dictates of conscience and pure religion, and doing that which we would not that others should do to us and ours." The discipline of the body of itinerants was conducted rigorously in accordance with this declaration.

It must not be supposed that the instances here cited represent exceptions to the general course of opinion in the church of those times. They are simply expressions of the universal judgment of those whose attention had been seriously fixed upon the subject. There appears no evidence of the existence of a contrary sentiment. The first beginnings of a party in the church in opposition to the common judgment of the Christian conscience on the subject of slavery are to be referred to a comparatively very recent date.

Another of the great conflicts of the modern church was impending. But it was only to prophetic minds in the middle of the eighteenth century that it was visible in the greatness of its proportions. The vice of drunkenness, which Isaiah had denounced in Samaria and Paul had denounced at Ephesus, was growing insensibly, since the introduction of distilled liquors as a common beverage, to a fatal prevalence. The trustees of the charitable colony of Georgia, consciously laying the foundations of many generations, endeavored to provide for the welfare of the nascent State by forbidding at once the importation of negro slaves and of spirituous liquors; but the salutary interdict was soon nullified in the interest of the crops and of the trade with the Indians. Dr. Hopkins "inculcated, at a very early day, the duty of entire abstinence from intoxicating liquids as a beverage."[206:1] But, as in the conflict with slavery, so in this conflict, the priority of leadership belongs easily to Wesley and his itinerants. The conference of 1783 declared against permitting the converts "to make spirituous liquors, sell and drink them in drams," as "wrong in its nature and consequences." To this course they were committed long in advance by the "General Rules" set forth by the two Wesleys in May, 1743, for the guidance of the "United Societies."[206:2]

An incident of the times immediately preceding the War of Independence requires to be noted in this place, not as being of great importance in itself, but as characteristic of the condition of the country and prophetic of changes that were about to take place. During the decade from 1760 to 1775 the national body of the Presbyterians—the now reunited synod of New York and Philadelphia—and the General Association of the Congregational pastors of Connecticut met together by their representatives in annual convention to take counsel over a grave peril that seemed to be impending. A petition had been urgently pressed, in behalf of the American Episcopalians, for the establishment of bishops in the colonies under the authority of the Church of England. The reasons for this measure were obvious and weighty; and the protestations of those who promoted it, that they sought no advantage before the law over their fellow-Christians, were doubtless sincere. Nevertheless, the fear that the bringing in of Church of England bishops would involve the bringing in of many of those mischiefs of the English church establishment which neither they nor their fathers had been able to bear was a perfectly reasonable fear both to the Puritans of New England and to the Presbyterians from Ireland. It was difficult for these, and it would have been even more difficult for the new dignitaries, in colonial days, to understand how bishops could be anything but lord bishops. The fear of such results was not confined to ecclesiastics. The movement was felt by the colonial statesmen to be dangerously akin to other British encroachments on colonial rights. The Massachusetts Assembly instructed its agent in London strenuously to oppose it. In Virginia, the Episcopalian clergy themselves at first refused to concur in the petition for bishops; and when at last the concurrence was voted, it was in the face of a formal protest of four of the clergy, for which they received a vote of thanks from the House of Burgesses.[207:1]

The alliance thus occasioned between the national synod of the Presbyterian Church and the Congregationalist clergy of the little colony of Connecticut seems like a disproportioned one. And so it was indeed; for the Connecticut General Association was by far the larger and stronger body of the two. By and by the disproportion was inverted, and the alliance continued, with notable results.

CHAPTER XIII. RECONSTRUCTION.

Seven years of war left the American people exhausted, impoverished, disorganized, conscious of having come into possession of a national existence, and stirred with anxious searchings of heart over the question what new institutions should succeed to those overthrown in the struggle for independence.

Like questions pervaded the commonwealth of American Christians through all its divisions. The interconfessional divisions of the body ecclesiastic were about to prove themselves a more effectual bar to union than the political and territorial divisions of the body politic. The religious divisions were nearly equal in number to the political. Naming them in the order in which they had settled themselves on the soil of the new nation, they were as follows: 1. The Protestant Episcopalians; 2. The Reformed Dutch; 3. The Congregationalists; 4. The Roman Catholics; 5. The Friends; 6. The Baptists; 7. The Presbyterians; 8. The Methodists; to which must be added three sects which up to this time had almost exclusively to do with the German language and the German immigrant population, to wit, 9. The German Reformed; 10. The Lutherans; 11. The Moravians. Some of these, as the Congregationalists and the Baptists, were of so simple and elastic a polity, so self-adaptive to whatever new environment, as to require no effort to adjust themselves. Others, as the Dutch and the Presbyterians, had already organized themselves as independent of foreign spiritual jurisdiction. Others still, as the German Reformed, the Moravians, and the Quakers, were content to remain for years to come in a relation of subordination to foreign centers of organization. But there were three communions, of great prospective importance, which found it necessary to address themselves to the task of reorganization to suit the changed political conditions. These were the Episcopalians, the Catholics, and the Methodists.

In one respect all the various orders of churches were alike. They had all suffered from the waste and damage of war. Pastors and missionaries had been driven from their cures, congregations had been scattered, houses of worship had been desecrated or destroyed. The Episcopalian and Methodist ministers were generally Tories, and their churches, and in some instances their persons, were not spared by the patriots. The Friends and the Moravians, principled against taking active part in warfare, were exposed to aggressions from both sides. All other sects were safely presumed to be in earnest sympathy with the cause of independence, which many of their pastors actively served as chaplains or as combatants, or in other ways; wherever the British troops held the ground, their churches were the object of spite. Nor were these the chief losses by the war. More grievous still were the death of the strong men and the young men of the churches, the demoralization of camp life, and, as the war advanced, the infection of the current fashions of unbelief from the officers both of the French and of the British armies. The prevalent diathesis of the American church in all its sects was one of spiritual torpor, from which, however, it soon began to be aroused as the grave exigencies of the situation disclosed themselves.

Perhaps no one of the Christian organizations of America came out of the war in a more forlorn condition than the Episcopalians. This condition was thus described by Bishop White, in an official charge to his clergy at Philadelphia in 1832:

"The congregations of our communion throughout the United States were approaching annihilation. Although within this city three Episcopal clergymen were resident and officiating, the churches over the rest of the State had become deprived of their clergy during the war, either by death or by departure for England. In the Eastern States, with two or three exceptions, there was a cessation of the exercises of the pulpit, owing to the necessary disuse of the prayers for the former civil rulers. In Maryland and Virginia, where the church had enjoyed civil establishments, on the ceasing of these, the incumbents of the parishes, almost without exception, ceased to officiate. Farther south the condition of the church was not better, to say the least."[210:1]

This extreme feebleness of Episcopalianism in the several States conspired with the tendencies of the time in civil affairs to induce upon the new organization a character not at all conformed to the ideal of episcopal government. Instead of establishing as the unit of organization the bishop in every principal town, governing his diocese at the head of his clergy with some measure of authority, it was almost a necessity of the time to constitute dioceses as big as kingdoms, and then to take security against excess of power in the diocesan by overslaughing his authority through exorbitant powers conferred upon a periodical mixed synod, legislating for a whole continent, even in matters confessedly variable and unessential. In the later evolution of the system, this superior limitation of the bishop's powers is supplemented from below by magnifying the authority of representative bodies, diocesan and parochial, until the work of the bishop is reduced as nearly as possible to the merely "ministerial" performance of certain assigned functions according to prescribed directions. Concerning this frame of government it is to be remarked: 1. That it was quite consciously and confessedly devised for the government of a sect, with the full and fraternal understanding that other "religious denominations of Christians" (to use the favorite American euphemism) "were left at full and equal liberty to model and organize their respective churches" to suit themselves.[211:1] 2. That, judged according to its professed purpose, it has proved itself a practically good and effective government. 3. That it is in no proper sense of the word an episcopal government, but rather a classical and synodical government, according to the common type of the American church constitutions of the period.[211:2]

The objections which only a few years before had withstood the importation into the colonies of lord bishops, with the English common and canon law at their backs, vanished entirely before the proposal for the harmless functionaries provided for in the new constitution. John Adams himself, a leader of the former opposition, now, as American minister in London, did his best to secure for Bishops-elect White and Provoost the coveted consecration from English bishops. The only hindrance now to this long-desired boon was in the supercilious dilatoriness of the English prelates and of the civil authorities to whom they were subordinate. They were evidently in a sulky temper over the overwhelming defeat of the British arms. If it had been in their power to blockade effectively the channels of sacramental grace, there is no sign that they would have consented to the American petition. Happily there were other courses open. 1. There was the recourse to presbyterial ordination, an expedient sanctioned, when necessary, by the authority of "the judicious Hooker," and actually recommended, if the case should require, by the Rev. William White, soon to be consecrated as one of the first American bishops. 2. Already for more than a half-century the Moravian episcopate had been present and most apostolically active in America. 3. The Lutheran Episcopal churches of Denmark and Sweden were fully competent and known to be not unwilling to confer the episcopal succession on the American candidates. 4. There were the Scotch nonjuring bishops, outlawed for political reasons from communion with the English church, who were tending their "persecuted remnant" of a flock in Scotland. Theirs was a not less valid succession than those of their better-provided English brethren, and fully as honorable a history. It was due to the separate initiative of the Episcopalian ministers of Connecticut, and to the persistence of their bishop-elect, Samuel Seabury, that the deadlock imposed by the Englishmen was broken. Inheriting the Puritan spirit, which sought a jus divinum in all church questions, they were men of deeper convictions and "higher" principles than their more southern brethren. In advance of the plans for national organization, without conferring with flesh and blood, they had met and acted, and their candidate for consecration was in London urging his claims, before the ministers in the Middle States had any knowledge of what was doing. After a year of costly and vexatious delay in London, finding no progress made and no hope of any, he proceeded to Aberdeen and was consecrated bishop November 14, 1784. It was more than two years longer before the English bishops succeeded in finding a way to do what their unrecognized Scotch brethren had done with small demur. But they did find it. So long as the Americans seemed dependent on English consecration they could not get it. When at last it was made quite plain that they could and would do without it if necessary, they were more than welcome to it. Dr. White for Pennsylvania, and Dr. Provoost for New York, were consecrated by the Archbishop of

Canterbury at the chapel of Lambeth Palace, February 4, 1787. Dr. Griffith, elected for Virginia, failed to be present; in all that great diocese there was not interest enough felt in the matter to raise the money to pay his passage to England and back.

The American Episcopal Church was at last in a condition to live. Some formidable dangers of division arising from the double derivation of the episcopate were happily averted by the tact and statesmanship of Bishop White, and liturgical changes incidental to the reconstitution of the church were made, on the whole with cautious judgment and good taste, and successfully introduced. But for many years the church lived only a languishing life. Bishop Provoost of New York, after fourteen years of service, demitted his functions in 1801, discouraged about the continuance of the church. He "thought it would die out with the old colonial families."[213:1] The large prosperity of this church dates only from the second decade of this century. It is the more notable for the brief time in which so much has been accomplished.

The difficulties in the way of the organization of the Catholic Church for the United States were not less serious, and were overcome with equal success, but not without a prolonged struggle against opposition from within. It is not easy for us, in view either of the antecedent or of the subsequent history, to realize the extreme feebleness of American Catholicism at the birth of our nation. According to an official "Relation on the State of Religion in the United States," presented by the prefect apostolic in 1785, the total number of Catholics in the entire Union was 18,200, exclusive of an unascertainable number, destitute of priests, in the Mississippi Valley. The entire number of the clergy was twenty-four, most of them former members of the Society of Jesuits, that had been suppressed in 1773 by the famous bull, Dominus ac Redemptor, of Clement XIV. Sorely against their will, these missionaries, hitherto subject only to the discipline of their own society, were transformed into secular priests, under the jurisdiction of the Vicar Apostolic of London. After the establishment of independence, with the intense jealousy felt regarding British influence, and by none more deeply and more reasonably felt than by the Catholics, this jurisdiction was impracticable. The providentially fit man for the emergency was found in the Rev. John Carroll, of an old Maryland family distinguished alike for patriotism and for faithfulness to Catholic principles. In June, 1784, he was made prefect apostolic over the Catholic Church in the United States, and the dependence on British jurisdiction was terminated.

When, however, it was proposed that this provisional arrangement should be superseded by the appointment of a bishop, objections not unexpected were encountered from among the clergy. Already we have had occasion to note the jealousy of episcopal authority that is felt by the clergy of the regular orders. The lately disbanded Jesuits, with characteristic flexibility of self-adaptation to circumstances, had at once reincorporated themselves under another name, thus to hold the not inconsiderable estates of their order in the State of Maryland. But the plans of these energetic men either to control the bishop or to prevent his appointment were unsuccessful. In December, 1790, Bishop Carroll, having been consecrated in England, arrived and entered upon his see of Baltimore.

Difficulties, through which there were not many precedents to guide him, thickened about the path of the new prelate. It was well both for the church and for the republic that he was a man not only versed in the theology and polity of his church, but imbued with American principles and feelings. The first conflict that vexed the church under his administration, and which for fifty years continued to vex his associates and successors, was a collision between the American sentiment for local and individual liberty and self-government, and the absolutist spiritual government of Rome. The Catholics of New York, including those of the Spanish and French legations, had built a church in Barclay Street, then on the northern outskirt of the city; and they had the very natural and just feeling that they had a right to do what they would with their own and with the building erected at their charges. They proceeded accordingly to put in charge of it priests of their own selection. But they had lost sight of the countervailing principle that if they had a right to do as they would with their building, the bishop, as representing the supreme authority in the church, had a like right to do as he would with his clergy. The building was theirs; but it was for the bishop to say what services should be held in it, or whether there should be any services in it at all, in the Roman Catholic communion. It is surprising how often this issue was made, and how repeatedly and obstinately it was fought out in various places, when the final result was so inevitable. The hierarchical power prevailed, of course, but after much irritation between priesthood and people, and "great loss of souls to the church."[216:1] American ideas and methods were destined profoundly and beneficially to affect the Roman Church in the United States, but not by the revolutionary process of establishing "trusteeism," or the lay control of parishes. The damaging results of such disputes to both parties and to their common interest in the church put the two parties under heavy bonds to deal by each other with mutual consideration. The tendency, as in some parallel cases, is toward an absolute government administered on republican principles, the authoritative command being given with cautious consideration of the disposition of the subject. The rights of the laity are sufficiently secured, first, by their holding the purse, and, secondly, in a community in which the Roman is only one of many churches held in like esteem and making like claims to divine authority, by their holding in reserve the right of withdrawal.

Other and unwonted difficulties for the young church lay in the Babel confusion of races and languages among its disciples, and in the lack of public resources, which could be supplied no otherwise than by free gift. Yet another difficulty was the scant supply of clergy; but events which about this time began to spread desolation among the institutions of Catholic Europe proved to be of inestimable benefit to the ill-provided Catholics of America. Rome might almost have been content to see the wasting and destruction in her ancient strongholds, for the opportune reinforcement which it brought, at a critical time, to the renascent church in the New World. More important than the priests of various orders and divers languages, who came all equipped for mission work among immigrants of different nationalities, was the arrival of the Sulpitians of Paris, fleeing from the persecutions of the French Revolution, ready for their special work of training for the parish priesthood. The founding of their seminary in Baltimore in 1791, for the training of a native clergy, was the best security that had yet been given for the permanence of the Catholic revival. The American Catholic Church was a small affair as yet, and for twenty years to come was to continue so; but the framework was preparing of an organization sufficient for the days of great things that were before it.

The most revolutionary change suffered by any religious body in America, in adjusting itself to the changed conditions after the War of Independence, was that suffered by the latest arrived and most rapidly growing of them all. We have seen the order of the Wesleyan preachers coming so tardily across the ocean, and propagated with constantly increasing momentum southward from the border of Maryland. Its congregations were not a church; its preachers were not a clergy. Instituted in England by a narrow, High-church clergyman of the established church, its preachers were simply a company of lay missionaries under the command of John Wesley; its adherents were members of the Church of England, bound to special fidelity to their duties as such in their several parish churches, but united in clubs and classes for the mutual promotion of holy living in an unholy age; and its chapels and other property, fruits of the self-denial of many poor, were held under iron-bound title-deeds, subject to the control of John Wesley and of the close corporation of preachers to whom he should demit them.

It seems hardly worthy of the immense practical sagacity of Wesley that he should have thought to transplant this system unchanged into the midst of circumstances so widely different as those which must surround it in America. And yet even here, where the best work of his preachers was to be done among populations not only churchless, but out of reach of church or ministry of whatever name, in those Southern States in which nine tenths of his penitents and converts were gained, his preachers were warned against the sacrilege of ministering to the craving converts the Christian ordinances of baptism and the holy supper, and bidden to send them to their own churches—when they had none. The wretched incumbents of the State parishes at the first sounds of war had scampered from the field like hirelings whose own the sheep are not, and the demand that the preachers of the word should also minister the comfort of the Christian ordinances became too strong to be resisted. The call of duty and necessity seemed to the preachers gathered at a conference at Fluvanna in 1779 to be a call from God; and, contrary to the strong objections of Wesley and Asbury, they chose from the older of their own number a committee who "ordained themselves, and proceeded to ordain and set apart other ministers for the same purpose—that they might minister the holy ordinances to the church of Christ."[218:1] The step was a bold one, and although it seemed to be attended by happy spiritual results, it threatened to precipitate a division of "the Society" into two factions. The progress of events, the establishment and acknowledgment of American independence, and the constant expansion of the Methodist work, brought its own solution of the divisive questions.

It was an important day in the history of the American church, that second day of September, 1784, when John Wesley, assisted by other presbyters of the Church of England, laid his hands in benediction upon the head of Dr. Thomas Coke, and committed to him the superintendency of the Methodist work in America, as colleague with Francis Asbury. On the arrival of Coke in America, the preachers were hastily summoned together in conference at Baltimore, and there, in Christmas week of the same year, Asbury was ordained successively as deacon, as elder, and as superintendent. By the two bishops thus constituted were ordained elders and deacons, and Methodism became a living church.

The two decades from the close of the War of Independence include the period of the lowest ebb-tide of vitality in the history of American Christianity. The spirit of half-belief or unbelief that prevailed on the other side of the sea, both in the church and out of it, was manifest also here. Happily the tide of foreign immigration at this time was stayed, and the church had opportunity to gather strength for the immense task that was presently to be devolved upon it. But the westward movement of our own population was now beginning to pour down the western slope of the Alleghanies into the great Mississippi basin. It was observed by the Methodist preachers that the members of their societies who had, through fear, necessity, or choice, moved into the back settlements and into new parts of the country, as soon as peace was settled and the way was open solicited the preachers to come among them, and so the work followed them to the west.[219:1] In the years 1791-1810 occurred the great movement of population from Virginia to Kentucky and from Carolina to Tennessee. It was reckoned that one fourth of the Baptists of Virginia had removed to Kentucky, and yet they hardly leavened the lump of early frontier barbarism. The Presbyterian Church, working in its favorite methods, devised campaigns of home missionary enterprise in its presbyteries and synods, detailing pastors from their parishes for temporary mission service in following the movement of the Scotch-Irish migration into the hill-country in which it seemed to find its congenial habitat, and from which its powerful influences were to flow in all directions. The Congregationalists of New England in like manner followed with Christian teaching and pastoral care their sons moving westward to occupy the rich lands of western New York and of Ohio. The General Association of the pastors of Connecticut, solicitous that the work of missions to the frontier should be carried forward without loss of power through division of forces, entered, in 1801, into the compact with the General Assembly of the Presbyterians known as the "Plan of Union," by which Christians of both polities might coöperate in the founding of churches and in maintaining the work of the gospel.

In the year 1803 the most important political event since the adoption of the Constitution, the purchase of Louisiana by President Jefferson, opened to the American church a new and immense field for missionary activity. This vast territory, stretching from the Mississippi westward to the summits of the Rocky Mountains and nearly doubling the domain of the United States, was the last remainder of the great projected French Catholic empire that had fallen in 1763. Passed back and forth with the vicissitudes of European politics between French and Spanish masters, it had made small progress in either civilization or Christianity.

But the immense possibilities of it to the kingdoms of this world and to the kingdom of heaven were obvious to every intelligent mind. Not many years were to pass before it was to become an arena in which all the various forces of American Christianity were to be found contending against all the powers of darkness, not without dealing some mutual blows in the melley.

The review of this period must not close without adverting to two important advances in public practical Christianity, in which (as often in like cases) the earnest endeavors of some among the Christians have been beholden for success to uncongenial reinforcements. As it is written, "The earth helped the woman."

In the establishment of the American principle of the non-interference of the state with religion, and the equality of all religious communions before the law, much was due, no doubt, to the mutual jealousies of the sects, no one or two of which were strong enough to maintain exceptional pretensions over the rest combined. Much also is to be imputed to the indifferentism and sometimes the anti-religious sentiment of an important and numerous class of doctrinaire politicians of which Jefferson may be taken as a type. So far as this work was a work of intelligent conviction and religious faith, the chief honor of it must be given to the Baptists. Other sects, notably the Presbyterians, had been energetic and efficient in demanding their own liberties; the Friends and the Baptists agreed in demanding liberty of conscience and worship, and equality before the law, for all alike. But the active labor in this cause was mainly done by the Baptists. It is to their consistency and constancy in the warfare against the privileges of the powerful "Standing Order" of New England, and of the moribund establishments of the South, that we are chiefly indebted for the final triumph, in this country, of that principle of the separation of church from state which is one of the largest contributions of the New World to civilization and to the church universal.

It is not surprising that a people so earnest as the Baptists showed themselves in the promotion of religious liberty should be forward in the condemnation of American slavery. We have already seen the vigor with which the Methodists, having all their strength at the South, levied a spiritual warfare against this great wrong. It was at the South that the Baptists, in 1789, "Resolved, That slavery is a violent deprivation of the rights of nature, and inconsistent with a republican government, and we therefore recommend it to our brethren to make use of every legal measure to extirpate this horrid evil from the land."[222:1] At the North, Jonathan Edwards the Younger is conspicuous in the unbroken succession of antislavery churchmen. His sermon on the "Injustice and Impolicy of the Slave-trade," preached in 1791 before the Connecticut Abolition Society, of which President Ezra Stiles was the head, long continued to be reprinted and circulated, both at the North and at the South, as the most effective argument not only against the slave-trade, but against the whole system of slavery.

It will not be intruding needlessly upon the difficult field of dogmatic history if we note here the widely important diversities of Christian teaching that belong to this which we may call the sub-Revolutionary period.

It is in contradiction to our modern association of ideas to read that the prevailing type of doctrine among the early Baptists of New England was Arminian.[222:2] The pronounced individualism of the Baptist churches, and the emphasis which they place upon human responsibility, might naturally have created a tendency in this direction; but a cause not less obvious was their antagonism to the established Congregationalism, with its sharply defined Calvinistic statements. The public challenging of these statements made a favorite issue on which to appeal to the people from their constituted teachers. But when the South and Southwest opened itself as the field of a wonderfully rapid expansion before the feet of the Baptist evangelists, the antagonism was quite of another sort. Their collaborators and sharp competitors in the great and noble work of planting the gospel and the church in old and neglected fields at the South, and carrying them westward to the continually advancing frontier of population, were to be found in the multiplying army of the Methodist itinerants and local exhorters, whose theology, enjoined upon them by their commission, was the Arminianism of John Wesley. No explanation is apparent for the revulsion of the great body of

American Baptists into a Calvinism exaggerated to the point of caricature, except the reaction of controversy with the Methodists. The tendency of the two parties to opposite poles of dogma was all the stronger for the fact that on both sides teachers and taught were alike lacking in liberalizing education. The fact that two by far the most numerous denominations of Christians in the United States were picketed thus over against each other in the same regions, as widely differing from each other in doctrine and organization as the Dominican order from the Jesuit, and differing somewhat in the same way, is a fact that invites our regret and disapproval, but at the same time compels us to remember its compensating advantages.

It is to this period that we trace the head-waters of several important existing denominations. At the close of the war the congregation of the "King's Chapel," the oldest Episcopal church in New England, had been thinned and had lost its rector in the general migration of leading Tory families to Nova Scotia. At the restoration of peace it was served in the capacity of lay reader by Mr. James Freeman, a young graduate of Harvard, who came soon to be esteemed very highly in love both for his work's sake and for his own. Being chosen pastor of the church, he was not many months in finding that many things in the English Prayer-book were irreconcilable with doubts and convictions concerning the Trinity and related doctrines, which about this time were widely prevalent among theologians both in the Church of England and outside of it. In June, 1785, it was voted in the congregation, by a very large majority, to amend the order of worship in accordance with these scruples. The changes were in a direction in which not a few Episcopalians were disposed to move,[224:1] and the congregation did not hesitate to apply for ordination for their pastor, first to Bishop Seabury, and afterward, with better hope of success, to Bishop Provoost. Failing here also, the congregation proceeded to induct their elect pastor into his office without waiting further upon bishops; and thus "the first Episcopal church in New England became the first Unitarian church in America." It was not the beginning of Unitarianism in America, for this had long been "in the air." But it was the first distinct organization of it. How rapidly and powerfully it spread within narrow geographical limits, and how widely it has affected the course of religious history, must appear in later chapters.

Close as might seem to be the kindred between Unitarianism and Universalism, coeval as they are in their origin as organized sects, they are curiously diverse in their origin. Each of them, at the present day, holds the characteristic tenet of the other; in general, Unitarians are Universalists, and Universalists are Unitarians.[225:1] But in the beginning Unitarianism was a bold reactionary protest against leading doctrines of the prevailing Calvinism of New England, notably against the doctrines of the Trinity, of expiatory atonement, and of human depravity; and it was still more a protest against the intolerant and intolerable dogmatism of the sanhedrim of Jonathan Edwards's successors, in their cock-sure expositions of the methods of the divine government and the psychology of conversion. Universalism, on the other hand, in its first setting forth in America, planted itself on the leading "evangelical" doctrines, which its leaders had earnestly preached, and made them the major premisses of its argument. Justification and salvation, said John Murray, one of Whitefield's Calvinistic Methodist preachers, are the lot of those for whom Christ died. But Christ died for the elect, said his Calvinistic brethren. Nay, verily, said Murray (in this following one of his colleagues, James Relly); what saith the Scripture? "Christ died for all." It was the pinch of this argument which brought New England theologians, beginning with Smalley and the second Edwards, to the acceptance of the rectoral theory of the atonement, and so prepared the way for much disputation among the doctors of the next century.[225:2]

Mr. Murray arrived in America in 1770, and after much going to and fro organized, in 1779, at Gloucester, Mass., the first congregation in America on distinctly Universalist principles. But other men, along other lines of thought, had been working their way to somewhat similar conclusions. In 1785 Elhanan Winchester, a thoroughly Calvinistic Baptist minister in Philadelphia, led forth his excommunicated brethren, one hundred strong, and organized them into a "Society of Universal Baptists," holding to the universal restoration of mankind to holiness and happiness. The two differing schools fraternized in a convention of Universalist churches at Philadelphia in 1794, at which articles of belief and a plan of organization were set forth, understood to be from the pen of Dr. Benjamin Rush; and a resolution was adopted declaring the holding of slaves to be "inconsistent with the union of the human race in a common Saviour, and the obligations to mutual and universal love which flow from that union."

It was along still another line of argument, proceeding from the assumed "rectitude of human nature," that the Unitarians came, tardily and hesitatingly, to the Universalist position. The long persistence of definite boundary lines between two bodies so nearly alike in their tenets is a subject worthy of study. The lines seem to be rather historical and social than theological. The distinction between them has been thus epigrammatically stated: that the Universalist holds that God is too good to damn a man; the Unitarian holds that men are too good to be damned.

No controversy in the history of the American church has been more deeply marked by a sincere and serious earnestness, over and above the competitive zeal and invidious acrimony that are an inevitable admixture in such debates, than the controversy that was at once waged against the two new sects claiming the title "Liberal." It was sincerely felt by their antagonists that, while the one abandoned the foundation of the Christian faith, the other destroyed the foundation of Christian morality. In the early propaganda of each of them was much to deepen this mistrust. When the standard of dissent is set up in any community, and men are invited to it in the name of liberality, nothing can hinder its becoming a rallying-point for all sorts of disaffected souls, not only the liberal, but the loose. The story of the controversy belongs to later chapters of this book. It is safe to say at this point that the early orthodox fears have at least not been fully confirmed by the sequel up to this date. It was one of the most strenuous of the early disputants against the "liberal" opinions[227:1] who remarked in his later years, concerning the Unitarian saints, that it seemed as if their exclusive contemplation of Jesus Christ in his human character as the example for our imitation had wrought in them an exceptional beauty and Christlikeness of living. As for the Universalists, the record of their fidelity, as a body, to the various interests of social morality is not surpassed by that of any denomination. But in the earlier days the conflict against the two sects called "liberal" was waged ruthlessly, not as against defective or erroneous schemes of doctrine, but as against distinctly antichristian heresies.

There is instruction to be gotten from studying, in comparison, the course of these opinions in the established churches of Great Britain and among the unestablished churches of America. Under the enforced comprehensiveness or tolerance of a national church, it is easier for strange doctrines to spread within the pale. Under the American plan of the organization of Christianity by voluntary mutual association according to elective affinity, with freedom to receive or exclude, the flock within the fold may perhaps be kept safer from contamination; as when the Presbyterian General Assembly in 1792, and again in 1794, decided that Universalists be not admitted to the sealing ordinances of the gospel;[228:1] but by this course the excluded opinion is compelled to intrench itself both for defense and for attack in a sectarian organization. It is a practically interesting question, the answer to which is by no means self-evident, whether Universalist opinions would have been less prevalent to-day in England and Scotland if they had been excluded from the national churches and erected into a sect with its partisan pulpits, presses, and propagandists; or whether they would have more diffused in America if, instead of being dealt with by process of excommunication or deposition, they had been dealt with simply by argument. This is one of the many questions which history raises, but which (happily for him) it does not fall within the function of the historian to answer.

To this period is to be referred the origin of some of the minor American sects.

The "United Brethren in Christ" grew into a distinct organization about the year 1800. It arose incidentally to the Methodist evangelism, in an effort on the part of Philip William Otterbein, of the German Reformed Church, and Martin Boehm, of the Mennonites, to provide for the shepherdless German-speaking people by an adaptation of the Wesleyan methods. Presently, in the natural progress of language, the English work outgrew the German. It is now doing an extensive and useful work by pulpit and press, chiefly in Pennsylvania and the States of that latitude. The reasons for its continued existence separate from the Methodist Church, which it closely resembles both in doctrine and in polity, are more apparent to those within the organization than to superficial observers from outside.

The organization just described arose from the unwillingness of the German Reformed Church to meet the craving needs of the German people by using the Wesleyan methods. From the unwillingness of the Methodist Church to use the German language arose another organization, "the Evangelical Association," sometimes known, from the name of its founder, by the somewhat grotesque title of "the Albrights." This also is both Methodist and Episcopal, a reduced copy of the great Wesleyan institution, mainly devoted to labors among the Germans.

In 1792 was planted at Baltimore the first American congregation of that organization of disciples of Emanuel Swedenborg which had been begun in London nine years before and called by the appropriately fanciful name of "the Church of the New Jerusalem."

CHAPTER XIV. THE SECOND AWAKENING.

The closing years of the eighteenth century show the lowest low-water mark of the lowest ebb-tide of spiritual life in the history of the American church. The demoralization of army life, the fury of political factions, the catchpenny materialist morality of Franklin, the philosophic deism of men like Jefferson, and the popular ribaldry of Tom Paine, had wrought, together with other untoward influences, to bring about a condition of things which to the eye of little faith seemed almost desperate.

From the beginning of the reaction from the stormy excitements of the Great Awakening, nothing had seemed to arouse the New England churches from a lethargic dullness; so, at least, it seemed to those who recalled those wonderful days of old, either in memory or by tradition. We have a gauge of the general decline of the public morals, in the condition of Yale College at the accession of President Dwight in 1795, as described in the reminiscences of Lyman Beecher, then a sophomore.

"Before he came, college was in a most ungodly state. The college church was almost extinct. Most of the students were skeptical, and rowdies were plenty. Wine and liquors were kept in many rooms; intemperance, profanity, gambling, and licentiousness were common. I hardly know how I escaped.... That was the day of the infidelity of the Tom Paine school. Boys that dressed flax in the barn, as I used to, read Tom Paine and believed him; I read and fought him all the way. Never had any propensity to infidelity. But most of the class before me were infidels, and called each other Voltaire, Rousseau, D'Alembert, etc."[231:1]

In the Middle States the aspect was not more promising. Princeton College had been closed for three years of the Revolutionary War. In 1782 there were only two among the students who professed themselves Christians. The Presbyterian General Assembly, representing the strongest religious force in that region, in 1798 described the then existing condition of the country in these terms:

"Formidable innovations and convulsions in Europe threaten destruction to morals and religion. Scenes of devastation and bloodshed unexampled in the history of modern nations have convulsed the world, and our country is threatened with similar calamities. We perceive with pain and fearful apprehension a general dereliction of religious principles and practice among our fellow-citizens, a visible and prevailing impiety and contempt for the laws and institutions of religion, and an abounding infidelity, which in many instances tends to atheism itself. The profligacy and corruption of the public morals have advanced with a progress proportionate to our declension in religion. Profaneness, pride, luxury, injustice, intemperance, lewdness, and every species of debauchery and loose indulgence greatly abound."

From the point of view of the Episcopalian of that day the prospect was even more disheartening. It was at this time that Bishop Provoost of New York laid down his functions, not expecting the church to continue much longer; and Bishop Madison of Virginia shared the despairing conviction of Chief-Justice Marshall that the church was too far gone ever to be revived.[232:1] Over all this period the historian of the Lutheran Church writes up the title "Deterioration."[232:2] Proposals were set on foot looking toward the merger of these two languishing denominations.

Even the Methodists, the fervor of whose zeal and vitality of whose organization had withstood what seemed severer tests, felt the benumbing influence of this unhappy age. For three years ending in 1796 the total membership diminished at the rate of about four thousand a year.

Many witnesses agree in describing the moral and religious condition of the border States of Kentucky and Tennessee as peculiarly deplorable. The autobiography of that famous pioneer preacher, Peter Cartwright, gives a lively picture of Kentucky society in 1793 as he remembered it in his old age:

"Logan County, when my father moved into it, was called 'Rogues' Harbor.' Here many refugees from all parts of the Union fled to escape punishment or justice; for although there was law, yet it could not be executed, and it was a desperate state of society. Murderers, horse-thieves, highway robbers, and counterfeiters fled there, until they combined and actually formed a majority. Those who favored a better state of morals were called 'Regulators.' But they encountered fierce opposition from the 'Rogues,' and a battle was fought with guns, pistols, dirks, knives, and clubs, in which the 'Regulators' were defeated."[233:1]

The people that walked in this gross darkness beheld a great light. In 1796 a Presbyterian minister, James McGready, who for more than ten years had done useful service in Pennsylvania and North Carolina, assumed charge of several Presbyterian churches in that very Logan County which we know through the reminiscences of Peter Cartwright. As he went the round of his scattered congregations his preaching was felt to have peculiar power "to arouse false professors, to awaken a dead church, and warn sinners and lead them to seek the new spiritual life which he himself had found." Three years later two brothers, William and John McGee, one a Presbyterian minister and the other a Methodist, came through the beautiful Cumberland country in Kentucky and Tennessee, speaking, as if in the spirit and power of John the Baptist, to multitudes that gathered from great distances to hear them. On one occasion, in the woods of Logan County, in July, 1800, the gathered families, many of whom came from far, tethered their teams and encamped for several days for the unaccustomed privilege of common worship and Christian preaching. This is believed to have been the first American camp-meeting—an era worth remembering in our history. Not without abundant New Testament antecedents, it naturalized itself at once on our soil as a natural expedient for scattered frontier populations unprovided with settled institutions. By a natural process of evolution, adapting itself to other environments and uses, the backwoods camp-meeting has grown into the "Chautauqua" assembly, which at so many places besides the original center at Chautauqua Lake has grown into an important and most characteristic institution of American civilization.

We are happy in having an account of some of these meetings from one who was personally and sympathetically interested in them. For in the spring of the next year Barton Warren Stone, a Presbyterian minister serving his two congregations of Concord and Cane Ridge in Bourbon County, and oppressed with a sense of the religious apathy prevailing about him, made the long journey across the State of Kentucky to see for himself the wonderful things of which he had heard, and afterward wrote his reminiscences.

"There, on the edge of a prairie in Logan County, Kentucky, the multitudes came together and continued a number of days and nights encamped on the ground, during which time worship was carried on in some part of the encampment. The scene was new to me and passing strange. It baffled description. Many, very many, fell down as men slain in battle, and continued for hours together in an apparently breathless and motionless state, sometimes for a few moments reviving and exhibiting symptoms of life by a deep groan or piercing shriek, or by a prayer for mercy fervently uttered. After lying there for hours they obtained deliverance. The gloomy cloud that had covered their faces seemed gradually and visibly to disappear, and hope, in smiles, brightened into joy. They would rise, shouting deliverance, and then would address the surrounding multitude in language truly eloquent and impressive. With astonishment did I hear men, women, and children declaring the wonderful works of God and the glorious mysteries of the gospel. Their appeals were solemn, heart-penetrating, bold, and free. Under such circumstances many others would fall down into the same state from which the speakers had just been delivered.

"Two or three of my particular acquaintances from a distance were struck down. I sat patiently by one of them, whom I knew to be a careless sinner, for hours, and observed with critical attention everything that passed, from the beginning to the end. I noticed the momentary revivings as from death, the humble confession of sins, the fervent prayer, and the ultimate deliverance; then the solemn thanks and praise to God, and affectionate exhortation to companions and to the people around to repent and come to Jesus. I was astonished at the knowledge of gospel truth displayed in the address. The effect was that several sank down into the same appearance of death. After attending to many such cases, my conviction was complete that it was a good work—the work of God; nor has my mind wavered since on the subject. Much did I see then, and much have I seen since, that I consider to be fanaticism; but this should not condemn the work. The devil has always tried to ape the works of God, to bring them into disrepute; but that cannot be a Satanic work which brings men to humble confession, to forsaking of sin, to prayer, fervent praise and thanksgiving, and a sincere and affectionate exhortation to sinners to repent and come to Jesus the Saviour."

Profoundly impressed by what he had seen and heard, Pastor Stone returned to his double parish in Bourbon County and rehearsed the story of it. "The congregation was affected with awful solemnity, and many returned home weeping." This was in the early spring. Not many months afterward there was a notable springing up of this seed.

"A memorable meeting was held at Cane Ridge in August, 1801. The roads were crowded with wagons, carriages, horses, and footmen moving to the solemn camp. It was judged by military men on the ground that between twenty and thirty thousand persons were assembled. Four or five preachers spoke at the same time in different parts of the encampment without confusion. The Methodist and Baptist preachers aided in the work, and all appeared cordially united in it. They were of one mind and soul: the salvation of sinners was the one object. We all engaged in singing the same songs, all united in prayer, all preached the same things.... The numbers converted will be known only in eternity. Many things transpired in the meeting which were so much like miracles that they had the same effect as miracles on unbelievers. By them many were convinced that Jesus was the Christ and were persuaded to submit to him. This meeting continued six or seven days and nights, and would have continued longer, but food for the sustenance of such a multitude failed.

"To this meeting many had come from Ohio and other distant parts. These returned home and diffused the same spirit in their respective neighborhoods. Similar results followed. So low had religion sunk, and such carelessness had universally prevailed, that I have thought that nothing common could have arrested and held the attention of the people."[236:1]

The sober and cautious tone of this narrative will already have impressed the reader. These are not the words of a heated enthusiast, or a man weakly credulous. We may hesitate to accept his judgment, but may safely accept his testimony, amply corroborated as it is, to facts which he has seen and heard.

But the crucial test of the work, the test prescribed by the Lord of the church, is that it shall be known by its fruits. And this test it seems to bear well. Dr. Archibald Alexander, had in high reverence in the Presbyterian Church as a wise counselor in spiritual matters, made scrupulous inquiry into the results of this revival, and received from one of his correspondents, Dr.

George A. Baxter, who made an early visit to the scenes of the revival, the following testimony:

"On my way I was informed by settlers on the road that the character of Kentucky travelers was entirely changed, and that they were as remarkable for sobriety as they had formerly been for dissoluteness and immorality. And indeed I found Kentucky to appearances the most moral place I had ever seen. A profane expression was hardly ever heard. A religious awe seemed to pervade the country. Upon the whole, I think the revival in Kentucky the most extraordinary that has ever visited the church of Christ; and, all things considered, it was peculiarly adapted to the circumstances of the country into which it came. Infidelity was triumphant and religion was on the point of expiring. Something extraordinary seemed necessary to arrest the attention of a giddy people who were ready to conclude that Christianity was a fable and futurity a delusion. This revival has done it. It has confounded infidelity and brought numbers beyond calculation under serious impressions."

A sermon preached in 1803 to the Presbyterian synod of Kentucky, by the Rev. David Rice, has the value of testimony given in the presence of other competent witnesses, and liable thus to be questioned or contradicted. In it he says:

"Neighborhoods noted for their vicious and profligate manners are now as much noted for their piety and good order. Drunkards, profane swearers, liars, quarrelsome persons, etc., are remarkably reformed.... A number of families who had lived apparently without the fear of God, in folly and in vice, without any religious instruction or any proper government, are now reduced to order and are daily joining in the worship of God, reading his word, singing his praises, and offering up their supplications to a throne of grace. Parents who seemed formerly to have little or no regard for the salvation of their children are now anxiously concerned for their salvation, are pleading for them, and endeavoring to lead them to Christ and train them up in the way of piety and virtue."

That same year the General Assembly of the Presbyterian Church, in its annual review of the state of religion, adverted with emphasis to the work in the Cumberland country, and cited remarkable instances of conversion—malignant opposers of vital piety convinced and reconciled, learned, active, and conspicuous infidels becoming signal monuments of that grace which they once despised; and in conclusion declared with joy that "the state and prospects of vital religion in our country are more favorable and encouraging than at any period within the last forty years."[238:1]

In order successfully to study the phenomena of this remarkable passage in the history of the church, it is necessary to bear in mind the social conditions that prevailed. A population perfervido ingenio, of a temper peculiarly susceptible of intense excitement, transplanted into a wild country, under little control either of conventionality or law, deeply ingrained from many generations with the religious sentiment, but broken loose from the control of it and living consciously in reckless disregard of the law of God, is suddenly aroused to a sense of its apostasy and wickedness. The people do not hear the word of God from Sabbath to Sabbath, or even from evening to evening, and take it home with them and ponder it amid the avocations of daily business; by the conditions, they are sequestered for days together in the wilderness for the exclusive contemplation of momentous truths pressed upon the mind with incessant and impassioned iteration; and they remain together, an agitated throng, not of men only, but of women and children. The student of psychology recognizes at once that here are present in an unusual combination the conditions not merely of the ready propagation of influence by example and persuasion, but of those nervous, mental, or spiritual infections which make so important a figure in the world's history, civil, military, or religious. It is wholly in accord with human nature that the physical manifestations attendant on religious excitement in these circumstances should be of an intense and extravagant sort.

And such indeed they were. Sudden outcries, hysteric weeping and laughter, faintings, catalepsies, trances, were customary concomitants of the revival preaching. Multitudes fell prostrate on the ground, "spiritually slain," as it was said. Lest the helpless bodies should be trampled on by the surging crowd, they were taken up and laid in rows on the floor of the neighboring meeting-house. "Some lay quiet, unable to move or speak. Some talked, but could not move. Some beat the floor with their heels. Some, shrieking in agony, bounded about, it is said, like a live fish out of water. Many lay down and rolled over and over for hours at a time. Others rushed wildly over the stumps and benches, and then plunged, shouting 'Lost! Lost!' into the forest."

As the revival went on and the camp-meeting grew to be a custom and an institution, this nervous epidemic took on certain recognizable forms, one of which was known as "the jerks." This malady "began in the head and spread rapidly to the feet. The head would be thrown from side to side so swiftly that the features would be blotted out and the hair made to snap. When the body was affected the sufferer was hurled over hindrances that came in his way, and finally dashed on the ground, to bounce about like a ball." The eccentric Lorenzo Dow, whose freaks of eloquence and humor are remembered by many now living, speaks from his own observation on the subject:

"I have passed a meeting-house where I observed the undergrowth had been cut for a camp-meeting, and from fifty to a hundred saplings were left breast-high on purpose for persons who were 'jerked' to hold on to. I observed where they had held on they had kicked up the earth as a horse stamping flies.... I believe it does not affect those naturalists who wish to get it to philosophize about it; and rarely those who are the most pious; but the lukewarm, lazy professor is subject to it. The wicked fear it and are subject to it; but the persecutors are more subject to it than any, and they have sometimes cursed and sworn and damned it while jerking."[240:1]

There is nothing improbable in the claim that phenomena like these, strange, weird, startling, "were so much like miracles that they had the same effect as miracles on unbelievers." They helped break up the apathetic torpor of the church and summon the multitudes into the wilderness to hear the preaching of repentance and the remission of sins. But they had some lamentable results. Those who, like many among the Methodists,[241:1] found in them the direct work of the Holy Spirit, were thereby started along the perilous incline toward enthusiasm and fanaticism. Those, on the other hand, repelled by the grotesqueness and extravagance of these manifestations, who were led to distrust or condemn the good work with which they were associated, fell into a graver error. This was the error into which, to its cost, the Presbyterian Church was by and by drawn in dealing with questions that emerged from these agitations. The revival gave rise to two new sects, both of them marked by the fervor of spirit that characterized the time, and both of them finding their principal habitat in the same western region. The Cumberland Presbyterians, now grown to large numbers and deserved influence and dignity in the fellowship of American sects, separated themselves from the main body of Presbyterians by refusing to accept, in face of the craving needs of the pastorless population all about them, the arbitrary rule shutting the door of access to the Presbyterian ministry to all candidates, how great soever their other qualifications, who lacked a classical education. Separating on this issue, they took the opportunity to amend the generally accepted doctrinal statements of the Presbyterian churches by mitigating those utterances which seemed to them, as they have seemed to many others, to err in the direction of fatalism.

About the same time there was manifested in various quarters a generous revolt against the existence and multiplication of mutually exclusive sects in the Christian family, each limited by humanly devised doctrinal articles and branded with partisan names. How these various protesting elements came together on the sole basis of a common faith in Christ and a common acceptance of the divine authority of the Bible; how, not intending it, they came to be themselves a new sect; and how, struggling in vain against the inexorable laws of language, they came to be distinguished by names, as Campbellite Baptist, Christ-ian (with a long i), and (κατ' ἐξόχην) Disciples, are points on which interesting and instructive light is shed in the history by Dr. B. B. Tyler.[242:1]

The great revival of the West and Southwest was not the only revival, and not even the earliest revival, of that time of crisis. As early as 1792 the long inertia of the eastern churches began to be broken here and there by signs of growing earnestness and attentiveness to spiritual things. There was little of excited agitation. There was no preaching of famous evangelists. There were no imposing convocations. Only in many and many of those country towns in which, at that time, the main strength of the population lay, the labors of faithful pastors began to be rewarded with large ingatherings of penitent believers. The languishing churches grew strong and hopeful, and the insolent infidelity of the times was abashed. With such sober simplicity was the work of the gospel carried forward, in the opening years of this century, among the churches and pastors that had learned wisdom from the mistakes made in the Great Awakening, that there are few striking incidents for the historian. Hardly any man is to be pointed out as a preëminent leader of the church at this period. If to any one, this place of honor belongs to Timothy Dwight, grandson of Jonathan Edwards, whose accession to the presidency of Yale College at the darkest hour in its history marked the turning-point. We have already learned from the reminiscences of Lyman Beecher how low the college had sunk in point of religious character, when most of the class above him were openly boastful of being infidels.[243:1] How the new president dealt with them is well described by the same witness:

"They thought the faculty were afraid of free discussion. But when they handed Dr. Dwight a list of subjects for class disputation, to their surprise, he selected this: 'Is the Bible the word of God?' and told them to do their best. He heard all they had to say, answered them, and there was an end. He preached incessantly for six months on the subject, and all infidelity skulked and hid its head. He elaborated his theological system in a series of forenoon sermons in the chapel; the afternoon discourses were practical. The original design of Yale College was to found a divinity school. To a mind appreciative, like mine, his preaching was a continual course of education and a continual feast. He was copious and polished in style, though disciplined and logical. There was a pith and power of doctrine there that has not been since surpassed, if equaled."[243:2]

It may be doubted whether to any man of his generation it was given to exercise a wider and more beneficent influence over the American church than that of President Dwight. His system of "Theology Explained and Defended in a Series of Sermons," a theology meant to be preached and made effective in convincing men and converting them to the service of God, was so constructed as to be completed within the four years of the college curriculum, so that every graduate should have heard the whole of it. The influence of it has not been limited by the boundaries of our country, nor has it expired with the century just completed since President Dwight's accession.

At the East also, as well as at the West, the quickening of religious thought and feeling had the common effect of alienating and disrupting. Diverging tendencies, which had begun to disclose themselves in the discussions between Edwards and Chauncy in their respective volumes of "Thoughts" on the Great Awakening, became emphasized in the revival of 1800. That liberalism which had begun as a protest against a too peremptory style of dogmatism was rapidly advancing toward a dogmatic denial of points deemed by the opposite party to be essential. Dogmatic differences were aggravated by differences of taste and temperament, and everything was working toward the schism by which some sincere and zealous souls should seek to do God service.

In one most important particular the revival of 1800 was happily distinguished from the Great Awakening of 1740. It was not done and over with at the end of a few years, and then followed by a long period of reaction. It was the beginning of a long period of vigorous and "abundant life," moving forward, not, indeed, with even and unvarying flow, yet with continuous current, marked with those alternations of exaltation and subsidence which seem, whether for evil or for good, to have become a fixed characteristic of American church history. The widespread revivals of the first decade of the nineteenth century saved the church of Christ in America from its low estate and girded it for stupendous tasks that were about to be devolved on it. In the glow of this renewed fervor, the churches of New England successfully made the difficult transition from establishment to self-support and to the costly enterprises of aggressive evangelization into which, in company with other churches to the South and West, they were about to enter. The Christianity of the country was prepared and equipped to attend with equal pace the prodigious rush of population across the breadth of the Great Valley, and to give welcome to the invading host of immigrants which before the end of a half century was to effect its entrance into our territory at the rate of a thousand a day. It was to accommodate itself to changing social conditions, as the once agricultural population began to concentrate itself in factory villages and commercial towns. It was to carry on systematic campaigns of warfare against instituted social wrong, such as the drinking usages of society, the savage code of dueling, the public sanction of slavery. And it was to enter the "effectual door" which from the beginning of the century opened wider and wider to admit the gospel and the church to every nation under heaven.

CHAPTER XV. ORGANIZED BENEFICENCE.

When the Presbyterian General Assembly, in 1803, made a studious review of the revivals which for several years had been in progress, especially at the South and West, it included in its "Narrative" the following observations:

"The Assembly observe with great pleasure that the desire for spreading the gospel among the blacks and among the savage tribes on our borders has been rapidly increasing during the last year. The Assembly take notice of this circumstance with the more satisfaction, as it not only affords a pleasing presage of the spread of the gospel, but also furnishes agreeable evidence of the genuineness and the benign tendency of that spirit which God has been pleased to pour out upon his people."

In New England the like result had already, several years before, followed upon the like antecedent. In the year 1798 the "Missionary Society of Connecticut" was constituted, having for its object "to Christianize the heathen in North America, and to support and promote Christian knowledge in the new settlements within the United States"; and in August, 1800, its first missionary, David Bacon, engaged at a salary of "one hundred and ten cents per day," set out for the wilderness south and west of Lake Erie, "afoot and alone, with no more luggage than he could carry on his person," to visit the wild tribes of that region, "to explore their situation, and learn their feelings with respect to Christianity, and, so far as he had opportunity, to teach them its doctrines and duties." The name forms a link in the bright succession from John Eliot to this day. But it must needs be that some suffer as victims of the inexperience of those who are first to take direction of an untried enterprise. The abandonment of its first missionary by one of the first missionary societies, leaving him helpless in the wilderness, was a brief lesson in the economy of missions opportunely given at the outset of the American mission work, and happily had no need to be repeated.[247:1]

David Bacon, like Henry Martyn, who at that same time, in far different surroundings, was intent upon his plans of mission work in India, was own son in the faith to David Brainerd. But they were elder sons in a great family. The pathetic story of that heroic youth, as told by Jonathan Edwards, was a classic at that time in almost every country parsonage; but its influence was especially felt in the colleges, now no longer, as a few years earlier, the seats of the scornful, but the homes of serious and religious learning which they were meant to be by their founders.

Of the advancement of Christian civilization in the first quarter-century from the achievement of independence there is no more distinguished monument than the increase, through those troubled and impoverished years, of the institutions of secular and sacred learning. The really successful and effective colleges that had survived from the colonial period were hardly a half-dozen. Up to 1810 these had been reinforced by as many more. By far the greater number of them were founded by the New England Congregationalists, to whom this has ever been a favorite field of activity. But special honor must be paid to the wise and courageous and nobly successful enterprise of large-minded and large-hearted men among the Baptists, who as early as 1764, boldly breasting a current of unworthy prejudice in their own denomination, began the work of Brown University at Providence, which, carried forward by a notable succession of great educators, has been set in the front rank of existing American institutions of learning. After the revivals of 1800 these Christian colleges were not only attended by students coming from zealous and fervid churches; they themselves became the foci from which high and noble spiritual influences were radiated through the land. It was in communities like these that the example of such lives as that of Brainerd stirred up generous young minds to a chivalrous and even ascetic delight in attempting great labors and enduring great sacrifices as soldiers under the Captain of salvation.

It was at Williams College, then just planted in the Berkshire hills, that a little coterie of students was formed which, for the grandeur of the consequences that flowed from it, is worthy to be named in history beside the Holy Club of Oxford in 1730, and the friends at Oriel College in 1830. Samuel J. Mills came to Williams College in 1806 from the parsonage of "Father Mills" of Torringford, concerning whom quaint traditions and even memories still linger in the neighboring parishes of Litchfield County, Connecticut. Around this young student gathered a circle of men like-minded. The shade of a lonely haystack was their oratory; the pledges by which they bound themselves to a life-work for the kingdom of heaven remind one of the mutual vows of the earliest friends of Loyola. Some of the youths went soon to the theological seminary, and at once leavened that community with their own spirit.

The seminary—there was only one in all Protestant America. As early as 1791 the Sulpitian fathers had organized their seminary at Baltimore. But it was not until 1808 that any institution for theological studies was open to candidates for the Protestant ministry. Up to that time such studies were made in the regular college curriculum, which was distinctly theological in character; and it was common for the graduate to spend an additional year at the college for special study under the president or the one professor of divinity. But many country parsonages that were tenanted by men of fame as writers and teachers were greatly frequented by young men preparing themselves for the work of preaching.

The change to the modern method of education for the ministry was a sudden one. It was precipitated by an event which has not even yet ceased to be looked on by the losing party with honest lamentation and with an unnecessary amount of sectarian acrimony. The divinity professorship in Harvard College, founded in 1722[249:1] by Thomas Hollis, of London, a Baptist friend of New England, was filled, after a long struggle and an impassioned protest, by the election of Henry Ware, an avowed and representative Unitarian. It was a distinct announcement that the government of the college had taken sides in the impending conflict, in opposition to the system of religious doctrine to the maintenance of which the college had from its foundation been devoted. The significance of the fact was not mistaken by either party. It meant that the two tendencies which had been recognizable from long before the Great Awakening were drawing asunder, and that thenceforth it must be expected that the vast influence of the venerable college, in the clergy and in society, would be given to the Liberal side. The dismay of one party and the exultation of the other were alike well grounded. The cry of the Orthodox was "To your tents, O Israel!" Lines of ecclesiastical non-intercourse were drawn. Church was divided from church, and family from family. When the forces and the losses on each side came to be reckoned up, there was a double wonder: First, at the narrow boundaries by which the Unitarian defection was circumscribed: "A radius of thirty-five miles from Boston as a center would sweep almost the whole field of its history and influence;"[250:1] and then at the sweeping completeness of it within these bounds; as Mrs. H. B. Stowe summed up the situation at Boston, "All the literary men of Massachusetts were Unitarian; all the trustees and professors of Harvard College were Unitarian; all the élite of wealth and fashion crowded Unitarian churches; the judges on the bench were Unitarian, giving decisions by which the peculiar features of church organization so carefully ordered by the Pilgrim Fathers had been nullified and all the power had passed into the hands of the congregation."[250:2]

The schism, with its acrimonies and heartburnings, was doubtless in some sense necessary. And it was attended with some beneficent consequences. It gave rise to instructive and illuminating debate. And on the part of the Orthodox it occasioned an outburst of earnest zeal which in a wonderfully short time had more than repaired their loss in numbers, and had started them on a career of wide beneficence, with a momentum that has been increasing to this day. But it is not altogether useless to put the question how much was lost to both parties and to the common cause by the separation. It is not difficult to conceive that such dogged polemics as Nathanael Emmons and Jedidiah Morse might have been none the worse for being held in some sort of fellowship, rather than in exasperated controversy, with such types of Christian sainthood as the younger Ware and the younger Buckminster; and it is easy to imagine the extreme culture and cool intellectual and spiritual temper of the Unitarian pulpit in general as finding its advantage in not being cut off from direct radiations from the fiery zeal of Lyman Beecher and Edward Dorr Griffin. Is it quite sure that New England Congregationalism would have been in all respects worse off if Channing and his friends had continued to be recognized as the Liberal wing of its clergy? or that the Unitarian ministers would not have been a great deal better off if they had remained in connection with a strong and conservative right wing, which might counterbalance the exorbitant leftward flights of their more impatient and erratic spirits?

The seating of a pronounced Unitarian in the Hollis chair of theology at Harvard took place in 1805. Three years later, in 1808, the doors of Andover Seminary were opened to students. Thirty-six were present, and the number went on increasing. The example was quickly followed. In 1810 the Dutch seminary was begun at New Brunswick, and in 1812 the Presbyterian at Princeton. In 1816 Bangor Seminary (Congregationalist) and Hartwick Seminary (Lutheran) were opened. In 1819 the Episcopalian "General Seminary" followed, and the Baptist "Hamilton Seminary" in 1820. In 1821 Presbyterian seminaries were begun at Auburn, N. Y., and Marysville, Tenn. In 1822 the Yale Divinity College was founded (Congregationalist); in 1823 the Virginia (Episcopalian) seminary at Alexandria; in 1824 the Union (Presbyterian) Seminary, also in Virginia, and the Unitarian seminary at Cambridge; in 1825 the Baptist seminary at Newton, Mass., and the German Reformed at York, Pa.; in 1826 the Lutheran at Gettysburg; in 1827 the Baptist at Rock Spring, Ill. Thus, within a period of twenty years, seventeen theological schools had come into existence where none had been known before. It was a swift and beneficent revolution, and the revolution has never gone backward. In 1880 were enumerated in the United States no less than one hundred and forty-two seminaries, representing all sects, orders, and schools of theological opinion, employing five hundred and twenty-nine resident professors.[252:1]

To Andover, in the very first years of its great history, came Mills and others of the little Williams College circle; and at once their infectious enthusiasm for the advancement of the kingdom of God was felt throughout the institution. The eager zeal of these young men brooked no delay. In June, 1810, the General Association of Massachusetts met at the neighboring town of Bradford; there four of the students, Judson, Nott, Newell, and Hall, presented themselves and their cause; and at that meeting was constituted the American Board of Commissioners for Foreign Missions. The little faith of the churches shrank from the responsibility of sustaining missionaries in the field, and Judson was sent to England to solicit the coöperation of the London Missionary Society. This effort happily failing, the burden came back upon the American churches and was not refused. At last, in February, 1812, the first American missionaries to a foreign country, Messrs. Judson, Rice, Newell, Nott, and Hall, with their wives, sailed, in two parties, for Calcutta.

And now befell an incident perplexing, embarrassing, and disheartening to the supporters of the mission, but attended with results for the promotion of the gospel to which their best wisdom never could have attained. Adoniram Judson, a graduate of Brown University, having spent the long months at sea in the diligent and devout study of the Scriptures, arrived at

Calcutta fully persuaded of the truth of Baptist principles. His friend, Luther Rice, arriving by the other vessel, came by and by to the same conclusion; and the two, with their wives, were baptized by immersion in the Baptist church at Calcutta. The announcement of this news in America was an irresistible appeal to the already powerful and rapidly growing Baptist denomination to assume the support of the two missionaries who now offered themselves to the service of the Baptist churches. Rice returned to urge the appeal on their immediate attention, while Judson remained to enter on that noble apostolate for which his praise is in all the churches.

To the widespread Baptist fellowship this sudden, unmistakable, and imperative providential summons to engage in the work of foreign missions was (it is hardly too much to say) like life from the dead. The sect had doubled its numbers in the decade just passed, and was estimated to include two hundred thousand communicants, all "baptized believers." But this multitude was without common organization, and, while abundantly endowed with sectarian animosities, was singularly lacking in a consciousness of common spiritual life. It was pervaded by a deadly fatalism, which, under the guise of reverence for the will of God, was openly pleaded as a reason for abstaining from effort and self-denial in the promotion of the gospel. Withal it was widely characterized not only by a lack of education in its ministry, but by a violent and brutal opposition to a learned clergy, which was particularly strange in a party the moiety of whose principles depends on a point in Greek lexicology. It was to a party—we may not say a body—deeply and widely affected by traits like these that the divine call was to be presented and urged. The messenger was well fitted for his work. To the zeal of a new convert to Baptist principles, and a missionary fervor deepened by recent contact with idolatry in some of its most repulsive forms, Luther Rice united a cultivated eloquence and a personal persuasiveness. Of course his first address was to pastors and congregations in the seaboard cities, unexcelled by any, of whatever name, for intelligent and reasonable piety; and here his task was easy and brief, for they were already of his mind. But the great mass of ignorance and prejudice had also to be reckoned with. By a work in which the influence of the divine Spirit was quite as manifest as in the convulsive agitations of a camp-meeting, it was dealt with successfully. Church history moved swiftly in those days. The news of the accession of Judson and Rice was received in January, 1813. In May, 1814, the General Missionary Convention of the Baptists was organized at Philadelphia, thirty-three delegates being present, from eleven different States. The Convention, which was to meet triennially, entered at once upon its work. It became a vital center to the Baptist denomination. From it, at its second meeting, proceeded effective measures for the promotion of education in the ministry, and, under the conviction that "western as well as eastern regions are given to the Son of God as an inheritance," large plans for home missions at the West.

Thus the great debt which the English Congregationalists had owed to the Baptists for heroic leadership in the work of foreign missions was repaid with generous usury by the Congregationalists to the Baptists of America. From this time forward the American Baptists came more and more to be felt as a salutary force in the religious life of the nation and the world. But against what bitter and furious opposition on the part of the ancient ignorance the new light had to struggle cannot easily be conceived by those who have only heard of the "Hard-Shell Baptist" as a curious fossil of a prehistoric period.[255:1]

The American Board of Commissioners for Foreign Missions continued for twenty-seven years to be the common organ of foreign missionary operations for the Congregationalists, the Presbyterians, and the Dutch and German Reformed churches. In the year 1837 an official Presbyterian Board of Missions was erected by the Old-School fragment of the disrupted Presbyterian Church; and to this, when the two fragments were reunited, in 1869, the contributions of the New-School side began to be transferred. In 1858 the Dutch church, and in 1879 the German church, instituted their separate mission operations. Thus the initiative of the Andover students in 1810 resulted in the erection, not of one mission board, timidly venturing to set five missionaries in the foreign field, but of five boards, whose total annual resources are counted by millions of dollars, whose evangelists, men and women, American and foreign-born, are a great army, and whose churches, schools, colleges, theological seminaries, hospitals, printing-presses, with the other equipments of a Christian civilization, and the myriads of whose faithful Christian converts, in every country under the whole heaven, have done more for the true honor of our nation than all that it has achieved in diplomacy and war.[255:2]

The Episcopalians entered on foreign mission work in 1819, and the Methodists, tardily but at last with signal efficiency and success, in 1832. No considerable sect of American Christians at the present day is unrepresented in the foreign field.

In order to complete the history of this organizing era in the church, we must return to the humble but memorable figure of Samuel J. Mills. It was his characteristic word to one of his fellows, as they stood ready to leave the seclusion of the seminary for active service, "You and I, brother, are little men, but before we die, our influence must be felt on the other side of the world." No one claimed that he was other than a "little man," except as he was filled and possessed with a great thought, and that the thought that filled the mind of Christ—the thought of the Coming Age and of the Reign of God on earth.[256:1] While his five companions were sailing for the remotest East, Mills plunged into the depth of the western wilderness, and between 1812 and 1815, in two toilsome journeys, traversed the Great Valley as far as New Orleans, deeply impressed everywhere with the famine of the word, and laboring, in coöperation with local societies at the East, to provide for the universal want by the sale or gift of Bibles and the organization of Bible societies. After his second return he proposed the organization of the American Bible Society, which was accomplished in 1816.

But already this nobly enterprising mind was intent on a new plan, of most far-reaching importance, not original with himself, but, on the contrary, long familiar to those who studied the extension of the church and pondered the indications of God's providential purposes. The earliest attempt in America toward the propagation of the gospel in foreign lands would seem to have been the circular letter sent out by the neighbor pastors, Samuel Hopkins and Ezra Stiles, in the year 1773, from Newport, chief seat of the slave-trade, asking contributions for the education of two colored men as missionaries to their native continent of Africa. To many generous minds at once, in this era of great Christian enterprises, the thought recurred of vast blessings to be wrought for the Dark Continent by the agency of colored men Christianized, civilized, and educated in America. Good men reverently hoped to see in this triumphant solution of the mystery of divine providence in permitting the curse of African slavery, through the cruel greed of men, to be inflicted on the American republic. In 1816 Mills successfully pressed upon the Presbyterian "Synod of New York and New Jersey" a plan for educating Christian men of color for the work of the gospel in their fatherland. That same year, in coöperation with an earnest philanthropist, Dr. Robert Finley, of New Jersey, he aided in the instituting of the American Colonization Society. In 1817 he sailed, in company with a colleague, the Rev. Ebenezer Burgess, to explore the coast of Africa in search of the best site for a colony. On the return voyage he died, and his body was committed to the sea: a "little man," to whom were granted only five years of what men call "active life"; but he had fulfilled his vow, and the ends of the earth had felt his influence for the advancement of the kingdom of the Lord Jesus Christ. The enterprise of African colonization, already dear to Christian hearts for the hopes that it involved of the redemption of a lost continent, of the elevation of an oppressed race in America, of the emancipation of slaves and the abolition of slavery, received a new consecration as the object of the dying labors and prayers of Mills. It was associated, in the minds of good men, not only with plans for the conversion of the heathen, and with the tide of antislavery sentiment now spreading and deepening both at the South and at the North, but also with "Clarkson societies" and other local organizations, in many different places, for the moral and physical elevation of the free colored people from the pitiable degradation in which they were commonly living in the larger towns. Altogether the watchmen on the walls of Zion saw no fairer sign of dawn, in that second decade of the nineteenth century, than the hopeful lifting of the cloud from Africa, the brightening prospects of the free negroes of the United States, and the growing hope of the abolition of American slavery.[258:1]

Other societies, national in their scope and constituency, the origin of which belongs in this organizing period, are the American Education Society (1815), the American Sunday-school Union (1824), the American Tract Society (1825), the Seamen's Friend Society (1826), and the American Home Missionary Society (1826), in which last the Congregationalists of New England coöperated with the Presbyterians on the basis of a Plan of Union entered into between the General Assembly and the General Association of Connecticut, the tendency of which was to reinforce the Presbyterian Church with the numbers and the vigor of the New England westward migration. Of course the establishment of these and other societies for beneficent work outside of sectarian lines did not hinder, but rather stimulated, sectarian organizations for the like objects. The whole American church, in all its orders, was girding itself for a work, at home and abroad, the immense grandeur of which no man of that generation could possibly have foreseen.

The grandeur of this work was to consist not only in the results of it, but in the resources of it. As never before, the sympathies, prayers, and personal coöperation of all Christians, even the feeblest, were to be combined and utilized for enterprises coextensive with the continent and the world and taking hold on eternity. The possibilities of the new era were dazzling to the prophetic imagination. A young minister then standing on the threshold of a long career exulted in the peculiar and excelling glory of the dawning day:

"Surely, if it is the noblest attribute of our nature that spreads out the circle of our sympathies to include the whole family of man, and sends forth our affections to embrace the ages of a distant futurity, it must be regarded as a privilege no less exalted that our means of doing good are limited by no remoteness of country or distance of duration, but we may operate, if we will, to assuage the miseries of another hemisphere, or to prevent the necessities of an unborn generation. The time has been when a man might weep over the wrongs of Africa, and he might look forward to weep over the hopelessness of her degradation, till his heart should bleed; and yet his tears would be all that he could give her. He might relieve the beggar at his door, but he could do nothing for a dying continent. He might provide for his children, but he could do nothing for the nations that were yet to be born to an inheritance of utter wretchedness. Then the privilege of engaging in schemes of magnificent benevolence belonged only to princes and to men of princely possessions; but now the progress of improvement has brought down this privilege to the reach of every individual. The institutions of our age are a republic of benevolence, and all may share in the unrestrained and equal democracy. This privilege is ours. We may stretch forth our hand, if we will, to enlighten the Hindu or to tame the savage of the wilderness. It is ours, if we will, to put forth our contributions and thus to operate not ineffectually for the relief and renovation of a continent over which one tide of misery has swept without ebb and without restraint for unremembered centuries. It is ours, if we will, to do something that shall tell on all the coming ages of a race which has been persecuted and enslaved, trodden down and despised, for a thousand generations. Our Father has made us the almoners of his love. He has raised us to partake, as it were, in the ubiquity of his own beneficence. Shall we be unworthy of the trust? God forbid!"[260:1]

CHAPTER XVI. CONFLICTS OF THE CHURCH WITH PUBLIC WRONGS.

The transition from establishment to the voluntary system for the support of churches was made not without some difficulty, but with surprisingly little. In the South the established churches were practically dead before the laws establishing them were repealed and the endowments disposed of. In New York the Episcopalian churches were indeed depressed and discouraged by the ceasing of State support and official patronage; and inasmuch as these, with the subsidies of the "S. P. G.," had been their main reliance, it was inevitable that they should pass through a period of prostration until the appreciation of their large endowments, and the progress of immigration and of conversion from other sects, and especially the awakening of religious earnestness and of sectarian ambition.

In New England the transition to the voluntary system was more gradual. Not till 1818 in Connecticut, and in Massachusetts not till 1834, was the last strand of connection severed between the churches of the standing order and the state, and the churches left solely to their own resources. The exaltation and divine inspiration that had come to these churches with the revivals which from the end of the eighteenth century were never for a long time intermitted, and the example of the dissenting congregations, Baptist, Episcopalian, and Methodist, successfully self-supported among them, made it easy for them, notwithstanding the misgivings of many good men, not only to assume the entire burden of their own expenses, but with this to undertake and carry forward great and costly enterprises of charity reaching to the bounds of the country and of the inhabited earth. It is idle to claim that the American system is at no disadvantage in comparison with that which elsewhere prevails almost throughout Christendom; but it may be safely asserted that the danger that has been most emphasized as a warning against the voluntary system has not attended this system in America. The fear that a clergy supported by the free gifts of the people would prove subservient and truckling to the hand by which it is fed has been proved groundless. Of course there have been time-servers in the American ministry, as in every other; but flagrant instances of the abasement of a whole body of clergy before the power that holds the purse and controls promotion are to be sought in the old countries rather than the new. Even selfish motives would operate against this temptation, since it has often been demonstrated that the people will not sustain a ministry which it suspects of the vice of subserviency. The annals of no established church can show such unsparing fidelity of the ministry in rebuking the sins of people and of rulers in the name of the Lord, as that which has been, on the whole, characteristic of the Christian ministers of the United States.

Among the conflicts of the American church with public wrongs strongly intrenched in law or social usage, two are of such magnitude and protracted through so long a period as to demand special consideration—the conflict with drunkenness and the conflict with slavery. Some less conspicuous illustrations of the fidelity of the church in the case of public and popular sins may be more briefly referred to.

The death of Alexander Hamilton, in July, 1804, in a duel with Aaron Burr, occasioned a wide and violent outburst of indignation against the murderer, now a fugitive and outcast, for the dastardly malignity of the details of his crime, and for the dignity and generosity as well as the public worth of his victim. This was the sort of explosion of excited public feeling which often loses itself in the air. It was a different matter when the churches and ministers of Christ took up the affair in the light of the law of God, and, dealing not with the circumstances but with the essence of it, pressed it inexorably on the conscience of the people. Some of the most memorable words in American literature were uttered on this occasion, notwithstanding that there were few congregations in which there were not sore consciences to be irritated or political anxieties to be set quaking by them. The names of Eliphalet Nott and John M. Mason were honorably conspicuous in this work. But one unknown young man of thirty, in a corner of Long Island, uttered words in his little country meeting-house that pricked the conscience of the nation. The words of Lyman Beecher on this theme may well be quoted as being a part of history, for the consequences that followed them.

"Dueling is a great national sin. With the exception of a small section of the Union, the whole land is defiled with blood. From the lakes of the North to the plains of Georgia is heard the voice of lamentation and woe—the cries of the widow and fatherless. This work of desolation is performed often by men in office, by the appointed guardians of life and liberty. On the floor of Congress challenges have been threatened, if not given, and thus powder and ball have been introduced as the auxiliaries of deliberation and argument.... We are murderers—a nation of murderers—while we tolerate and reward the perpetrators of the crime."

Words such as these resounding from pulpit after pulpit, multiplied and disseminated by means of the press, acted on by representative bodies of churches, becoming embodied in anti-dueling societies, exorcised the foul spirit from the land. The criminal folly of dueling did not, indeed, at once and altogether cease. Instances of it continue to be heard of to this day. But the conscience of the nation was instructed, and a warning was served upon political parties to beware of proposing for national honors men whose hands were defiled with blood.[264:1] Another instance of the fidelity of the church in resistance to public wrong was its action in the matter of the dealing of the State of Georgia and the national government toward the Georgia Indians. This is no place for the details of the shameful story of perfidy and oppression. It is well told by Helen Hunt Jackson in the melancholy pages of "A Century of Dishonor." The wrongs inflicted on the Cherokee nation were deepened by every conceivable aggravation. "In the whole history of our government's dealings with the Indian tribes there is no record so black as the record of its perfidy to this nation. There will come a time in the remote future when to the student of American history it will seem well-nigh incredible. From the beginning of the century they had been steadily advancing in civilization. As far back as 1800 they had begun the manufacture of cotton cloth, and in 1820 there was scarcely a family in that part of the nation living east of the Mississippi but what understood the use of the card and spinning-wheel. Every family had its farm under cultivation. The territory was laid off into districts, with a council-house, a judge, and a marshal in each district. A national committee and council were the supreme authority in the nation. Schools were flourishing in all the villages. Printing-presses were at work.... They were enthusiastic in their efforts to establish and perfect their own system of jurisprudence. Missions of several sects were established in their country, and a large number of them had professed Christianity and were leading exemplary lives. There is no instance in all history of a race of people passing in so short a space of time from the barbarous stage to the agricultural and civilized."[265:1]

We do well to give authentic details of the condition of the Cherokee nation in the early part of the century, for the advanced happy and peaceful civilization of this people was one of the fairest fruits of American Christianity working upon exceptionally noble race-qualities in the recipients of it. An agent of the War Department in 1825 made official report to the Department on the rare beauty of the Cherokee country, secured to them by the most sacred pledges with which it was possible for the national government to bind itself, and covered by the inhabitants, through their industry and thrift, with flocks and herds, with farms and villages; and goes on to speak of the Indians themselves:

"The natives carry on considerable trade with the adjoining States; some of them export cotton in boats down the Tennessee to the Mississippi, and down that river to New Orleans. Apple and peach orchards are quite common, and gardens are cultivated and much attention paid to them. Butter and cheese are seen on Cherokee tables. There are many public roads in the nation, and houses of entertainment kept by natives. Numerous and flourishing villages are seen in every section of the country. Cotton and woolen cloths are manufactured; blankets of various dimensions, manufactured by Cherokee hands, are very common. Almost every family in the nation grows cotton for its own consumption. Industry and commercial enterprise are extending themselves in every part. Nearly all the merchants in the nation are native Cherokees. Agricultural pursuits engage the chief attention of the people. Different branches in mechanics are pursued. The population is rapidly increasing.... The Christian religion is the religion of the nation. Presbyterians, Methodists, Baptists, and Moravians are the most numerous sects. Some of the most influential characters are members of the church and live consistently with their professions. The whole nation is penetrated with gratitude for the aid it has received from the United States government and from different religious societies. Schools are increasing every year; learning is encouraged and rewarded; the young class acquire the English and those of mature age the Cherokee system of learning."[266:1]

This country, enriched by the toil and thrift of its owners, the State of Georgia resolved not merely to subjugate to its jurisdiction, but to steal from its rightful and lawful owners, driving them away as outlaws. As a sure expedient for securing popular consent to the intended infamy, the farms of the Cherokees were parceled out to be drawn for in a lottery, and the lottery tickets distributed among the white voters. Thus fortified, the brave State of Georgia went to all lengths of outrage. "Missionaries were arrested and sent to prison for preaching to Cherokees; Cherokees were sentenced to death by Georgia courts and hung by Georgia executioners." But the great crime could not be achieved without the connivance, and at last the active consent, of the national government. Should this consent be given? Never in American history has the issue been more squarely drawn between the kingdom of Satan and the kingdom of Christ. American Christianity was most conspicuously represented in this conflict by an eminent layman, Jeremiah Evarts, whose fame for this public service, and not for this alone, will in the lapse of time outshine even that of his illustrious son. In a series of articles in the "National Intelligencer," under the signature of "William Penn," he cited the sixteen treaties in which the nation had pledged its faith to defend the Cherokees in the possession of their lands, and set the whole case before the people as well as the government. But his voice was not solitary. From press and pulpit and from the platforms of public meetings all over the country came petitions, remonstrances, and indignant protests, reinforcing the pathetic entreaties of the Cherokees themselves to be protected from the cruelty that threatened to tear them from their homes. In Congress the honor of leadership among many faithful and able advocates of right and justice was conceded to Theodore Frelinghuysen, then in the prime of a great career of Christian service. By the majority of one vote the bill for the removal of the Cherokees passed the United States Senate. The gates of hell triumphed for a time with a fatal exultation. The authors and abettors of the great crime were confirmed in their delusion that threats of disunion and rebellion could be relied on to carry any desired point. But the mills of God went on grinding. Thirty years later, when in the battle of Missionary Ridge the chivalry of Georgia went down before the army that represented justice and freedom and the authority of national law, the vanquished and retreating soldiers of a lost cause could not be accused of superstition if they remembered that the scene of their humiliating defeat had received its name from the martyrdom of Christian missionaries at the hands of their fathers.

In earlier pages we have already traced the succession of bold protests and organized labors on the part of church and clergy against the institution of slavery.[268:1] If protest and argument against it seem to be less frequent in the early years of the new century, it is only because debate must needs languish when there is no antagonist. Slavery had at that time no defenders in the church. No body of men in 1818 more unmistakably represented the Christian citizenship of the whole country, North, South, and West, outside of New England, than the General Assembly of the then undivided Presbyterian Church. In that year the Assembly set forth a full and unanimous expression of its sentiments on the subject of slavery, addressed "to the churches and people under its care." This monumental document is too long to be cited here in full. The opening paragraphs of it exhibit the universally accepted sentiment of American Christians of that time:

"We consider the voluntary enslaving of one part of the human race by another as a gross violation of the most precious and sacred rights of human nature; as utterly inconsistent with the law of God, which requires us to love our neighbor as ourselves; and as totally irreconcilable with the spirit and principles of the gospel of Christ, which enjoin that 'all things whatsoever ye would that men should do to you, do ye even so to them.' Slavery creates a paradox in the moral system. It exhibits rational, accountable, and immortal beings in such circumstances as scarcely to leave them the power of moral action. It exhibits them as dependent on the will of others whether they shall receive religious instruction; whether they shall know and worship the true God; whether they shall enjoy the ordinances of the gospel; whether they shall perform the duties and cherish the endearments of husbands and wives, parents and children, neighbors and friends; whether they shall preserve their chastity and purity or regard the dictates of justice and humanity. Such are some of the consequences of slavery—consequences not imaginary, but which connect themselves with its very existence. The evils to which the slave is always exposed often take place in fact, and in their worst degree and form; and where all of them do not take place, as we rejoice to say that in many instances, through the influence of the principles of humanity and religion on the minds of masters, they do not, still the slave is deprived of his natural right, degraded as a human being, and exposed to the danger of passing into the hands of a master who may inflict upon him all the hardships and injuries which inhumanity and avarice may suggest.

"From this view of the consequences resulting from the practice into which Christian people have most inconsistently fallen of enslaving a portion of their brethren of mankind,—for 'God hath made of one blood all nations of men to dwell on the face of the earth,'—it is manifestly the duty of all Christians who enjoy the light of the present day, when the inconsistency of slavery both with the dictates of humanity and religion has been demonstrated and is generally seen and acknowledged, to use their honest, earnest, and unwearied endeavors to correct the errors of former times, and as speedily as possible to efface this blot on our holy religion and to obtain the complete abolition of slavery throughout Christendom, and if possible throughout the world."

It was not strange that while sentiments like these prevailed without contradiction in all parts of the country, while in State after State emancipations were taking place and acts of abolition were passing, and even in the States most deeply involved in slavery "a great, and the most virtuous, part of the community abhorred slavery and wished its extermination,"[270:1] there should seem to be little call for debate. But that the antislavery spirit in the churches was not dead was demonstrated with the first occasion.

In the spring of 1820, at the close of two years of agitating discussion, the new State of Missouri was admitted to the Union as a slave State, although with the stipulation that the remaining territory of the United States north of the parallel of latitude bounding Missouri on the south should be consecrated forever to freedom. The opposition to this extension of slavery was taken up by American Christianity as its own cause. It was the impending danger of such an extension that prompted that powerful and unanimous declaration of the Presbyterian General Assembly in 1818. The arguments against the Missouri bill, whether in the debates of Congress or in countless memorials and resolutions from public meetings both secular and religious, were arguments from justice and duty and the law of Christ. These were met by constitutional objections and considerations of expediency and convenience, and by threats of disunion and civil war. The defense of slavery on principle had not yet begun to be heard, even among politicians.

The successful extension of slavery beyond the Mississippi River was disheartening to the friends of justice and humanity, but only for the moment. Already, before the two years' conflict had been decided by "the Missouri Compromise," a powerful series of articles by that great religious leader, Jeremiah Evarts, in the "Panoplist" (Boston, 1820), rallied the forces of the church to renew the battle. The decade that opened with that defeat is distinguished as a period of sustained antislavery activity on the part of the united Christian citizenship of the nation in all quarters.[271:1] In New England the focus of antislavery effort was perhaps the theological seminary at Andover. There the leading question among the students in their "Society of Inquiry concerning Missions" was the question, what could be done, and especially what they could do, for the uplifting of the colored population of the country, both the enslaved and the free. Measures were concerted there for the founding of "an African college where youth were to be educated on a scale so liberal as to place them on a level with other men";[271:2] and the plan was not forgotten or neglected by these young men when from year to year they came into places of effective influence. With eminent fitness the Fourth of July was taken as an antislavery holiday, and into various towns within reach from Andover their most effective speakers went forth to give antislavery addresses on that day. Beginning with the Fourth of July, 1823, the annual antislavery address at Park Street Church, Boston, before several united churches of that city, continued for the rest of that decade at least to be an occasion for earnest appeal and practical effort in behalf of the oppressed. Neither was the work of the young men circumscribed by narrow local boundaries. The report of their committee, in the year 1823, on "The Condition of the Black Population of the United States," could hardly be characterized as timid in its utterances on the moral character of American slavery. A few lines will indicate the tone of it in this respect:

"Excepting only the horrible system of the West India Islands, we have never heard of slavery in any country, ancient or modern, pagan, Mohammedan, or Christian, so terrible in its character, so pernicious in its tendency, so remediless in its anticipated results, as the slavery which exists in these United States.... When we use the strong language which we feel ourselves compelled to use in relation to this subject, we do not mean to speak of animal suffering, but of an immense moral and political evil.... In regard to its influence on the white population the most lamentable proof of its deteriorating effects may be found in the fact that, excepting the pious, whose hearts are governed by the Christian law of reciprocity between man and man, and the wise, whose minds have looked far into the relations and tendencies of things, none can be found to lift their voices against a system so utterly repugnant to the feelings of unsophisticated humanity—a system which permits all the atrocities of the domestic slave trade—which permits the father to sell his children as he would his cattle—a system which consigns one half of the community to hopeless and utter degradation, and which threatens in its final catastrophe to bring down the same ruin on the master and the slave."[272:1]

The historical value of the paper from which these brief extracts are given, as illustrating the attitude of the church at the time, is enhanced by the use that was made of it. Published in the form of a review article in a magazine of national circulation, the recognized organ of the orthodox Congregationalists, it was republished in a pamphlet for gratuitous distribution and extensively circulated in New England by the agency of the Andover students. It was also republished at Richmond, Va. Other laborers at the East in the same cause were Joshua Leavitt, Bela B. Edwards, and Eli Smith, afterward illustrious as a missionary,[273:1] and Ralph Randolph Gurley, secretary of the Colonization Society, whose edition of the powerful and uncompromising sermon of the younger Edwards on "The Injustice and Impolicy of the Slave Trade and of the Slavery of the Africans" was published at Boston for circulation at the South, in hopes of promoting the universal abolition of slavery. The list might be indefinitely extended to include the foremost names in the church in that period. There was no adverse party.

At the West an audacious movement of the slavery extension politicians, flushed with their success in Missouri, to introduce slavery into Illinois, Indiana, and even Ohio, was defeated largely by the aid of the Baptist and Methodist clergy, many of whom had been southern men and had experienced the evils of the system.[273:2] In Kentucky and Tennessee the abolition movement was led more distinctively by the Presbyterians and the Quakers. It was a bold effort to procure the manumission of slaves and the repeal of the slave code in those States by the agreement of the citizens. The character of the movement is indicated in the constitution of the "Moral Religious Manumission Society of West Tennessee," which declares that slavery "exceeds any other crime in magnitude" and is "the greatest act of practical infidelity," and that "the gospel of Christ, if believed, would remove personal slavery at once by destroying the will in the tyrant to enslave."[274:1] A like movement in North Carolina and in Maryland, at the same time, attained to formidable dimensions. The state of sentiment in Virginia may be judged from the fact that so late as December, 1831, in the memorable debate in the legislature on a proposal for the abolition of slavery, a leading speaker, denouncing slavery as "the most pernicious of all the evils with which the body politic can be afflicted," could say, undisputed, "By none is this position denied, if we except the erratic John Randolph."[274:2] The conflict in Virginia at that critical time was between Christian principle and wise statesmanship on the one hand, and on the other hand selfish interest and ambition, and the prevailing terror resulting from a recent servile insurrection. Up to this time there appears no sign of any division in the church on this subject. Neither was there any sectional division; the opponents of slavery, whether at the North or at the South, were acting in the interest of the common country, and particularly in the interest of the States that were still afflicted with slavery. But a swift change was just impending.

We have already recognized the Methodist organization as the effective pioneer of systematic abolitionism in America.[275:1] The Baptists, also having their main strength in the southern States, were early and emphatic in condemning the institutions by which they were surrounded.[275:2] But all the sects found themselves embarrassed by serious difficulties when it came to the practical application of the principles and rules which they enunciated. The exacting of "immediate emancipation" as a condition of fellowship in the ministry or communion in the church, and the popular cries of "No fellowship with slave-holders," and "Slave-holding always and every where a sin," were found practically to conflict with frequent undeniable and stubborn facts. The cases in which conscientious Christians found themselves, by no fault of their own, invested by inhuman laws with an absolute authority over helpless fellow-men, which it would not be right for them suddenly to abdicate, were not few nor unimportant.[275:3] In dealing with such cases several different courses were open to the church: (1) To execute discipline rigorously according to the formula, on the principle, Be rid of the tares at all hazards; never mind the wheat. This course was naturally favored by some of the minor Presbyterian sects, and was apt to be vigorously urged by zealous people living at a distance and not well acquainted with details of fact. (2) To attempt to provide for all cases by stated exceptions and saving clauses. This course was entered on by the Methodist Church, but without success. (3) Discouraged by the difficulties, to let go all discipline. This was the point reached at last by most of the southern churches. (4) Clinging to the formulas, "Immediate emancipation," "No communion with slave-holders," so to "palter in a double sense" with the words as to evade the meaning of them. According to this method, slave-holding did not consist in the holding of slaves, but in holding them with evil purpose and wrong treatment; a slave who was held for his own advantage, receiving from his master "that which is just and equal," was said, in this dialect, to be "morally emancipated." This was the usual expedient of a large and respectable party of antislavery Christians at the North, when their principle of "no communion with slave-holders" brought them to the seeming necessity of excommunicating an unquestionably Christian brother for doing an undeniable duty. (5) To lay down, broadly and explicitly, the principles of Christian morality governing the subject, leaving the application of them in individual cases to the individual church or church-member. This was the course exemplified with admirable wisdom and fidelity in the Presbyterian "deliverance" of 1818. (6) To meet the postulate, laid down with so much assurance, as if an axiom, that "slave-holding is always and everywhere a sin, to be immediately repented of and forsaken," with a flat and square contradiction, as being irreconcilable with facts and with the judgment of the Christian Scriptures; and thus to condemn and oppose to the utmost the system of slavery, without imputing the guilt of it to persons involved in it by no fault of their own. This course commended itself to many lucid and logical minds and honest consciences, including some of the most consistent and effective opponents of slavery. (7) Still another course must be mentioned, which, absurd as it seems, was actually pursued by a few headlong reformers, who showed in various ways a singular alacrity at playing into the hands of their adversaries. It consisted in enunciating in the most violent and untenable form and the most offensive language the proposition that all slave-holding is sin and every slave-holder a criminal, and making the whole attack on slavery to turn on this weak pivot and fail if this failed. The argument of this sort of abolitionist was: If there can be found anywhere a good man holding a bond-servant unselfishly, kindly, and for good reason justifiably, then the system of American slavery is right.[277:1] It is not strange that men in the southern churches, being offered such an argument ready made to their hand, should promptly accept both the premiss and the conclusion, and that so at last there should begin to be a pro-slavery party in the American church.

The disastrous epoch of the beginning of what has been called "the southern apostasy" from the universal moral sentiment of Christendom on the subject of slavery may be dated at about the year 1833. A year earlier began to be heard those vindications on political grounds of what had just been declared in the legislature of Virginia to be by common consent the most pernicious of political evils—vindications which continued for thirty years to invite the wonder of the civilized world. When (about 1833) a Presbyterian minister in Mississippi, the Rev. James Smylie, made the "discovery," which "surprised himself," that the system of American slavery was sanctioned and approved by the Scriptures as good and righteous, he found that his brethren in the Presbyterian ministry at the extreme South were not only surprised, but shocked and offended, at the proposition.[278:1] And yet such was the swift progress of this innovation that in surprisingly few years, we might almost say months, it had become not only prevalent, but violently and exclusively dominant in the church of the southern States, with the partial exception of Kentucky and Tennessee. It would be difficult to find a precedent in history for so sudden and sweeping a change of sentiment on a leading doctrine of moral theology. Dissent from the novel dogma was suppressed with more than inquisitorial rigor. It was less perilous to hold Protestant opinions in Spain or Austria than to hold, in Carolina or Alabama, the opinions which had but lately been commended to universal acceptance by the unanimous voice of great religious bodies, and proclaimed as undisputed principles by leading statesmen. It became one of the accepted evidences of Christianity at the South that infidelity failed to offer any justification for American slavery equal to that derived from the Christian Scriptures. That eminent leader among the Lutheran clergy, the Rev. Dr. Bachman, of Charleston, referred "that unexampled unanimity of sentiment that now exists in the whole South on the subject of slavery" to the confidence felt by the religious public in the Bible defense of slavery as set forth by clergymen and laymen in sermons and pamphlets and speeches in Congress.[278:2]

The historian may not excuse himself from the task of inquiring into the cause of this sudden and immense moral revolution. The explanation offered by Dr. Bachman is the very thing that needs to be explained. How came the Christian public throughout the slave-holding States, which so short a time before had been unanimous in finding in the Bible the condemnation of their slavery, to find all at once in the Bible the divine sanction and defense of it as a wise, righteous, and permanent institution? Doubtless there was mixture of influences in bringing about the result. The immense advance in the market value of slaves consequent on Whitney's invention of the cotton-gin had its unconscious effect on the moral judgments of some. The furious vituperations of a very small but noisy faction of antislavery men added something to the swift current of public opinion. But demonstrably the chief cause of this sudden change of religious opinion—one of the most remarkable in the history of the church—was panic terror. In August, 1831, a servile insurrection in Virginia, led by a crazy negro, Nat Turner by name, was followed (as always in such cases) by bloody vengeance on the part of the whites.

"The Southampton insurrection, occurring at a time when the price of slaves was depressed in consequence of a depression in the price of cotton, gave occasion to a sudden development of opposition to slavery in the legislature of Virginia. A measure for the prospective abolition of the institution in that ancient commonwealth was proposed, earnestly debated, eloquently urged, and at last defeated, with a minority ominously large in its favor. Warned by so great a peril, and strengthened soon afterward by an increase in the market value of cotton and of slaves, the slave-holding interest in all the South was stimulated to new activity. Defenses of slavery more audacious than had been heard before began to be uttered by southern politicians at home and by southern representatives and senators in Congress. A panic seized upon the planters in some districts of the Southwest. Conspiracies and plans of insurrection were discovered. Negroes were tortured or terrified into confessions. Obnoxious white men were put to death without any legal trial and in defiance of those rules of evidence which are insisted on by southern laws. Thus a sudden and convincing terror was spread through the South. Every man was made to know that if he should become obnoxious to the guardians of the great southern 'institution' he was liable to be denounced and murdered. It was distinctly and imperatively demanded that nobody should be allowed to say anything anywhere against slavery. The movement of the societies which had then been recently formed at Boston and New York, with 'Immediate abolition' for their motto, was made use of to stimulate the terror and the fury of the South.... The position of political parties and of candidates for the Presidency, just at that juncture, gave special advantage to the agitators—an advantage that was not neglected. Everything was done that practiced demagogues could contrive to stimulate the South into a frenzy and to put down at once and forever all opposition to slavery. The clergy and the religious bodies were summoned to the patriotic duty of committing themselves on the side of 'southern institutions.' Just then it was, if we mistake not, that their apostasy began. They dared not say that slavery as an institution in the State is essentially an organized injustice, and that, though the Scriptures rightly and wisely enjoin justice and the recognition of the slaves' brotherhood upon masters, and conscientious meekness upon slaves, the organized injustice of the institution ought to be abolished by the shortest process consistent with the public safety and the welfare of the enslaved. They dared not even keep silence under the plea that the institution is political and therefore not to be meddled with by religious bodies or religious persons. They yielded to the demand. They were carried along in the current of the popular frenzy; they joined in the clamor, 'Great is Diana of the Ephesians;' they denounced the fanaticism of abolition and permitted themselves to be understood as certifying, in the name of religion and of Christ, that the entire institution of slavery 'as it exists' is chargeable with no injustice and is warranted by the word of God."[281:1]

There is no good reason to question the genuineness and sincerity of the fears expressed by the slave-holding population as a justification of their violent measures for the suppression of free speech in relation to slavery; nor of their belief that the papers and prints actively disseminated from the antislavery press in Boston were fitted, if not distinctly intended, to kindle bloody insurrections. These terrors were powerfully pleaded in the great debate in the Virginia legislature as an argument for the abolition of slavery.[281:2] This failing, they became throughout the South a constraining power for the suppression of free speech, not only on the part of outsiders, but among the southern people themselves. The régime thus introduced was, in the strictest sense of the phrase, "a reign of terror." The universal lockjaw which thenceforth forbade the utterance of what had so recently and suddenly ceased to be the unanimous religious conviction of the southern church soon produced an "unexampled unanimity" on the other side, broken only when some fiery and indomitable abolitionist like Dr. Robert J. Breckinridge, of the Presbyterian Church in Kentucky, delivered his soul with invectives against the system of slavery and the new-fangled apologies that had been devised to defend it, declaring it "utterly indefensible on every correct human principle, and utterly abhorrent from every law of God," and exclaiming, "Out upon such folly! The man who cannot see that involuntary domestic slavery, as it exists among us, is founded on the principle of taking by force that which is another's has simply no moral sense.... Hereditary slavery is without pretense, except in avowed rapacity."[282:1] Of course the antislavery societies which, under various names, had existed in the South by hundreds were suddenly extinguished, and manumissions, which had been going on at the rate of thousands in a year, almost entirely ceased.

The strange and swiftly spreading moral epidemic did not stop at State boundary lines. At the North the main cause of defection was not, indeed, directly operative. There was no danger there of servile insurrection. But there was true sympathy for those who lived under the shadow of such impending horrors, threatening alike the guilty and the innocent. There was a deep passion of honest patriotism, now becoming alarmed lest the threats of disunion proceeding from the terrified South should prove a serious peril to the nation in whose prosperity the hopes of the world seemed to be involved. There was a worthy solicitude lest the bonds of intercourse between the churches of North and South should be ruptured and so the integrity of the nation be the more imperiled. Withal there was a spreading and deepening and most reasonable disgust at the reckless ranting of a little knot of antislavery men having their headquarters at Boston, who, exulting in their irresponsibility, scattered loosely appeals to men's vindictive passions and filled the unwilling air with clamors against church and ministry and Bible and law and government, denounced as "pro-slavery" all who declined to accept their measures or their persons, and, arrogating to themselves exclusively the name of abolitionist, made that name, so long a title of honor, to be universally odious.[282:2]

These various factors of public opinion were actively manipulated. Political parties competed for the southern vote. Commercial houses competed for southern business. Religious sects, parties, and societies were emulous in conciliating southern adhesions or contributions and averting schisms. The condition of success in any of these cases was well understood to be concession, or at least silence, on the subject of slavery. The pressure of motives, some of which were honorable and generous, was everywhere, like the pressure of the atmosphere. It was not strange that there should be defections from righteousness. Even the enormous effrontery of the slave power in demanding for its own security that the rule of tyrannous law and mob violence by which freedom of speech and of the press had been extinguished at the South should be extended over the so-called free States did not fail of finding citizens of reputable standing so base as to give the demand their countenance, their public advocacy, and even their personal assistance. As the subject emerged from time to time in the religious community, the questions arising were often confused and embarrassed by false issues and illogical statements, and the state of opinion was continually misrepresented through the incurable habit of the over-zealous in denouncing as "pro-slavery" those who dissented from their favorite formulas. But after all deductions, the historian who shall by and by review this period with the advantage of a longer perspective will be compelled to record not a few lamentable defections, both individual and corporate, from the cause of freedom, justice, and humanity. And, nevertheless, that later record will also show that while the southern church had been terrified into "an unexampled unanimity" in renouncing the principles which it had unanimously held, and while like causes had wrought potently upon northern sentiment, it was the steadfast fidelity of the Christian people that saved the nation from ruin. At the end of thirty years from the time when the soil of Missouri was devoted to slavery the "Kansas-Nebraska Bill" was proposed, which should open for the extension of slavery the vast expanse of national territory which, by the stipulation of the "Missouri Compromise," had been forever consecrated to freedom. The issue of the extension of slavery was presented to the people in its simplicity. The action of the clergy of New England was prompt, spontaneous, emphatic, and practically unanimous. Their memorial, with three thousand and fifty signatures, protested against the bill, "in the name of Almighty God and in his presence," as "a great moral wrong; as a breach of faith eminently injurious to the moral principles of the community and subversive of all confidence in national engagements; as a measure full of danger to the peace and even the existence of our beloved Union, and exposing us to the just judgments of the Almighty." In like manner the memorial of one hundred and fifty-one clergymen of various denominations in New York City and vicinity protested in like terms, "in the name of religion and humanity," against the guilt of the extension of slavery. Perhaps there has been no occasion on which the consenting voice of the entire church has been so solemnly uttered on a question of public morality, and this in the very region in which church and clergy had been most stormily denounced by the little handful of abolitionists who gloried in the name of infidel[285:1] as recreant to justice and humanity.

The protest of the church was of no avail to defeat the machination of demagogues. The iniquitous measure was carried through. But this was not the end; it was only the beginning of the end. Yet ten years, and American slavery, through the mad folly of its advocates and the steadfast fidelity of the great body of the earnestly religious people of the land, was swept away by the tide of war.

The long struggle of the American church against drunkenness as a social and public evil begins at an early date. One of the thirteen colonies, Georgia, had the prohibition of slavery and of the importation of spirituous liquors incorporated by Oglethorpe in its early and short-lived constitution. It would be interesting to discover, if we could, to what extent the rigor of John Wesley's discipline against both these mischiefs was due to his association with Oglethorpe in the founding of that latest of the colonies. Both the imperious nature of Wesley and the peculiar character of his fraternity as being originally not a church, but a voluntary society within the church, predisposed to a policy of arbitrary exclusiveness by hard and fast lines drawn according to formula, which might not have been ventured on by one who was consciously drawing up the conditions of communion in the church. In the Puritan colonies the public morals in respect to temperance were from the beginning guarded by salutary license laws devised to suppress all dram-shops and tippling-houses, and to prevent, as far as law could wisely undertake to prevent, all abusive and mischievous sales of liquor. But these indications of a sound public sentiment did not prevent the dismal fact of a wide prevalence of drunkenness as one of the distinguishing characteristics of American society at the opening of the nineteenth century. Two circumstances had combined to aggravate the national vice. Seven years of army life, with its exhaustion and exposure and military social usage, had initiated into dangerous drinking habits many of the most justly influential leaders of society, and the example of these had set the tone for all ranks. Besides this, the increased importation and manufacture of distilled spirits had made it easy and common to substitute these for the mild fermented liquors which had been the ordinary drink of the people. Gradually and unobserved the nation had settled down into a slough of drunkenness of which it is difficult for us at this date to form a clear conception. The words of Isaiah concerning the drunkards of Ephraim seem not too strong to apply to the condition of American society, that "all tables were full of vomit and filthiness." In the prevalence of intemperate drinking habits the clergy had not escaped the general infection. "The priest and the prophet had gone astray through strong drink." Individual words of warning, among the earliest of which was the classical essay of Dr. Benjamin Rush (1785), failed to arouse general attention. The new century was well advanced before the stirring appeals of Ebenezer Porter, Lyman Beecher, Heman Humphrey, and Jeremiah Evarts had awakened in the church any effectual conviction of sin in the matter. The appointment of a strong committee, in 1811, by the Presbyterian General Assembly was promptly followed by like action by the clergy of Massachusetts and Connecticut, leading to the formation of State societies. But general concerted measures on a scale commensurate with the evil to be overcome must be dated from the organization of the "American Society for the Promotion of Temperance," in 1826. The first aim of the reformers of that day was to break down those domineering social usages which almost enforced the habit of drinking in ordinary social intercourse. The achievement of this object was wonderfully swift and complete. A young minister whose pastorate had begun at about the same time with the organizing of the national temperance society was able at the end of five years to bear this testimony in the presence of those who were in a position to recognize any misstatement or exaggeration: "The wonderful change which the past five years have witnessed in the manners and habits of this people in regard to the use of ardent spirits—the new phenomenon of an intelligent people rising up, as it were, with one consent, without law, without any attempt at legislation, to put down by the mere force of public opinion, expressing itself in voluntary associations, a great social evil which no despot on earth could have put down among his subjects by any system of efforts—has excited admiration and roused to imitation not only in our sister country of Great Britain, but in the heart of continental Europe."[287:1]

It is worthy of remark, for any possible instruction there may be in it, that the first, greatest, and most permanent of the victories of the temperance reformation, the breaking down of almost universal social drinking usages, was accomplished while yet the work was a distinctively religious one, "without law or attempt at legislation," and while the efforts at suppression were directed at the use of ardent spirits. The attempt to combine the friends of temperance on a basis of "teetotal" abstinence, putting fermented as well as distilled liquors under the ban, dates from as late as 1836.

But it soon appeared that the immense gain of banishing ardent spirits from the family table and sideboard, the social entertainment, the haying field, and the factory had not been attained without some corresponding loss. Close upon the heels of the reform in the domestic and social habits of the people there was spawned a monstrous brood of obscure tippling-shops—a nuisance, at least in New England, till then unknown. From the beginning wise and effective license laws had interdicted all dram-shops; even the taverner might sell spirits only to his transient guests, not to the people of the town. With the suppression of social drinking there was effected, in spite of salutary law to the contrary, a woeful change. The American "saloon" was, in an important sense, the offspring of the American temperance reformation. The fact justified the reformer in turning his attention to the law. From that time onward the history of the temperance reformation has included the history of multitudinous experiments in legislation, none of which has been so conclusive as to satisfy all students of the subject that any later law is, on the whole, more usefully effective than the original statutes of the Puritan colonies.[288:1]

In 1840 the temperance reformation received a sudden forward impulse from an unexpected source. One evening a group of six notoriously hard drinkers, coming together greatly impressed from a sermon of that noted evangelist, Elder Jacob Knapp, pledged themselves by mutual vows to total abstinence; and from this beginning went forward that extraordinary agitation known as "the Washingtonian movement." Up to this time the aim of the reformers had been mainly directed to the prevention of drunkenness by a change in social customs and personal habits. Now there was suddenly opened a door of hope to the almost despair of the drunkard himself. The lately reformed drunkards of Baltimore set themselves to the reforming of other drunkards, and these took up the work in their turn, and reformation was extended in a geometrical progression till it covered the country. Everywhere meetings were held, to be addressed by reformed drunkards, and new recruits from the gutter were pushed forward to tell their experience to the admiring public, and sent out on speaking tours. The people were stirred up as never before on the subject of temperance. There was something very Christian-like in the method of this propagation, and hopeful souls looked forward to a temperance millennium as at hand. But fatal faults in the work soon discovered themselves. Among the new evangelists were not a few men of true penitence and humility, like John Hawkins, and one man at least of incomparable eloquence as well as Christian earnestness, John B. Gough. But the public were not long in finding that merely to have wallowed in vice and to be able to tell ludicrous or pathetic stories from one's experience was not of itself sufficient qualification for the work of a public instructor in morals. The temperance platform became infested with swaggering autobiographers, whose glory was in their shame, and whose general influence was distinctly demoralizing. The sudden influx of the tide of enthusiasm was followed by a disastrous ebb. It was the estimate of Mr. Gough that out of six hundred thousand reformed drunkards not less than four hundred and fifty thousand had relapsed into vice. The same observer, the splendor of whose eloquence was well mated with an unusual sobriety of judgment, is credited with the statement that he knew of no case of stable reformation from drunkenness that was not connected with a thorough spiritual renovation and conversion. Certainly good was accomplished by the transient whirlwind of the "Washingtonian" excitement. But the evil that it did lived after it. Already at the time of its breaking forth the temperance reformation had entered upon that period of decadence in which its main interest was to be concentrated upon law and politics. And here the vicious ethics of the reformed-drunkard school became manifest. The drunkard, according to his own account of himself (unless he was not only reformed, but repentant), had been a victim of circumstances. Drunkenness, instead of a base and beastly sin, was an infirmity incident to a high-strung and generous temperament. The blame of it was to be laid, not upon the drunkard, whose exquisitely susceptible organization was quite unable to resist temptation coming in his way, but on those who put intoxicating liquor where he could get at it, or on the State, whose duty it was to put the article out of the reach of its citizens. The guilt of drunkenness must rest, not on the unfortunate drunkard who happened to be attacked by that disease, but on the sober and well-behaving citizen, and especially the Christian citizen, who did not vote the correct ticket. What may be called the Prohibition period of the temperance reformation begins about 1850 and still continues. It is characterized by the pursuit of a type of legislation of variable efficacy or inefficacy, the essence of which is that the sale of intoxicating liquors shall be a monopoly of the government.[290:1] Indications begin to appear that the disproportionate devotion to measures of legislation and politics is abating. Some of the most effective recent labor for the promotion of temperance has been wrought independently of such resort. If the cycle shall be completed, and the church come back to the methods by which its first triumphs in this field were won, it will come back the wiser and the stronger for its vicissitudes of experience through these threescore years and ten.

CHAPTER XVII. A DECADE OF CONTROVERSIES AND SCHISMS.

During the period from 1835 to 1845 the spirit of schism seemed to be in the air. In this period no one of the larger organizations of churches was free from agitating controversies, and some of the most important of them were rent asunder by explosion.

At the time when the Presbyterian Church suffered its great schism, in 1837, it was the most influential religious body in the United States. In 120 years its solitary presbytery had grown to 135 presbyteries, including 2140 ministers serving 2865 churches and 220,557 communicants. But these large figures are an inadequate measure of its influence. It represented in its ministry and membership the two most masterful races on the continent, the New England colonists and the Scotch-Irish immigrants; and the tenacity with which it had adhered to the tradition derived through both these lines, of admitting none but liberally educated men to its ministry, had given it exceptional social standing and control over men of intellectual strength and leadership. In the four years beginning with 1831 the additions to its roll of communicants "on examination" had numbered nearly one hundred thousand. But this spiritual growth was chilled and stunted by the dissensions that arose. The revivals ceased and the membership actually dwindled.

The contention had grown (a fact not without parallel in church history) out of measures devised in the interest of coöperation and union. In 1801, in the days of its comparative feebleness, the General Assembly had proposed to the General Association of Connecticut a "Plan of Union" according to which the communities of New England Christians then beginning to move westward between the parallels that bound "the New England zone," and bringing with them their accustomed Congregational polity, might coöperate on terms of mutual concession with Presbyterian churches in their neighborhood. The proposals had been fraternally received and accepted, and under the terms of this compact great accessions had been made to the strength of the Presbyterian Church, of pastors and congregations marked with the intellectual activity and religious enterprise of the New England churches, who, while cordially conforming to the new methods of organization and discipline, were not in the least penetrated with the traditionary Scotch veneration for the Westminster standards. For nearly thirty years the great reinforcements from New England and from men of the New England way of thinking had been ungrudgingly bestowed and heartily welcomed. But the great accessions which in the first four years of the fourth decade of this century had increased the roll of the communicants of the Presbyterian Church by more than fifty per cent. had come in undue proportion from the New Englandized regions of western New York and Ohio. It was inevitable that the jealousy of hereditary Presbyterians, "whose were the fathers," should be aroused by the perfectly reasonable fear lest the traditional ways of the church which they felt to be in a peculiar sense their church might be affected by so large an element from without. The grounds of explicit complaint against the party called "New School" were principally twofold—doctrine and organization.

In the Presbyterian Church at this time were three pretty distinct types of theological thought. First, there was the unmitigated Scotch Calvinism; secondly, there was the modification of this system, which became naturalized in the church after the Great Awakening, when Jonathan Dickinson and Jonathan Edwards, from neighbor towns in Massachusetts, came to be looked upon as the great Presbyterian theologians; thirdly, there was the "consistent Calvinism," that had been still further evolved by the patient labor of students in direct succession from Edwards, and that was known under the name of "Hopkinsianism." Just now the latest and not the least eminent in this school, Dr. Nathaniel W. Taylor, of New Haven, was enunciating to large and enthusiastic classes in Yale Divinity School new definitions and forms of statement giving rise to much earnest debate. The alarm of those to whom the very phrase "improvement in theology" was an abomination expressed itself in futile indictments for heresy brought against some of the most eminently godly and useful ministers in all the church. Lyman Beecher, of Lane Seminary, Edward Beecher, J. M. Sturtevant, and William Kirby, of Illinois College, and George Duffield, of the presbytery of Carlisle, Pa., were annoyed by impeachments for heresy, which all failed before reaching the court of last resort. But repeated and persistent prosecutions of Albert Barnes, of Philadelphia, were destined to more conspicuous failure, by reason of their coming up year after year before the General Assembly, and also by reason of the position of the accused as pastor of the mother church of the denomination, the First Church of Philadelphia, which was the customary meeting-place of the Assembly; withal by reason of the character of the accused, the honor and love in which he was held for his faithful and useful work as pastor, his world-wide fame as a devoted and believing student of the Scriptures, and the Christlike gentleness and meekness with which he endured the harassing of church trials continuing through a period of seven years, and compelling him, under an irregular and illegal sentence of the synod, to sit silent in his church for the space of a year, as one suspended from the ministry.

The earliest leaders in national organization for the propagation of Christianity at home and abroad were the Congregationalists of New England and men like-minded with them. But the societies thus originated were organized on broad and catholic principles, and invited the coöperation of all Christians. They naturally became the organs of much of the active beneficence of Presbyterian congregations, and the Presbyterian clergy and laity were largely represented in the direction of them. They were recognized and commended by the representative bodies of the Presbyterian Church. As a point of high-church theory it was held by the rigidly Presbyterian party that the work of the gospel in all its departments and in all lands is the proper function of "the church as such"—meaning practically that each sect ought to have its separate propaganda. There was logical strength in this position as reached from their premises, and there were arguments of practical convenience to be urged in favor of it. But the demand to sunder at once the bonds of fellowship which united Christians of different names in the beneficent work of the great national societies was not acceptable even to the whole of the Old-School party. To the New Englanders it was intolerable.

There were other and less important grounds of difference that were discussed between the parties. And in the background, behind them all, was the slavery question. It seems to have been willingly kept in the background by the leaders of debate on both sides; but it was there. The New-School synods and presbyteries of the North were firm in their adherence to the antislavery principles of the church. On the other hand, the Old-School party relied, in the coup d'église that was in preparation, on the support of "an almost solid South."[296:1]

It was an unpardonable offense of the New-School party that it had grown to such formidable strength, intellectually, spiritually, and numerically. The probability that the church might, with the continued growth and influence of this party, become Americanized and so lose the purity of its thoroughgoing Scotch traditions was very real, and to some minds very dreadful. To these the very ark of God seemed in danger. Arraignments for heresy in presbytery and synod resulted in failure; and when these and other cases involving questions of orthodoxy or of the policy of the church were brought into the supreme judicature of the church, the solemn but unmistakable fact disclosed itself that even the General Assembly could not be relied on for the support of measures introduced by the Old-School leaders. In fact, every Assembly from 1831 to 1836, with a single exception, had shown a clear New-School majority. The foundations were destroyed, and what should the righteous do?

History was about to repeat itself with unwonted preciseness of detail. On the gathering of the Assembly of 1837 a careful count of noses revealed what had been known only once before in seven years, and what might never be again—a clear Old-School majority in the house. To the pious mind the neglecting of such an opportunity would have been to tempt Providence. Without notice, without complaint or charges or specifications, without opportunity of defense, 4 synods, including 533 churches and more than 100,000 communicants, were excommunicated by a majority vote. The victory of pure doctrine and strict church order, though perhaps not exactly glorious, was triumphant and irreversible. There was no more danger to the church from a possible New-School majority.

When the four exscinded synods, three in western New York and one in Ohio, together with a great following of sympathizing congregations in all parts of the country, came together to reconstruct their shattered polity, they were found to number about four ninths of the late Presbyterian Church. For thirty years the American church was to present to Christendom the strange spectacle of two great ecclesiastical bodies claiming identically the same name, holding the same doctrinal standards, observing the same ritual and governed by the same discipline, and occupying the same great territory, and yet completely dissevered from each other and at times in relations of sharp mutual antagonism.[297:1]

The theological debate which had split the Presbyterian Church from end to end was quite as earnest and copious in New England. But owing to the freer habit of theological inquiry and the looser texture of organization among the Congregationalist churches, it made no organic schism beyond the setting up of a new theological seminary in Connecticut to offset what were deemed the "dangerous tendencies" of the New Haven theology. After a few years the party lines had faded out and the two seminaries were good neighbors.

The unlikeliest place in all American Christendom for a partisan controversy and a schism would have seemed to be the Unitarian denomination in and about Boston. Beginning with the refusal not only of any imposed standard of belief, but of any statement of common opinions, and with unlimited freedom of opinion in every direction, unless, perhaps, in the direction of orthodoxy, it was not easy to see how a splitting wedge could be started in it. But the infection of the time was not to be resisted. Even Unitarianism must have its heresies and heresiarchs to deal with. No sooner did the pressure of outside attack abate than antagonisms began pretty sharply to declare themselves. In 1832 Mr. Ralph Waldo Emerson, pastor of the Second Church in Boston, proposed to the church to abandon or radically change the observance of the Lord's Supper. When the church demurred at this extraordinary demand he resigned his office, firing off an elaborate argument against the usage of the church by way of a parting salute. Without any formal demission of the ministry, he retired to his literary seclusion at Concord, from which he brought forth in books and lectures the oracular utterances which caught more and more the ear of a wide public, and in which, in casual-seeming parentheses and obiter dicta, Christianity and all practical religion were condemned by sly innuendo and half-respectful allusion by which he might "without sneering teach the rest to sneer." In 1838 he was still so far recognized in the ministry as to be invited to address the graduating class of the Harvard Divinity School. The blank pantheism which he then enunciated called forth from Professor Henry Ware, Jr., a sermon in the college chapel on the personality of God, which he sent with a friendly note to Mr. Emerson. The gay and Skimpolesque reply of the sage is an illustration of that flippancy with which he chose to toy in a literary way with momentous questions, and which was so exasperating to the earnest men of positive religious convictions with whom he had been associated in the Christian ministry.

"It strikes me very oddly that good and wise men at Cambridge should think of raising me into an object of criticism. I have always been, from my incapacity of methodical writing, 'a chartered libertine,' free to worship and free to rail, lucky when I could make myself understood, but never esteemed near enough to the institutions and mind of society to deserve the notice of masters of literature and religion.... I could not possibly give you one of the 'arguments' you so cruelly hint at on which any doctrine of mine stands, for I do not know what arguments mean in reference to any expression of thought. I delight in telling what I think, but if you ask me how I dare say so, or why it is so, I am the most helpless of mortal men. I do not even see that either of these questions admits of an answer. So that in the present droll posture of my affairs, when I see myself suddenly raised into the importance of a heretic, I am very uneasy when I advert to the supposed duties of such a personage who is to make good his thesis against all comers. I certainly shall do no such thing."

The issue was joined and the controversy began. Professor Andrews Norton in a pamphlet denounced "the latest form of infidelity," and the Rev. George Ripley replied in a volume, to which Professor Norton issued a rejoinder. But there was not substance enough of religious dogma and sentiment in the transcendentalist philosophers to give them any permanent standing in the church. They went into various walks of secular literature, and have powerfully influenced the course of opinions; but they came to be no longer recognizable as a religious or theological party.

Among the minor combatants in the conflict between the Unitarians and the pantheists was a young man whose name was destined to become conspicuous, not within the Unitarian fellowship, but on the outskirts of it. Theodore Parker was a man of a different type from the men about him of either party. The son of a mechanic, he fought his way through difficulties to a liberal education, and was thirty years old before his very great abilities attracted general attention. A greedy gormandizer of books in many languages, he had little of the dainty scholarship so much prized at the neighboring university. But the results of his vast reading were stored in a quick and tenacious memory as ready rhetorical material wherewith to convince or astonish. Paradox was a passion with him, that was stimulated by complaints, and even by deprecations, to the point of irreverence. He liked to "make people's flesh crawl." Even in his advocacy of social and public reforms, which was strenuous and sincere, he delighted so to urge his cause as to inflame prejudice and opposition against it. With this temper it is not strange that when he came to enunciate his departure from some of the accepted tenets of his brethren, who were habitually reverent in their discipleship toward Jesus Christ, he should do this in a way to offend and shock. The immediate reaction of the Unitarian clergy from the statements of his sermon, in 1841, on "The Transient and the Permanent in Christianity," in which the supernatural was boldly discarded from his belief, was so general and so earnest as to give occasion to Channing's exclamation, "Now we have a Unitarian orthodoxy!" Channing did not live to see the characteristic tenets of the heresiarch to whom he hesitated to give the name of Christian not only widely accepted in the Unitarian churches, but some of them freely discussed as open questions among some orthodox scholars. Two very great events in this period of schism may be dispatched with a brevity out of all proportion to their importance, on account of the simplicity of motive and action by which they are characterized.

In the year 1844 the slavery agitation in the Methodist Episcopal Church culminated, not in the rupture of the church, but in the well-considered, deliberate division of it between North and South. The history of the slavery question among the Methodists was a typical one. From the beginning the Methodist Society had been committed by its founder and his early successors to the strictest (not the strongest) position on this question. Not only was the system of slavery denounced as iniquitous, but the attempt was made to enforce the rigid rule that persons involved under this system in the relation of master to slave should be excluded from the ministry, if not from the communion. But the enforcement of this rule was found to be not only difficult, but wrong, and difficult simply because it was wrong. Then followed that illogical confusion of ideas studiously fostered by zealots at either extreme: If the slave-holder may be in some circumstances a faithful Christian disciple, fulfilling in righteousness and love a Christian duty, then slavery is right; if slavery is wrong, then every slave-holder is a manstealer, and should be excommunicated as such without asking any further questions. Two statements more palpably illogical were never put forth for the darkening of counsel. But each extreme was eager to sustain the unreason of the opposite extreme as the only alternative of its own unreason, and so, what with contrary gusts from North and South, they fell into a place where two seas met and ran the ship aground. The attempts made from 1836 to 1840, by stretching to the utmost the authority of the General Conference and the bishops, for the suppression of "modern abolitionism" in the church (without saying what they meant by the phrase) had their natural effect: the antislavery sentiment in the church organized and uttered itself more vigorously and more extravagantly than ever on the basis, "All slave-holding is sin; no fellowship with slave-holders." In 1843 an antislavery secession took place, which drew after it a following of six thousand, increased in a few months to fifteen thousand. The paradoxical result of this movement is not without many parallels in church history: After the drawing off of fifteen thousand of the most zealous antislavery men in the church, the antislavery party in the church was vastly stronger, even in numbers, than it had been before. The General Conference of 1836 had pronounced itself, without a dissenting vote, to be "decidedly opposed to modern abolitionism." The General Conference of 1844, on the first test vote on the question of excluding from the ministry one who had become a slave-holder through marriage, revealed a majority of one hundred and seventeen to fifty-six in favor of the most rigorous antislavery discipline. The graver question upon the case of Bishop Andrew, who was in the like condemnation, could not be decided otherwise. The form of the Conference's action in this case was studiously inoffensive. It imputed no wrong and proposed no censure, but, simply on the ground that the circumstances would embarrass him in the exercise of his office, declared it as "the sense of this General Conference that he desist from the exercise of this office so long as this impediment remains." The issue could not have been simpler and clearer. The Conference was warned that the passage of the resolution would be followed by the secession of the South. The debate was long, earnest, and tender. At the end of it the resolution was passed, one hundred and eleven to sixty-nine. At once notice was given of the intended secession. Commissioners were appointed from both parties to adjust the conditions of it, and in the next year (1845) was organized the "Methodist Episcopal Church, South."

Under the fierce tyranny then dominant at the South the southern Baptists might not fall behind their Methodist neighbors in zeal for slavery. This time it was the South that forced the issue. The Alabama Baptist Convention, without waiting for a concrete case, demanded of the national missionary boards "the distinct, explicit avowal that slave-holders are eligible and entitled equally with non-slave-holders to all the privileges and immunities of their several unions." The answer of the Foreign Mission Board was perfectly kind, but, on the main point, perfectly unequivocal: "We can never be a party to any arrangement which would imply approbation of slavery." The result had been foreseen. The great denomination was divided between North and South. The Southern Baptist Convention was organized in May, 1845, and began its home and foreign missionary work without delay.

This dark chapter of our story is not without its brighter aspects. (1) Amid the inevitable asperities attendant on such debate and division there were many and beautiful manifestations of brotherly love between the separated parties. (2) These strifes fell out to the furtherance of the gospel. Emulations, indeed, are not among the works of the Spirit. In the strenuous labors of the two divided denominations, greatly exceeding what had gone before, it is plain that sometimes Christ was preached of envy and strife. Nevertheless Christ was preached, with great and salutary results; and therein do we rejoice, yea, and will rejoice.

Two important orders in the American church, which for a time had almost faded out from our field of vision, come back, from about this epoch of debate and division, into continually growing conspicuousness and strength. Neither of them was implicated in that great debate involving the fundamental principles of the kingdom of heaven,—the principles of righteousness and love to men,—by which other parts of the church had been agitated and sometimes divided. Whether to their discredit or to their honor, it is part of history that neither the Protestant Episcopal Church nor the Roman Catholic Church took any important part, either corporately or through its representative men, in the agonizing struggle of the American church to maintain justice and humanity in public law and policy. But standing thus aloof from the great ethical questions that agitated the conscience of the nation, they were both of them disturbed by controversies internal or external, which demand mention at least in this chapter. The beginning of the resuscitation of the Protestant Episcopal Church from the dead-and-alive condition in which it had so long been languishing is dated from the year 1811.[304:1] This year was marked by the accession to the episcopate of two eminent men, representing two strongly divergent parties in that church—Bishop Griswold, of Massachusetts, Evangelical, and Bishop Hobart, of New York, High-churchman. A quorum of three bishops having been gotten together, not without great difficulty, the two were consecrated in Trinity Church, New York, May 29, 1811.

The time was opportune and the conjuncture of circumstances singularly favorable. The stigma of Toryism, which had marked the church from long before the War of Independence, was now more than erased. In New England the Episcopal Church was of necessity committed to that political party which favored the abolition of the privileges of the standing order; and this was the anti-English party, which, under the lead of Jefferson, was fast forcing the country into war with England. The Episcopalians were now in a position to retort the charge of disloyalty under which they had not unjustly suffered. At the same time their church lost nothing of the social prestige incidental to its relation to the established Church of England. Politicians of the Democratic party, including some men of well-deserved credit and influence, naturally attached themselves to a religious party having many points of congeniality.[305:1] In another sense, also, the time was opportune for an advance of the Episcopal Church. In the person of Bishop Hobart it had now a bold, energetic, and able representative of principles hitherto not much in favor in America—the thoroughgoing High-church principles of Archbishop Laud. Before this time the Episcopal Church had had very little to contribute by way of enriching the diversity of the American sects. It was simply the feeblest of the communions bearing the common family traits of the Great Awakening, with the not unimportant differentia of its settled ritual of worship and its traditions of order and decorum. But when Bishop Hobart put the trumpet to his lips and prepared himself to sound, the public heard a very different note, and no uncertain one. The church (meaning his own fragment of the church) the one channel of saving grace; the vehicles of that grace, the sacraments, valid only when ministered by a priesthood with the right pedigree of ordination; submission to the constituted authorities of the church absolutely unlimited, except by clear divine requirements; abstinence from prayer-meetings; firm opposition to revivals of religion; refusal of all coöperation with Christians outside of his own sect in endeavors for the general advancement of religion—such were some of the principles and duties inculcated by this bishop of the new era as of binding force.[306:1] The courage of this attitude was splendid and captivating. It requires, even at the present time, not a little force of conviction to sustain one in publicly enunciating such views; but at the time of the accession of Hobart, when the Episcopal Church was just beginning to lift up its head out of the dust of despair, it needed the heroism of a martyr. It was not only the vast multitude of American Christians outside of the Episcopal Church, comprising almost all the learning, the evangelistic zeal, and the charitable activity and self-denial of the American church of that time, that heard these unwonted pretensions with indignation or with ridicule; in the Episcopal Church itself they were disclaimed, scouted, and denounced with (if possible) greater indignation still. But the new party had elements of growth for which its adversaries did not sufficiently reckon. The experience of other orders in the church confirms this principle: that steady persistence and iteration in assuring any body of believers that they are in some special sense the favorites of Heaven, and in assuring any body of clergy that they are endued from on high with some special and exceptional powers, will by and by make an impression on the mind. The flattering assurance may be coyly waived aside; it may even be indignantly repelled; but in the long run there will be a growing number of the brethren who become convinced that there is something in it. It was in harmony with human nature that the party of high pretensions to distinguished privileges for the church and prerogatives for the "priesthood" should in a few years become a formidable contestant for the control of the denomination. The controversy between the two parties rose to its height of exacerbation during the prevalence of that strange epidemic of controversy which ran simultaneously through so many of the great religious organizations of the country at once. No denomination had it in a more malignant form than the Episcopalians. The war of pamphlets and newspapers was fiercely waged, and the election of bishops sometimes became a bitter party contest, with the unpleasant incidents of such competitions. In the midst of the controversy at home the publication of the Oxford Tracts added new asperity to it. A distressing episode of the controversy was the arraignment of no less than four of the twenty bishops on charges affecting their personal character. In the morbid condition of the body ecclesiastic every such hurt festered. The highest febrile temperature was reached when, at an ordination in 1843, two of the leading presbyters in the diocese of New York rose in their places, and, reading each one his solemn protest against the ordaining of one of the candidates on the ground of his Romanizing opinions, left the church.

The result of the long conflict was not immediately apparent. It was not only that "high" opinions, even the highest of the Tractarian school, were to be tolerated within the church, but that the High-church party was to be the dominant party. The Episcopal Church was to stand before the public as representing, not that which it held in common with the other churches of the country, but that which was most distinctive. From this time forth the "Evangelical" party continued relatively to decline, down to the time, thirty years later, when it was represented in the inconsiderable secession of the "Reformed Episcopal Church." The combination of circumstances and influences by which this party supremacy was brought about is an interesting study, for which, however, there is no room in this brief compendium of history. A more important fact is this: that in spite of these agitating internal strifes, and even by reason of them, the growth of the denomination was wonderfully rapid and strong. No fact in the external history of the American church at this period is more imposing than this growth of the Episcopal Church from nothing to a really commanding stature. It is easy to enumerate minor influences tending to this result, some of which are not of high spiritual dignity; but these must not be overestimated. The nature of this growth, as well as the numerical amount of it, requires to be considered. This strongly distinguished order in the American church has been aggrandized, not, to any great degree, by immigration, nor by conquest from the ranks of the irreligious, but by a continual stream of accessions both to its laity and to its clergy from other sects of the church. These accessions have of course been variable in quality, but they have included many such as no denomination could afford to lose, and such as any would be proud to receive. Without judging of individual cases, it is natural and reasonable to explain so considerable a current setting so steadily for two generations toward the Episcopal Church as being attracted by the distinctive characteristics of that church. Foremost among these we may reckon the study of the dignity and beauty of public worship, and the tradition and use of forms of devotion of singular excellence and value. A tendency to revert to the ancient Calvinist doctrine of the sacraments has prepossessed some in favor of that sect in which the old Calvinism is still cherished. Some have rejoiced to find a door of access to the communion of the church not beset with revivalist exactions of examination and scrutiny of the sacred interior experiences of the soul. Some have reacted from an excessive or inquisitive or arbitrary church discipline, toward a default of discipline. Some, worthily weary of sectarian division and of the "evangelical" doctrine that schism is the normal condition of the church of Christ, have found real comfort in taking refuge in a sect in which, closing their eyes, they can say, "There are no schisms in the church; the church is one and undivided, and we are it." These and other like considerations, mingled in varying proportions, have been honorable motives impelling toward the Episcopal denomination; and few that have felt the force of them have felt constrained stubbornly to resist the gentle assurances offered by the "apostolic succession" theory of a superior authority and prerogative with which they had become invested. The numerous accessions to the Episcopal Church from other communions have, of course, been in large part reinforcements to the already dominant party.

In the Roman Catholic Church of the United States, during this stormy period, there was by no means a perfect calm. The ineradicable feeling of the American citizen—however recent his naturalization—that he has a right to do what he will with his own, had kept asserting itself in that plausible but untenable claim of the laity to manage the church property acquired by their own contributions, which is known to Catholic writers as "trusteeism." Through the whole breadth of the country, from Buffalo to New Orleans, sharp conflicts over this question between clergy and laity had continued to vex the peace of the church, and the victory of the clergy had not been unvarying and complete. When, in 1837, Bishop John Hughes took the reins of spiritual power in New York, he resolved to try conclusions with the trustees who attempted to overrule his authority in his own cathedral. Sharply threatening to put the church under interdict, if necessary, he brought the recalcitrants to terms at last by a less formidable process. He appealed to the congregation to withhold all further contributions from the trustees. The appeal, for conscience' sake, to refrain from giving has always a double hope of success. And the bishop succeeded in ousting the trustees, at the serious risk of teaching the people a trick which has since been found equally effective when applied on the opposite side of a dispute between clergyman and congregation. In Philadelphia the long struggle was not ended without the actual interdicting of the cathedral of St. Mary's, April, 1831. In Buffalo, so late as 1847, even this extreme measure, applied to the largest congregation in the newly erected diocese, did not at once enforce submission.

The conflict with trusteeism was only one out of many conflicts which gave abundant exercise to the administrative abilities of the American bishops. The mutual jealousies of the various nationalities and races among the laity, and of the various sects of the regular clergy, menaced, and have not wholly ceased to menace, the harmony of the church, if not its unity.

One disturbing element by which the Roman Catholic Church in some European countries has been sorely vexed makes no considerable figure in the corresponding history in America. There has never been here any "Liberal Catholic" party. The fact stands in analogy with many like facts. Visitors to America from the established churches of England or Scotland or Germany have often been surprised to find the temper of the old-country church so much broader and less rigid than that of the daughter church in the new and free republic. The reason is less recondite than might be supposed. In the old countries there are retained in connection with the state-church, by constraint of law or of powerful social or family influences, many whose adhesion to its distinctive tenets and rules is slight and superficial. It is out of such material that the liberal church party grows. In the migration it is not that the liberal churchman becomes more strict, but that, being released from outside pressure, he becomes less of a churchman. He easily draws off from his hereditary communion and joins himself to some other, or to none at all. This process of evaporation leaves behind it a strong residuum in which all characteristic elements are held as in a saturated solution.

A further security of the American Catholic Church against the growth of any "Liberal Catholic" party like those of continental Europe is the absolutist organization of the hierarchy under the personal government of the pope. In these last few centuries great progress has been made by the Roman see in extinguishing the ancient traditions of local or national independence in the election of bishops. Nevertheless in Catholic Europe important relics of this independence give an effective check to the absolute power of Rome. In America no trace of this historic independence has ever existed. The power of appointing and removing bishops is held absolutely and exclusively by the pope and exercised through the Congregation of the Propaganda. The power of ordaining and assigning priests is held by the bishop, who also holds or controls the title to the church property in his diocese. The security against partisan division within the church is as complete as it can be made without gravely increasing the risks of alienating additional multitudes from the fellowship of the church.[312:1]

During the whole of this dreary decade there were "fightings without" as well as within for the Catholic Church in the United States. Its great and sudden growth solely by immigration had made it distinctively a church of foreigners, and chiefly of Irishmen. The conditions were favorable for the development of a race prejudice aggravated by a religious antipathy. It was a good time for the impostor, the fanatic, and the demagogue to get in their work. In Boston, in 1834, the report that a woman was detained against her will in the Ursuline convent at Charlestown, near Boston, led to the burning of the building by a drunken mob. The Titus Oates of the American no-popery panic, in 1836, was an infamous woman named Maria Monk, whose monstrous stories of secret horrors perpetrated in a convent in Montreal, in which she claimed to have lived as a nun, were published by a respectable house and had immense currency. A New York pastor of good standing, Dr. Brownlee, made himself sponsor for her character and her stories; and when these had been thoroughly exposed, by Protestant ministers and laymen, for the shameless frauds that they were, there were plenty of zealots to sustain her still. A "Protestant Society" was organized in New York, and solicited the contributions of the benevolent and pious to promote the dissemination of raw-head-and-bloody-bones literature on the horrors of popery. The enterprise met with reprobation from sober-minded Protestants, but it was not without its influence for mischief. The presence of a great foreign vote, easily manipulated and cast in block, was proving a copious source of political corruption. Large concessions of privilege or of public property to Catholic institutions were reasonably suspected to have been made in consideration of clerical services in partisan politics.[313:1] The conditions provoked, we might say necessitated, a political reform movement, which took the name and character of "Native American." In Philadelphia, a city notorious at that time for misgovernment and turbulence, an orderly "American" meeting was attacked and broken up by an Irish mob. One act of violence led to another, the excitement increasing from day to day; deadly shots were exchanged in the streets, houses from which balls had been fired into the crowd were set in flames, which spread to other houses, churches were burned, and the whole city dominated by mobs that were finally suppressed by the State militia. It was an appropriate climax to the ten years of ecclesiastical and social turmoil.[314:1]

CHAPTER XVIII. THE GREAT IMMIGRATION.

At the taking of the first census of the United States, in 1790, the country contained a population of about four millions in its territory of less than one million of square miles. Sixty years later, at the census of 1850, it contained a population of more than twenty-three millions in its territory of about three millions of square miles.

The vast expansion of territory to more than threefold the great original domain of the United States had been made by honorable purchase or less honorable conquest. It had not added largely to the population of the nation; the new acquisitions were mainly of unoccupied land. The increase of the population, down to about 1845, was chiefly the natural increase of a hardy and prolific stock under conditions in the highest degree favorable to such increase. Up to the year 1820 the recent immigration had been inconsiderable. In the ten years 1820-29 the annual arrival of immigrants was nine thousand. In the next decade, 1830-39, the annual arrival was nearly thirty-five thousand, or a hundred a day. For forty years the total immigration from all quarters was much less than a half-million. In the course of the next three decades, from 1840 to 1869, there arrived in the United States from the various countries of Europe five and a half millions of people. It was more than the entire population of the country at the time of the first census;—

A multitude like which the populous North
Poured never from her frozen loins to pass
Rhene or the Danaw, when her barbarous sons
Came like a deluge on the South and spread
Beneath Gibraltar to the Libyan sands.

Under the pressure of a less copious flood of incursion the greatest empire in all history, strongest in arts and polity as well as arms, had perished utterly. If Rome, with her population of one hundred and twenty millions, her genius for war and government, and her long-compacted civilization, succumbed under a less sudden rush of invasion, what hope was there for the young American Republic, with its scanty population and its new and untried institutions?[316:1]

An impressive providential combination of causes determined this great historic movement of population at this time. It was effected by attractions in front of the emigrant, reinforced by impulses from behind. The conclusion of the peace of 1815 was followed by the beginning of an era of great public works, one of the first of which was the digging of the Erie Canal. This sort of enterprise makes an immediate demand for large forces of unskilled laborers; and in both hemispheres it has been observed to occasion movements of population out of Catholic countries into Protestant countries. The westward current of the indigenous population created a vacuum in the seaboard States, and a demand for labor that was soon felt in the labor-markets of the Old World. A liberal homestead policy on the part of the national government, and naturalization laws that were more than liberal, agencies for the encouragement of settlers organized by individual States and by railroad corporations and other great landed proprietors, and the eager competition of steamship companies drumming for steerage passengers in all parts of Europe—all these coöperated with the growing facility and cheapness of steam transportation to swell the current of migration. The discovery of gold in California quickened the flow of it.

As if it had been the divine purpose not only to draw forth, but to drive forth, the populations of the Old World to make their homes in the New, there was added to all these causes conducive to migration the Irish famine of 1846-47, and the futile revolutions of 1848, with the tyrannical reactions which followed them. But the great stimulus to migration was the success and prosperity that attended it. It was "success that succeeded." The great emigration agent was the letter written to his old home by the new settler, in multitudes of cases inclosing funds to pay the passage of friends whom he had left behind him.

The great immigration that began about 1845 is distinguished from some of the early colonizations in that it was in no sense a religious movement. Very grave religious results were to issue from it; but they were to be achieved through the unconscious coöperation of a multitude of individuals each intent with singleness of vision on his own individual ends. It is by such unconscious coöperation that the directing mind and the overruling hand of God in history are most signally illustrated.

In the first rush of this increased immigration by far the greatest contributor of new population was Ireland. It not only surpassed any other country in the number of its immigrants, but in the height of the Irish exodus, in the decade 1840-50, it nearly equaled all other countries of the world together. The incoming Irish millions were almost solidly Roman Catholic. The measures taken by the British government for many generations to attach the Irish people to the crown and convert them to the English standard of Protestantism had had the result of discharging upon our shores a people distinguished above all Christendom besides for its ardent and unreserved devotion to the Roman Church, and hardly less distinguished for its hatred to England.

After the first flood-tide the relative number of the Irish immigrants began to decrease, and has kept on decreasing until now. Since the Civil War the chief source of immigration has been Germany; and its contributions to our population have greatly aggrandized the Lutheran denomination, once so inconsiderable in numbers, until in many western cities it is the foremost of the Protestant communions, and in Chicago outnumbers the communicants of the Episcopalian, the Presbyterian, and the Methodist churches combined.[318:1] The German immigration has contributed its share, and probably more than its share, to our non-religious and churchless population. Withal, in a proportion which it is not easy to ascertain with precision, it added multitudinous thousands to the sudden and enormous growth of the Roman

Catholic Church. But there is an instructive contrast between the German immigrations, whether Catholic or Protestant, and the Irish immigration. The Catholicism of the Irish, held from generation to generation in the face of partisan and sometimes cruelly persecuting laws, was held with the ardor, if not of personal conviction, at least of strong hereditary animosity. To the Germans, their religious sect, whether Catholic, Lutheran, or Reformed, is determined for them by political arrangement, under the principle cujus regio, ejus religio. It is matter of course that tenets thus acquired should be held by a tenure so far removed from fanaticism as to seem to more zealous souls much like lukewarmness. Accustomed to have the cost of religious institutions provided for in the budget of public expenses, the wards of the Old World state-churches find themselves here in strange surroundings, untrained in habits of self-denial for religious objects. The danger is a grave and real one that before they become acclimated to the new conditions a large percentage will be lost, not only from their hereditary communion, but from all Christian fellowship, and lapse into simple indifferentism and godlessness. They have much to learn and something to teach. The indigenous American churches are not likely to be docile learners at the feet of alien teachers; but it would seem like the slighting of a providential opportunity if the older sects should fail to recognize that one of the greatest and by far the most rapidly growing of the Protestant churches of America, the Lutheran, growing now with new increments not only from the German, but also from the Scandinavian nations, is among us in such force to teach us somewhat by its example of the equable, systematic, and methodical ways of a state-church, as well as to learn something from the irregular fervor of that revivalism which its neighbors on every hand have inherited from the Great Awakening. It would be the very extravagance of national self-conceit if the older American churches should become possessed of the idea that four millions of German Christians and one million of Scandinavians, arriving here from 1860 to 1890, with their characteristic methods in theology and usages of worship and habits of church organization and administration, were here, in the providence of God, only to be assimilated and not at all to assimilate.

The vast growth of the Roman Catholic Church in America could not but fill its clergy and adherents with wonder and honest pride. But it was an occasion of immense labors and not a little anxiety. One effect of the enormous immigration was inevitably to impose upon this church, according to the popular apprehension, the character of a foreign association, and, in the earlier periods of the influx, of an Irish association. It was in like manner inevitable, from the fact that the immigrant class are preponderantly poor and of low social rank, that it should for two or three generations be looked upon as a church for the illiterate and unskilled laboring class. An incident of the excessive torrent rush of the immigration was that the Catholic Church became to a disproportionate extent an urban institution, making no adequate provision for the dispersed in agricultural regions.

Against these and other like disadvantages the hierarchy of the Catholic Church have struggled heroically, with some measure of success. The steadily rising character of the imported population in its successive generations has aided them. If in the first generations the churches were congregations of immigrants served by an imported clergy, the most strenuous exertions were made for the founding of institutions that should secure to future congregations born upon the soil the services of an American-trained priesthood. One serious hindrance to the noble advances that have nevertheless been made in this direction has been the fanatical opposition levied against even the most beneficent enterprises of the church by a bigoted Native-Americanism. It is not a hopeful method of conciliating and naturalizing a foreign element in the community to treat them with suspicion and hostility as alien enemies. The shameful persecution which the mob was for a brief time permitted to inflict on Catholic churches and schools and convents had for its chief effect to confirm the foreigner in his adherence to his church and his antipathy to Protestantism, and to provoke a twofold ferocity in return. At a time when there was reason to apprehend a Know-nothing riot in New York, in 1844, a plan was concerted and organized by "a large Irish society with divisions throughout the city," by which, "in case a single church was attacked, buildings should be fired in all quarters and the great city should be involved in a general conflagration."[321:1]

The utmost that could have been hoped for by the devoted but inadequate body of the Roman Catholic clergy in America, overwhelmed by an influx of their people coming in upon them in increasing volume, numbering millions per annum, was that they might be able to hold their own. But this hope was very far from being attained. How great have been the losses to the Roman communion through the transplantation of its members across the sea is a question to which the most widely varying answers have been given, and on which statistical exactness seems unattainable. The various estimates, agreeing in nothing else, agree in representing them as enormously great.[321:2] All good men will also agree that in so far as these losses represent mere lapses into unbelief and irreligion they are to be deplored. Happily there is good evidence of a large salvage, gathered into other churches, from what so easily becomes a shipwreck of faith with total loss.

It might seem surprising, in view of the many and diverse resources of attractive influence which the Roman Church has at its command, that its losses have not been to some larger extent compensated by conversions from other sects. Instances of such conversion are by no means wanting; but so far as a popular current toward Catholicism is concerned, the attractions in that direction are outweighed by the disadvantages already referred to. It has not been altogether a detriment to the Catholic Church in America that the social status and personal composition of its congregations, in its earlier years, have been such that the transition into it from any of the Protestant churches could be made only at the cost of a painful self-denial. The number of accessions to it has been thereby lessened, but (leaving out the case of the transition of politicians from considerations of expediency) the quality of them has been severely sifted. Incomparably the most valuable acquisition which the American Catholic Church has received has been the company of devoted and gifted young men, deeply imbued with the principles and sentiments of the High-church party in the Episcopal Church, who have felt constrained in conscience and in logic to take the step, which seems so short, from the highest level in the Anglican Church into the Roman, and who, organized into the Order of the Paulist Fathers, have exemplified in the Roman Church so many of the highest qualities of Protestant preaching.

He is a bold man who will undertake to predict in detail the future of the Roman Church in America. To say that it will be modified by its surroundings is only to say what is true of it in all countries. To say that it will be modified for the better is to say what is true of it in all Protestant countries. Nowhere is the Roman Church so pure from scandal and so effective for good as where it is closely surrounded and jealously scrutinized by bodies of its fellow-Christians whom it is permitted to recognize only as heretics. But when the influence of surrounding heresy is seen to be an indispensable blessing to the church, the heretic himself comes to be looked upon with a mitigated horror. Not with the sacrifice of any principle, but through the application of some of those provisions by which the Latin theology is able to meet exigencies like this,—the allowance in favor of "invincible ignorance" and prejudice, the distinction between the body and "the soul of the church,"—the Roman Catholic, recognizing the spirit of Christ in his Protestant fellow-Christian, is able to hold him in spiritual if not formal communion, so that the Catholic Church may prove itself not dissevered from the Church Catholic. In the common duties of citizenship and of humanity, in the promotion of the interests of morality, even in those religious matters that are of common concern to all honest disciples of Jesus Christ, he is at one with his heretic brethren. Without the change of a single item either of doctrine or of discipline, the attitude and temper of the church, as compared with the church of Spain or Italy or Mexico, is revolutionized. The change must needs draw with it other changes, which may not come without some jar and conflict between progressive and conservative, but which nevertheless needs must come. Out of many indications of the spirit of fellowship with all Christians now exemplified among American Catholics, I quote one of the most recent and authoritative from an address of Archbishop Ryan at the Catholic Congress in

Chicago in 1893. Speaking on Christian union, he said:

"If there is any one thing more than another upon which people agree, it is respect and reverence for the person and the character of the Founder of Christianity. How the Protestant loves his Saviour! How the Protestant eye will sometimes grow dim when speaking of our Lord! In this great center of union is found the hope of human society, the only means of preserving Christian civilization, the only point upon which Catholic and Protestant may meet. As if foreseeing that this should be, Christ himself gave his example of fraternal charity, not to the orthodox Jew, but to the heretical Samaritan, showing that charity and love, while faith remains intact, can never be true unless no distinction is made between God's creatures."[325:1]

Herein is fellowship higher than that of symbols and sacraments. By so far as it receives this spirit of love the American Catholic Church enters into its place in that greater Catholic Church of which we all make mention in the Apostles' Creed—"the Holy Universal Church, which is the fellowship of holy souls."

The effect of the Great Immigration on the body of the immigrant population is not more interesting or more important than the effect of it on the religious bodies already in occupation of the soil. The impression made on them by what seemed an irruption of barbarians of strange language or dialect, for the most part rude, unskilled, and illiterate, shunning as profane the Christian churches of the land, and bowing in unknown rites as devotees of a system known, and by no means favorably known, only through polemic literature and history, and through the gruesome traditions of Puritan and Presbyterian and Huguenot, was an impression not far removed from horror; and this impression was deepened as the enormous proportions of this invasion disclosed themselves from year to year. The serious and not unreasonable fear that these armies of aliens, handled as they manifestly were by a generalship that was quick to seize and fortify in a conspicuous way the strategic points of influence, especially in the new States, might imperil or ruin the institutions and liberties of the young Republic, was stimulated and exploited in the interest of enterprises of evangelization that might counter-work the operations of the invading church. The appeals of the Bible and tract societies, and of the various home mission agencies of the different denominations, as well as of the distinctively antipopery societies, were pointed with the alarm lest "the great West" should fall under the domination of the papal hierarchy. Naturally the delineations of the Roman system and of its public and social results that were presented to the public for these purposes were of no flattering character. Not history only, but contemporary geography gave warnings of peril. Canada on one hand, and Mexico and the rest of Spanish America on the other, were cited as living examples of the fate which might befall the free United States. The apocalyptic prophecies were copiously drawn upon for material of war. By processes of exegesis which critical scholarship regards with a smile or a shudder, the helpless pope was made to figure as the Antichrist, the Man of Sin and Son of Perdition, the Scarlet Woman on the Seven Hills, the Little Horn Speaking Blasphemies, the Beast, and the Great Red Dragon. That moiety of Christendom which, sorely as its history has been deformed by corruption and persecution, violently as it seems to be contrasted with the simplicity of the primeval church, is nevertheless the spiritual home of multitudes of Christ's well-approved servants and disciples, was held up to gaze as being nothing but the enemy of Christ and his cause. The appetite of the Protestant public for scandals at the expense of their fellow-Christians was stimulated to a morbid greediness and then overfed with willful and wicked fabrications. The effect of this fanaticism on some honest but illogical minds was what might have been looked for. Brought by and by into personal acquaintance with Catholic ministers and institutions, and discovering the fraud and injustice that had been perpetrated, they sprang by a generous reaction into an attitude of sympathy for the Roman Catholic system. A more favorable preparation of the way of conversion to Rome could not be desired by the skillful propagandist. One recognizes a retributive justice in the fact, when notable gains to the Catholic Church are distinctly traced to the reaction of honest men from these fraudulent polemics.[327:1]

The danger to the Republic, which was thus malignantly or ignorantly exaggerated and distorted, was nevertheless real and grave. No sincerely earnest and religious Protestant, nor even any well-informed patriotic citizen, with the example of French and Spanish America before his eyes, could look with tolerance upon the prospect of a possible Catholicizing of the new States at the West; and the sight of the incessant tide of immigration setting westward, the reports of large funds sent hither from abroad to aid the propagation of the Roman Church, and the accounts of costly and imposing ecclesiastical buildings rising at the most important centers of population, roused the Christian patriotism of the older States to the noblest enterprises of evangelization. There was no wasting of energy in futile disputation. In all the Protestant communions it was felt that the work called for was a simple, peaceful, and positive one—to plant the soil of the West, at the first occupation of it by settlers, with Christian institutions and influences. The immensity of the task stimulated rather than dismayed the zeal of the various churches. The work undertaken and accomplished in the twenty years from 1840 to 1860 in providing the newly settled regions with churches, pastors, colleges, and theological seminaries, with Sunday-schools, and with Bibles and other religious books, was of a magnitude which will never be defined by statistical figures. How great it was, and at what cost it was effected in gifts of treasure and of heroic lives of toil and self-denial, can only be a matter of vague wonder and thanksgiving.

The work of planting the church in the West exhibits the voluntary system at its best—and at its worst. A task so vast and so momentous has never been imposed on the resources of any state establishment. It is safe to say that no established church has ever existed, however imperially endowed, that would have been equal to the undertaking of it. With no imposing combination of forces, and no strategic concert of action, the work was begun spontaneously and simultaneously, like some of the operations of nature, by a multitude of different agencies, and went forward uninterrupted to something as nearly like completeness as could be in a work the exigencies of which continually widened beyond all achievements. The planting of the church in the West is one of the wonders of church history.

But this noble act of religious devotion was by no means a sacrifice without blemish. The sacred zeal for advancing God's reign and righteousness was mingled with many very human motives in the progress of it. Conspicuous among these was the spirit of sectarian competition. The worthy and apostolic love for kindred according to the flesh separated from home and exposed to the privations and temptations of the frontier, the honest anxiety to forestall the domination of a dangerously powerful religious corporation propagating perverted views of truth, even the desire to advance principles and forms of belief deemed to be important, were infused with a spirit of partisanship as little spiritual as the enthusiasm which animates the struggles and the shouters at a foot-ball game. The devoted pioneer of the gospel on the frontier, seeing his work endangered by that of a rival denomination, writes to the central office of his sect; the board of missions makes its appeal to the contributing churches; the churches respond with subsidies; and the local rivalry in the mission field is pressed, sometimes to a good result, on the principle that "competition is the life of business." Thus the fragrance of the precious ointment of loving sacrifice is perceptibly tainted, according to the warning of Ecclesiastes or the Preacher. And yet it is not easy for good men, being men, sternly to rebuke the spirit that seems to be effective in promoting the good cause that they have at heart.

If the effect of these emulations on the contributing churches was rather carnal than spiritual, the effect in the mission field was worse. The effect was seen in the squandering of money and of priceless service of good men and women, in the debilitating and demoralizing division and subdivision of the Christian people, not of cities and large towns, but of villages and hamlets and of thinly settled farming districts. By the building of churches and other edifices for sectarian uses, schism was established for coming time as a vested interest. The gifts and service bestowed in this cause with a truly magnificent liberality would have sufficed to establish the Christian faith and fellowship throughout the new settlements in strength and dignity, in churches which, instead of lingering as puny and dependent nurslings, would have grown apace to be strong and healthy nursing mothers to newer churches yet.

There is an instructive contrast, not only between the working of the voluntary system and that of the Old World establishments, but between the methods of the Catholic Church and the Protestant no-method. Under the control of a strong coördinating authority the competitions of the various Catholic orders, however sharp, could never be allowed to run into wasteful extravagance through cross-purposes. It is believed that the Catholics have not erected many monuments of their own unthrift in the shape of costly buildings begun, but left unfinished and abandoned. A more common incident of their work has been the buying up of these expensive failures, at a large reduction from their cost, and turning them to useful service. And yet the principle of sectarian competition is both recognized and utilized in the Roman system. The various clerical sects, with their characteristic names, costumes, methods, and doctrinal differences, have their recognized aptitudes for various sorts of work, with which their names are strongly associated: the Dominican for pulpit eloquence, the Capuchin for rough-and-ready street-preaching, the Benedictine for literary work, the Sulpitian for the training of priests, and the ubiquitous Jesuit for shifty general utility with a specialty of school-keeping. These and a multitude of other orders, male and female, have been effectively and usefully employed in the arduous labor Romanam condere gentem. But it would seem that the superior stability of the present enterprise of planting Catholicism in the domain of the United States, as compared with former expensive failures, was due in some part to the larger employment of a diocesan parish clergy instead of a disproportionate reliance on the "regulars."

On the whole, notwithstanding its immense armies of immigrants and the devoted labors of its priests, and notwithstanding its great expansion, visible everywhere in conspicuous monuments of architecture, the Catholic advance in America has not been, comparatively speaking, successful. For one thing, the campaign was carried on too far from its base of supplies. The subsidies from Lyons and Vienna, liberal as they were, were no match for the home missionary zeal of the seaboard States in following their own sons westward with church and gospel and pastor. Even the conditions which made possible the superior management and economy of resources, both material and personal, among the Catholics, were attended with compensating drawbacks. With these advantages they could not have the immense advantage of the popular initiative. In Protestantism the people were the church, and the minister was chief among the people only by virtue of being servant of all; the people were incited to take up the work for their own and carry it on at their best discretion; and they were free to make wasteful and disastrous blunders and learn therefrom by experience. With far greater expenditure of funds, they make no comparison with their brethren of the Roman obedience in stately and sumptuous buildings at great centers of commerce and travel. But they have covered the face of the land with country meeting-houses, twice as many as there was any worthy use for, in which faithful service is rendered to subdivided congregations by underpaid ministers, enough in number, if they were wisely distributed, for the evangelization of the whole continent; and each country meeting-house is a mission station, and its congregation, men, women, and children, are missionaries. Thus it has come about, in the language of the earnest Catholic from the once Catholic city of New Orleans, that "the nation, the government, the whole people, remain solidly Protestant."[331:1] Great territories originally discovered by Catholic explorers and planted in the name of the church by Catholic missionaries and colonists, and more lately occupied by Catholic immigrants in what seemed overwhelming numbers, are now the seat of free and powerful commonwealths in which the Catholic Church is only one of the most powerful and beneficent of the Christian sects, while the institutions and influences which characterize their society are predominantly Protestant. In the westward propagation of Protestantism, as well as of Catholicism, the distinctive attributes of the several sects or orders is strikingly illustrated.

Foremost in the pioneer work of the church are easily to be recognized the Methodists and the Baptists, one the most solidly organized of the Protestant sects, the other the most uncompact and individualist; the first by virtue of the supple military organization of its great corps of itinerants, the other by the simplicity and popular apprehensibleness of its distinctive tenets and arguments and the aggressive ardor with which it inspires all its converts, and both by their facility in recruiting their ministry from the rank and file of the church, without excluding any by arbitrarily imposed conditions. The Presbyterians were heavily cumbered for advance work by traditions and rules which they were rigidly reluctant to yield or bend, even when the reason for the rule was superseded by higher reasons. The argument for a learned ministry is doubtless a weighty one; but it does not suffice to prove that when college-bred men are not to be had it is better that the people have no minister at all. There is virtue in the rule of ministerial parity; but it should not be allowed to hinder the church from employing in humbler spiritual functions men who fall below the prescribed standard. This the church, in course of time, discovered, and instituted a "minor order" of ministers, under the title of colporteurs. But it was timidly and tardily done, and therefore ineffectively. The Presbyterians lost their place in the skirmish-line; but that which had been their hindrance in the advance work gave them great advantage in settled communities, in which for many years they took precedence in the building up of strong and intelligent congregations.

To the Congregationalists belongs an honor in the past which, in recent generations, they have not been jealous to retain. Beyond any sect, except the Moravians, they have cherished that charity which seeketh not her own. The earliest leaders in the organization of schemes of national beneficence in coöperation with others, they have sustained them with unselfish liberality, without regard to returns of sectarian advantage. The results of their labor are largely to be traced in the upbuilding of other sects. Their specialty in evangelization has been that of the religious educators of the nation. They have been preëminently the builders of colleges and theological seminaries. To them, also, belongs the leadership in religious journalism. Not only the journals of their own sect and the undenominational journals, but also to a notable extent the religious journals of other denominations, have depended for their efficiency on men bred in the discipline of Congregationalism.

It is no just reproach to the Episcopalians that they were tardy in entering the field of home missions. When we remember that it is only since 1811 that they have emerged from numerical insignificance, we find their contribution to the planting of the church in the new settlements to be a highly honorable one. By a suicidal compact the guileless Evangelical party agreed, in 1835, to take direction of the foreign missions of the church, and leave the home field under the direction of the aggressive High-church party. It surrendered its part in the future of the church, and determined the type of Episcopalianism that was to be planted in the West.[333:1] Entering thus late into the work, and that with stinted resources, the Episcopal Church wholly missed the apostolic glory of not building on other men's foundations. Coming with the highest pretensions to exclusive authority, its work was very largely a work of proselyting from other Christian sects. But this work was prosperously carried on; and although not in itself a work of the highest dignity, and although the methods of it often bore a painfully schismatic character, there is little room for doubt that the results of it have enriched and strengthened the common Christianity of America. Its specialties in the planting work have been the setting of a worthy example of dignity and simplicity in the conduct of divine worship, and in general of efficiency in the administration of a parish, and, above all, the successful handling of the immensely difficult duties imposed upon Christian congregations in great cities, where the Episcopal Church has its chief strength and its most effective work.

One must needs ascend to a certain altitude above the common level in order to discern a substantial resultant unity of movement in the strenuous rivalries and even antagonisms of the many sects of the one church of Christ in America in that critical quarter-century from the year 1835 to the outbreak of the Civil War, in which the work of the church was suddenly expanded by the addition of a whole empire of territory on the west, and the bringing in of a whole empire of alien population from the east, and when no one of the Christian forces of the nation could be spared from the field. The unity is very real, and is visible enough, doubtless, from "the circle of the heavens." The sharers in the toil and conflict and the near spectators are not well placed to observe it. It will be for historians in some later century to study it in a truer perspective.

It is not only as falling within this period of immigration, but as being largely dependent on its accessions from foreign lands, that the growth of Mormonism is entitled to mention in this chapter. In its origin Mormonism is distinctly American—a system of gross, palpable imposture contrived by a disreputable adventurer, Joe Smith, with the aid of three confederates, who afterward confessed the fraud and perjury of which they had been guilty. It is a shame to human nature that the silly lies put forth by this precious gang should have found believers. But the solemn pretensions to divine revelation, mixed with elements borrowed from the prevalent revivalism, and from the immediate adventism which so easily captivates excitable imaginations, drew a number of honest dupes into the train of the knavish leaders, and made possible the pitiable history which followed. The chief recruiting-grounds for the new religion were not in America, but in the manufacturing and mining regions of Great Britain, and in some of the countries, especially the Scandinavian countries, of continental Europe. The able handling of an emigration fund, and the dexterous combination of appeals to many passions and interests at once, have availed to draw together in the State of Utah and neighboring regions a body of fanatics formidable to the Republic, not by their number, for they count only about one hundred and fifty thousand, but by the solidity with which they are compacted into a political, economical, religious, and, at need, military community, handled at will by unscrupulous chiefs. It is only incidentally that the strange story of the Mormons, a story singularly dramatic and sometimes tragic, is connected with the history of American Christianity.[335:1]

To this same period belongs the beginning of the immigration of the Chinese, which, like that of the Mormons, becomes by and by important to our subject as furnishing occasion for active and fruitful missionary labors.

In the year 1843 culminated the panic agitation of Millerism. From the year 1831 an honest Vermont farmer named William Miller had been urging upon the public, in pamphlets and lectures, his views of the approaching advent of Christ to judgment and the destruction of the world. He had figured it out on the basis of prophecies in Daniel and the Revelation, and the great event was set down for April 23, 1843. As the date drew near the excitement of many became intense. Great meetings were held, in the open air or in tents, of those who wished to be found waiting for the Lord. Some nobly proved their sincerity by the surrender of their property for the support of their poorer brethren until the end should come. The awful day was awaited with glowing rapture of hope, or by some with terror. When it dawned there was eager gazing upon the clouds of heaven to descry the sign of the Son of man. And when the day had passed without event there were various revulsions of feeling. The prophets set themselves to going over their figures and fixing new dates; earnest believers, sobered by the failure of their pious expectations, held firmly to the substance of their faith and hope, while no longer attempting to "know times and seasons, which the Father hath put within his own power"; weak minds made shipwreck of faith; and scoffers cried in derision, "Where is the promise of his coming?" A monument of this honest delusion still exists in the not very considerable sect of Adventists, with its subdivisions; but sympathizers with their general scheme of prophetical interpretation are to be found among the most earnest and faithful members of other churches. Such has been the progress of Scriptural knowledge since the days when Farmer Miller went to work with his arithmetic and slate upon the strange symbols and enigmatic figures of the Old and New Testament Apocalypses, that plain Christians everywhere have now the means of knowing that the lines of calculation along which good people were led into delusion a half-century ago started from utterly fallacious premises. It is to the fidelity of critical scholars that we owe it that hereafter, except among the ignorant and unintelligent, these two books, now clearly understood, will not again be used to minister to the panic of a Millerite craze, nor to furnish vituperative epithets for antipopery agitators.

To this period also must be referred the rise of that system of necromancy which, originating in America, has had great vogue in other countries, and here in its native land has taken such form as really to constitute a new cult. Making no mention of sporadic instances of what in earlier generations would have been called (and properly enough) by the name of witchcraft, we find the beginning of so-called "spiritualism" in the "Rochester rappings," produced, to the wonder of many witnesses, by "the Fox girls" in 1849. How the rappings and other sensible phenomena were produced was a curious question, but not important; the main question was, Did they convey communications from the spirits of the dead, as the young women alleged, and as many persons believed (so they thought) from demonstrative evidence? The mere suggestion of the possibility of this of course awakened an inquisitive and eager interest everywhere. It became the subject of universal discussion and experiment in society. There was demand for other "mediums" to satisfy curiosity or aid investigation; and the demand at once produced a copious supply. The business of medium became a regular profession, opening a career especially to enterprising women. They began to draw together believers and doubters into "circles" and "séances," and to organize permanent associations. At the end of ten years the "Spiritual Register" for 1859, boasting great things, estimated the actual spiritualists in America at 1,500,000, besides 4,000,000 more partly converted. The latest census gives the total membership of their associations as 45,030. But this moderate figure should not be taken as the measure of the influence of their leading tenet. There are not a few honest Christians who are convinced that communications do sometimes take place between the dead and the living; there are a great multitude who are disposed, in a vague way, to think there must be something in it. But there are few even of the earnest devotees of the spiritualist cult who will deny that the whole business is infested with fraud, whether of dishonest mediums or of lying spirits. Of late years the general public has come into possession of material for independent judgment on this point. An earnest spiritualist, a man of wealth, named Seybert, dying, left to the University of Pennsylvania a legacy of sixty thousand dollars, on condition that the university should appoint a commission to investigate the claims of spiritualism. A commission was appointed which left nothing to be desired in point of ability, integrity, and impartiality. Under the presidency of the renowned Professor Joseph Leidy, and with the aid and advice of leading believers in spiritualism, they made a long, patient, faithful investigation, the processes and results of which are published in a most amusing little volume.[338:1] The gist of their report may be briefly summed up. Every case of alleged communication from the world of departed spirits that was investigated by the commission (and they were guided in their selection of cases by the advice of eminent and respectable believers in spiritualism) was discovered and demonstrated to be a case of gross, willful attempted fraud. The evidence is strong that the organized system of spiritualism in America, with its associations and lyceums and annual camp-meetings, and its itinerancy of mediums and trance speakers, is a system of mere imposture. In the honest simplicity of many of its followers, and in the wicked mendacity of its leaders, it seems to be on a par with the other American contribution to the religions of the world, Mormonism.

CHAPTER XIX. THE CIVIL WAR—ANTECEDENTS AND CONSEQUENCES.

It has been observed that for nearly half a generation after the reaction began from the fervid excitement of the Millerite agitation no season of general revival was known in the American church.

These were years of immense material prosperity, "the golden age of our history."[340:1] The wealth of the nation in that time far more than doubled; its railroad mileage more than threefolded; population moved westward with rapidity and volume beyond precedent.

Between 1845 and 1860 there were admitted seven new States and four organized Territories. Withal it was a time of continually deepening intensity of political agitation. The patchwork of compromises and settlements contrived by make-shift politicians like Clay and Douglas would

not hold; they tore out, and the rent was made worse. Part of the Compromise of 1850, which was to be something altogether sempiternal, was a Fugitive Slave Law so studiously base and wicked in its provisions as to stir the indignation of just and generous men whenever it was enforced, and to instruct and strengthen and consolidate an intelligent and conscientious opposition to slavery as not a century of antislavery lecturing and pamphleteering could have done. Four years later the sagacious Stephen Douglas introduced into Congress his ingenious permanent pacification scheme for taking the slavery question "out of politics" by perfidiously repealing the act under which the western Territories had for the third part of a century been pledged to freedom, and leaving the question of freedom or slavery to be decided by the first settlers upon the soil. It was understood on both sides that the effect of this measure would be to turn over the soil of Kansas to slavery; and for a moment there was a calm that did almost seem like peace. But the providential man for the emergency, Eli Thayer, boldly accepted the challenge under all the disadvantageous conditions, and appealed to the friends of freedom and righteousness to stand by him in "the Kansas Crusade." The appeal was to the same Christian sentiment which had just uttered its vain protest, through the almost unanimous voice of the ministers of the gospel, against the opening of the Territories to the possibility of slavery. It was taken up in the solemn spirit of religious duty. None who were present are likely to forget the scene when the emigrants from New Haven assembled in the North Church to be sped on their way with prayer and benediction; how the vast multitude were thrilled by the noble eloquence of Beecher, and how money came out of pocket when it was proposed to equip the colonists with arms for self-defense against the ferocity of "border ruffians." There were scenes like this in many a church and country prayer-meeting, where Christian hearts did not forget to pray "for them in bonds, as bound with them." There took place such a religious emigration as America had not known since the days of the first colonists. They went forth singing the words of Whittier:
We cross the prairies as of old
Our fathers crossed the sea,
To make the West, as they the East,
The empire of the free.
Those were choice companies; it was said that in some of their settlements every third man was a college graduate. Thus it was that, not all at once, but after desperate tribulations, Kansas was saved for freedom. It was the turning-point in the "irrepressible conflict." The beam of the scales, which politicians had for forty years been trying to hold level, dipped in favor of liberty and justice, and it was hopeless thenceforth to restore the balance.[342:1]
Neither of the two characteristics of this time, the abounding material prosperity or the turbid political agitation, was favorable to that fixed attention to spiritual themes which promotes the revival of religion. But the conditions were about to be suddenly changed.
Suddenly, in the fall of 1857, came a business revulsion. Hard times followed. Men had leisure for thought and prayer, and anxieties that they were fain to cast upon God, seeking help and direction. The happy thought occurred to a good man, Jeremiah Lanphier, in the employ of the old North Dutch Church in New York, to open a room in the "consistory building" in Fulton Street as an oratory for the common prayer of so many business men as might be disposed to gather there in the hour from twelve to one o'clock, "with one accord to make their common supplications." The invitation was responded to at first by hardly more than "two or three." The number grew. The room overflowed. A second room was opened, and then a third, in the same building, till all its walls resounded with prayer and song. The example was followed until at one time, in the spring of 1858, no fewer than twenty "daily union prayer-meetings" were sustained in different parts of the city. Besides these, there was preaching at unwonted times and places. Burton's Theater, on Chambers Street, in the thick of the business houses, was thronged with eager listeners to the rudimental truths of personal religion, expounded and applied by great preachers. Everywhere the cardinal topics of practical religious duty, repentance and Christian faith, were themes of social conversation. All churches and ministers

were full of activity and hope. "They that feared the Lord spake often one with another." What was true of New York was true, in its measure, of every city, village, and hamlet in the land. It was the Lord's doing, marvelous in men's eyes. There was no human leadership or concert of action in bringing it about. It came. Not only were there no notable evangelists traveling the country; even the pastors of churches did little more than enter zealously into their happy duty in things made ready to their hand. Elsewhere, as at New York, the work began with the spontaneous gathering of private Christians, stirred by an unseen influence. Two circumstances tended to promote the diffusion of the revival. The Young Men's Christian Association, then a recent but rapidly spreading institution, furnished a natural center in each considerable town for mutual consultation and mutual incitement among young men of various sects. For this was another trait of the revival, that it went forward as a tide movement of the whole church, in disregard of the dividing-lines of sect. I know not what Christian communion, if any, was unaffected by it. The other favorable circumstance was the business interest taken in the revival by the secular press. Up to this time the church had been little accustomed to look for coöperation to the newspaper, unless it was the religious weekly. But at this time that was fulfilled which was spoken of the prophet, that "holiness to the Lord" should be written upon the trains of commerce and upon all secular things. The sensation head-lines in enterprising journals proclaimed "Revival News," and smart reporters were detailed to the prayer-meeting or the sermon, as having greater popular interest, for the time, than the criminal trial or the political debate. Such papers as the "Tribune" and the "Herald," laying on men's breakfast-tables and counting-room desks the latest pungent word from the noon prayer-meeting or the evening sermon, did the work of many tract societies.

As the immediate result of the revival of 1857-58 it has been estimated that one million of members were added to the fellowship of the churches. But the ulterior result was greater. This revival was the introduction to a new era of the nation's spiritual life. It was the training-school for a force of lay evangelists for future work, eminent among whom is the name of Dwight Moody. And, like the Great Awakening of 1740, it was the providential preparation of the American church for an immediately impending peril the gravity of which there were none at the time far-sighted enough to predict. Looking backward, it is instructive for us to raise the question how the church would have passed through the decade of the sixties without the spiritual reinforcement that came to it amid the pentecostal scenes of 1857 and 1858.

And yet there were those among the old men who were ready to weep as they compared the building of the Lord's house with what they had known in their younger days: no sustained enforcement on the mind and conscience of alarming and heart-searching doctrines; no "protracted meetings" in which from day to day the warnings and invitations of the gospel were set forth before the hesitating mind; in the converts no severe and thorough "law-work," from the agonizing throes of which the soul was with no brief travail born to newness of life; but the free invitation, the ready and glad acceptance, the prompt enrollment on the Lord's side. Did not these things betoken a superficial piety, springing up like seed in the thin soil of rocky places? It was a question for later years to answer, and perhaps we have not the whole of the answer yet. Certainly the work was not as in the days of Edwards and Brainerd, nor as in the days of Nettleton and Finney; was it not, perhaps, more like the work in the days of Barnabas and Paul and Peter?

It does not appear that the spiritual quickening of 1857 had any effect in allaying the sharp controversy between northern and southern Christians on the subject of slavery. Perhaps it may have deepened and intensified it. The "southern apostasy," from principles universally accepted in 1818, had become complete and (so far as any utterance was permitted to reach the public) unanimous. The southern Methodists and the southern Baptists had, a dozen years before, relieved themselves from liability to rebuke, whether express or implied, from their northern brethren for complicity with the crimes involved in slavery, by seceding from fellowship. Into the councils of the Episcopalians and the Catholics this great question of public morality was never allowed to enter. The Presbyterians were divided into two bodies, each having its northern and its southern presbyteries; and the course of events in these two bodies may be taken as an indication of the drift of opinion and feeling. The Old-School body, having a strong southern element, remained silent, notwithstanding the open nullification of its declaration of 1818 by the presbytery of Harmony, S. C., resolving that "the existence of slavery is not opposed to the will of God," and the synod of Virginia declaring that "the General Assembly had no right to declare that relation sinful which Christ and his apostles teach to be consistent with the most unquestionable piety." The New-School body, patient and considerate toward its southern presbyteries, did not fail, nevertheless, to reassert the principles of righteousness, and in 1850 it declared slave-holding to be prima facie a subject of the discipline of the church. In 1853 it called upon its southern presbyteries to report what had been done in the case. One of them replied defiantly that its ministers and church-members were slave-holders by choice and on principle. When the General Assembly condemned this utterance, the entire southern part of the church seceded and set up a separate jurisdiction.[346:1]

There seems no reason to doubt the entire sincerity with which the southern church, in all its sects, had consecrated itself with religious devotion to the maintenance of that horrible and inhuman form of slavery which had drawn upon itself the condemnation of the civilized world. The earnest antislavery convictions which had characterized it only twenty-five years before, violently suppressed from utterance, seem to have perished by suffocation. The common sentiment of southern Christianity was expressed in that serious declaration of the Southern Presbyterian Church, during the war, of its "deep conviction of the divine appointment of domestic servitude," and of the "peculiar mission of the southern church to conserve the institution of slavery."[346:2]

At the North, on the other hand, with larger liberty, there was wider diversity of opinion. In general, the effect of continued discussion, of larger knowledge of facts, and of the enforcement on the common conscience, by the course of public events, of a sense of responsibility and duty in the matter, had been to make more intelligent, sober, and discriminating, and therefore more strong and steadfast, the resolution to keep clear of all complicity with slavery. There were few to assume the defense of that odious system, though there were some. There were many to object to scores of objectionable things in the conduct of abolitionists. And there were a very great number of honest, conscientious men who were appalled as they looked forward to the boldly threatened consequences of even the mildest action in opposition to slavery—the rending of the church, the ruin of the country, the horrors of civil war, and its uncertain event, issuing perhaps in the wider extension and firmer establishment of slavery itself. It was an immense power that the bold, resolute, rule-or-ruin supporters of the divine right of slavery held over the Christian public of the whole country, so long as they could keep these threats suspended in the air. It seemed to hold in the balance against a simple demand to execute righteousness toward a poor, oppressed, and helpless race, immense interests of patriotism, of humanity, of the kingdom of God itself. Presently the time came when these threats could no longer be kept aloft. The compliance demanded was clearly, decisively refused. The threats must either be executed or must fall to the ground amid general derision. But the moment that the threat was put in execution its power as a threat had ceased. With the first stroke against the life of the nation all great and noble motives, instead of being balanced against each other, were drawing together in the same direction. It ought not to have been a surprise to the religious leaders of disunion, ecclesiastical and political, to find that those who had most anxiously deprecated the attack upon the government should be among the most earnest and resolute to repel the attack when made.

No man can read the history of the American church in the Civil War intelligently who does not apprehend, however great the effort, that the Christian people of the South did really and sincerely believe themselves to be commissioned by the providence of God to "conserve the institution of slavery" as an institution of "divine appointment." Strange as the conviction seems, it is sure that the conviction of conscience in the southern army that it was right in waging war against the government of the country was as clear as the conviction, on the other side, of the duty of defending the government. The southern regiments, like the northern, were sent forth with prayer and benediction, and their camps, as well as those of their adversaries, were often the seats of earnest religious life.[348:1]

At the South the entire able-bodied population was soon called into military service, so that almost the whole church was in the army. At the North the churches at home hardly seemed diminished by the myriads sent to the field. It was amazing to see the charities and missions of the churches sustained with almost undiminished supplies, while the great enterprises of the Sanitary and Christian Commissions were set on foot and magnificently carried forward, for the physical, social, and spiritual good of the soldiers. Never was the gift of giving so abundantly bestowed on the church as in these stormy times. There was a feverish eagerness of life in all ways; if there was a too eager haste to make money among those that could be spared for business, there was a generous readiness in bestowing it. The little faith that expected to cancel and retrench, especially in foreign missions, in which it took sometimes three dollars in the collection to put one dollar into the work, was rebuked by the rising of the church to the height of the exigency.

One religious lesson that was learned as never before, on both sides of the conflict, was the lesson of Christian fellowship as against the prevailing folly of sectarian divisions, emulations, and jealousies. There were great drawings in this direction in the early days of the war, when men of the most unlike antecedents and associations gathered on the same platform, intent on the same work, and mutual aversions and partisan antagonisms melted away in the fervent heat of a common religious patriotism. But the lesson which was commended at home was enforced in the camp and the regiment by constraint of circumstances. The army chaplain, however one-sided he might have been in his parish, had to be on all sides with his kindly sympathy as soon as he joined his regiment. He learned in a right apostolic sense to become all things to all men, and, returning home, he did not forget the lesson. The delight of a fellowship truly catholic in the one work of Christ, once tasted, was not easily foregone. Already the current, perplexed with eddies, had begun to set in the direction of Christian unity. How much the common labors of Christian men and women and Christian ministers of every different name, through the five years of bloody strife, contributed to swell and speed the current, no one can measure.

According to a well-known law of the kingdom of heaven, the intense experiences of the war, both in the army and out of it, left no man just as he was before. To "them that were exercised thereby" they brought great promotion in the service of the King. The cases are not few nor inconspicuous of men coming forth from the temptations and the discipline of the military service every way stronger and better Christians than they entered it. The whole church gained higher conceptions of the joy and glory of self-sacrifice, and deeper and more vivid insight into the significance of vicarious suffering and death. The war was a rude school of theology, but it taught some things well. The church had need of all that it could learn, in preparation for the tasks and trials that were before it.

There were those, on the other hand, who emerged from the military service depraved and brutalized; and those who, in the rush of business incidental to the war, were not trained to self-sacrifice and duty, but habituated to the seeking of selfish interests in the midst of the public peril and affliction. We delight in the evidences that these cases were a small proportion of the whole. But even a small percentage of so many hundreds of thousands mounts up to a formidable total. The early years of the peace were so marked by crimes of violence that a frequent heading in the daily newspapers was "The Carnival of Crime." Prosperity, or the semblance of it, came in like a sudden flood. Immigration of an improved character poured into the country in greater volume than ever. Multitudes made haste to be rich, and fell into temptations and snares. The perilous era of enormous fortunes began.

CHAPTER XX. AFTER THE WAR.

When the five years of rending and tearing had passed, in which slavery was dispossessed of its hold upon the nation, there was much to be done in reconstructing and readjusting the religious institutions of the country.

Throughout the seceding States buildings and endowments for religious uses had suffered in the general waste and destruction of property. Colleges and seminaries, in many instances, had seen their entire resources swept away through investment in the hopeless promises of the defeated government. Churches, boards, and like associations were widely disorganized through the vicissitudes of military occupation and the protracted absence or the death of men of experience and capacity.

The effect of the war upon denominational organizations had been various. There was no sect of all the church the members and ministers of which had not felt the sweep of the currents of popular opinion all about them. But the course of events in each denomination was in some measure illustrative of the character of its polity.

In the Roman Catholic Church the antagonisms of the conflict were as keenly felt as anywhere. Archbishop Hughes of New York, who, with Henry Ward Beecher and Bishop McIlvaine of Ohio, accepted a political mission from President Lincoln, was not more distinctly a Union man than Bishop Lynch of Charleston was a secessionist. But the firm texture of the hierarchical organization, held steadily in place by a central authority outside of the national boundaries, prevented any organic rupture. The Catholic Church in America was eminently fortunate at one point: the famous bull Quanta Cura, with its appended "Syllabus" of damnable errors, in which almost all the essential characteristics of the institutions of the American Republic are anathematized, was fulminated in 1864, when people in the United States had little time to think of ecclesiastical events taking place at such a distance. If this extraordinary document had been first published in a time of peace, and freely discussed in the newspapers of the time, it could hardly have failed to inflict the most serious embarrassment on the interests of Catholicism in America. Even now it keeps the Catholic clergy in a constantly explanatory attitude to show that the Syllabus does not really mean what to the ordinary reader it unmistakably seems to mean; and the work of explanation is made the more necessary and the more difficult by the decree of papal infallibility, which followed the Syllabus after a few years.

Simply on the ground of a de facto political independence, the southern dioceses of the Protestant Episcopal Church, following the principles and precedents of 1789, organized themselves into a "Church in the Confederate States." One of the southern bishops, Polk, of Louisiana, accepted a commission of major-general in the Confederate army, and relieved his brethren of any disciplinary questions that might have arisen in consequence by dying on the field from a cannon-shot. With admirable tact and good temper, the "Church in the United States" managed to ignore the existence of any secession; and when the alleged de facto independence ceased, the seceding bishops and their dioceses dropped quietly back into place without leaving a trace of the secession upon the record.

The southern organizations of the Methodists and Baptists were of twenty years' standing at the close of the war in 1865. The war had abolished the original cause of these divisions, but it had substituted others quite as serious. The exasperations of the war, and the still more acrimonious exasperations of the period of the political reconstruction and of the organization of northern missions at the South, gendered strifes that still delay the reintegration which is so visibly future of both of these divided denominations.

At the beginning of the war one of the most important of the denominations that still retained large northern and southern memberships in the same fellowship was the Old-School Presbyterian Church; and no national sect had made larger concessions to avert a breach of unity. When the General Assembly met at Philadelphia in May, 1861, amid the intense excitements of the opening war, it was still the hope of the habitual leaders and managers of the Assembly to avert a division by holding back that body from any expression of sentiment on the question on which the minds of Christians were stirred at that time with a profound and most religious fervor. But the Assembly took the matter out of the hands of its leaders, and by a great majority, in the words of a solemn and temperate resolution drawn by the venerable and conservative Dr. Gardiner Spring, declared its loyalty to the government and constitution of the country. With expressions of horror at the sacrilege of taking the church into the domain of politics, southern presbyteries one after another renounced the jurisdiction of the General Assembly that could be guilty of so shocking a profanation, and, uniting in a General Assembly of their own, proceeded with great promptitude to make equally emphatic deliverances on the opposite side of the same political question.[354:1] But nice logical consistency and accurate working within the lines of a church theory were more than could reasonably be expected of a people in so pitiable a plight. The difference on the subject of the right function of the church continued to be held as the ground for continuing the separation from the General Assembly after the alleged ground in political geography had ceased to be valid; the working motive for it was more obvious in the unfraternal and almost wantonly exasperating course of the national General Assembly during the war; but the best justification for it is to be found in the effective and useful working of the Southern Presbyterian Church. Considering the impoverishment and desolation of the southern country, the record of useful and self-denying work accomplished by this body, not only at home, but in foreign fields, is, from its beginning, an immensely honorable one.

Another occasion of reconstruction was the strong disposition of the liberated negroes to withdraw themselves from the tutelage of the churches in which they had been held, in the days of slavery, in a lower-caste relation. The eager entrance of the northern churches upon mission work among the blacks, to which access had long been barred by atrocious laws and by the savage fury of mobs, tended to promote this change. The multiplication and growth of organized negro denominations is a characteristic of the period after the war. There is reason to hope that the change may by and by, with the advance of education and moral training among this people, inure to their spiritual advantage. There is equal reason to fear that at present, in many cases, it works to their serious detriment.

The effect of the war was not exclusively divisive. In two instances, at least, it had the effect of healing old schisms. The southern secession from the New-School Presbyterian Church, which had come away in 1858 on the slavery issue, found itself in 1861 side by side with the southern secession from the Old School, and in full agreement with it in morals and politics. The two bodies were not long in finding that the doctrinal differences which a quarter-century before had seemed so insuperable were, after all, no serious hindrance to their coming together.

Even after the war was over, its healing power was felt, this time at the North. There was a honeycomb for Samson in the carcass of the monster. The two great Presbyterian sects at the North had found a common comfort in their relief from the perpetual festering irritation of the slavery question; they had softened toward each other in the glow of a religious patriotism; they had forgotten old antagonisms in common labors; and new issues had obscured the tenuous doctrinal disputes that had agitated the continent in 1837. Both parties grew tired and ashamed of the long and sometimes ill-natured quarrel. With such a disposition on both sides, terms of agreement could not fail in time to be found. For substance, the basis of reunion was this: that the New-School church should yield the point of organization, and the Old-School church should yield the point of doctrine; the New-School men should sustain the Old-School boards, and the Old-School men should tolerate the New-School heresies. The consolidation of the two sects into one powerful organization was consummated at Pittsburg, November 12, 1869, with every demonstration of joy and devout thanksgiving.

One important denomination, the Congregationalists, had had the distinguished advantage, through all these turbulent years, of having no southern membership. Out of all proportion to its numerical strength was the part which it took in those missions to the neglected populations of the southern country into which the various denominations, both of the South and of the North, entered with generous emulation while yet the war was still waging. Always leaders in advanced education, they not only, acting through the American Missionary Association, provided for primary and secondary schools for the negroes, but promoted the foundation of institutions of higher, and even of the highest, grade at Hampton, at Atlanta, at Tuskegee, at New Orleans, at Nashville, and at Washington. Many noble lives have been consecrated to this most Christlike work of lifting up the depressed. None will grudge a word of exceptional eulogy to the memory of that splendid character, General Samuel C. Armstrong, son of one of the early missionaries to the Sandwich Islands, who poured his inspiring soul into the building up of the "Normal Institute" at Hampton, Va., thus not only rearing a visible monument of his labor in the enduring buildings of that great and useful institution, but also establishing his memory, for as long as human gratitude can endure, in the hearts of hundreds of young men and young women, negro and Indian, whose lives are the better and nobler for their having known him as their teacher.

It cannot be justly claimed for the Congregationalists of the present day that they have lost nothing of that corporate unselfishness, seeking no sectarian aggrandizement, but only God's reign and righteousness, which had been the glory of their fathers. The studious efforts that have been made to cultivate among them a sectarian spirit, as if this were one of the Christian virtues, have not been fruitless. Nevertheless it may be seen that their work of education at the South has been conducted in no narrow spirit. The extending of their sect over new territory has been a most trivial and unimportant result of their widespread and efficient work. A far greater result has been the promotion among the colored people of a better education, a higher standard of morality, and an enlightened piety, through the influence of the graduates of these institutions, not only as pastors and as teachers, but in all sorts of trades and professions and as mothers of families.

This work of the Congregationalists is entitled to mention, not as exceptional, but only as eminent among like enterprises, in which few of the leading sects have failed to be represented. Extravagant expectations were at first entertained of immediate results in bringing the long-depressed race up to the common plane of civilization. But it cannot be said that reasonable and intelligent expectations have been disappointed. Experience has taught much as to the best conduct of such missions. The gift of a fund of a million dollars by the late John F. Slater, of Norwich, has through wise management conduced to this end. It has encouraged in the foremost institutions the combination of training to skilled productive labor with education in literature and science.

The inauguration of these systems of religious education at the South was the most conspicuously important of the immediate sequels of the Civil War. But this time was a time of great expansion of the activities of the church in all directions. The influx of immigration, temporarily checked by the hard times of 1857 and by the five years of war, came in again in such floods as never before.[357:1] The foreign immigration is always attended by a westward movement of the already settled population. The field of home missions became greater and more exacting than ever. The zeal of the church, educated during the war to higher ideas of self-sacrifice, rose to the occasion. The average yearly receipts of the various Protestant home missionary societies, which in the decade 1850-59 had been $808,000, rose in the next decade to more than $2,000,000, in the next to nearly $3,000,000, and for the seven years 1881-87 to $4,000,000.[358:1]

In the perils of abounding wealth by which the church after the war was beset, it was divine fatherly kindness that opened before it new and enlarged facilities of service to the kingdom of heaven among foreign nations. From the first feeble beginnings of foreign missions from America in India and in the Sandwich Islands, they had been attended by the manifest favor of God. When the convulsion of the Civil War came on, with prostrations of business houses, and enormous burdens of public obligation, and private beneficence drawn down, as it seemed, to its "bottom dollar" for new calls of patriotism and charity, and especially when the dollar in a man's pocket shrank to a half or a third of its value in the world's currency, it seemed as if the work of foreign missions would have to be turned over to Christians in lands less burdened with accumulated disadvantages. But here again the grandeur of the burden gave an inspiration of strength to the burden-bearer. From 1840 to 1849 the average yearly receipts of the various foreign missionary societies of the Protestant churches of the country had been a little more than a half-million. In the decade 1850-59 they had risen to $850,000; for the years of distress, 1860-69, they exceeded $1,300,000; for the eleven years 1870-80 the annual receipts in this behalf were $2,200,000; and in the seven years 1881-87 they were $3,000,000.[359:1]

We have seen how, only forty years before the return of peace, in the days of a humble equality in moderate estates, ardent souls exulted together in the inauguration of the era of democracy in beneficence, when every humblest giver might, through association and organization, have part in magnificent enterprises of Christian charity such as had theretofore been possible "only to princes or to men of princely possessions."[359:2] But with the return of civil peace we began to recognize that among ourselves was growing up a class of "men of princely possessions"—a class such as the American Republic never before had known.[359:3] Among those whose fortunes were reckoned by many millions or many tens of millions were men of sordid nature, whose wealth, ignobly won, was selfishly hoarded, and to whose names, as to that of the late Jay Gould, there is attached in the mind of the people a distinct note of infamy. But this was not in general the character of the American millionaire. There were those of nobler strain who felt a responsibility commensurate with the great power conferred by great riches, and held their wealth as in trust for mankind. Through the fidelity of men of this sort it has come to pass that the era of great fortunes in America has become conspicuous in the history of the whole world as the era of magnificent donations to benevolent ends. Within a few months of each other, from the little State of Connecticut, came the fund of a million given by John F. Slater in his lifetime for the benefit of the freedmen, the gift of a like sum for the like purpose from Daniel Hand, and the legacy of a million and a half for foreign missions from Deacon Otis of New London. Great gifts like these were frequently directed to objects which could not easily have been attained by the painful process of accumulating small donations. It was a period not only of splendid gifts to existing institutions, but of foundations for new universities, libraries, hospitals, and other institutions of the highest public service, foundations without parallel in human history for large munificence. To this period belong the beginnings of the Johns Hopkins University and Hospital at Baltimore, the University of Chicago, the Clarke University at Worcester, the Vanderbilt University at Nashville, the Leland Stanford, Jr., University of California, the Peabody and Enoch Pratt Libraries at Baltimore, the Lenox Library at New York, the great endowed libraries of Chicago, the Drexel Institute at Philadelphia, and the Armour Institute at Chicago. These are some of the names that most readily occur of foundations due mainly to individual liberality, set down at the risk of omitting others with equal claim for mention. Not all of these are to be referred to a religious spirit in the founders, but none of them can fail of a Christian influence and result. They prepare a foothold for such a forward stride of Christian civilization as our continent has never before known.

The sum of these gifts of millions, added to the great aggregates of contribution to the national missionary boards and societies, falls far short of the total contributions expended in cities, towns, and villages for the building of churches and the maintenance of the countless charities that cluster around them. The era following the war was preëminently a "building era." Every one knows that religious devotion is only one of the mingled motives that work together in such an enterprise as the building of a church; but, after all deductions, the voluntary gifts of Christian people for Christ's sake in the promotion of such works, when added to the grand totals already referred to, would make an amount that would overtax the ordinary imagination to conceive.

And yet it is not certain that this period of immense gifts of money is really a period of increased liberality in the church from the time, thirty or forty years before, when a millionaire was a rarity to be pointed out on the streets, and the possession of a hundred thousand dollars gave one a place among "The Rich Men of New York." In 1850 the total wealth of the United

States was reported in the census as seven billions of dollars. In 1870, after twenty years, it had more than fourfolded, rising to thirty billions. Ten years later, according to the census, it had sixfolded, rising to forty-three billions.[361:1] From the point of view of One "sitting over against the treasury" it is not likely that any subsequent period has equaled in its gifts that early day when in New England the people "were wont to build a fine church as soon as they had houses for themselves,"[361:2] and when the messengers went from cabin to cabin to gather the gifts of "the college corn."

The greatest addition to the forces of the church in the period since the war has come from deploying into the field hitherto unused resources of personal service. The methods under which the personal activity of private Christians has formerly been organized for service have increased and multiplied, and old agencies have taken on new forms.

The earliest and to this day the most extensive of the organizations for utilizing the non-professional ministry in systematic religious labors is the Sunday-school. The considerable development of this instrumentality begins to be recognized after the Second Awakening in the early years of the present century. The prevailing characteristic of the American Sunday-school as distinguished from its British congener is that it is commonly a part of the equipment of the local church for the instruction of its own children, and incidentally one of the most important resources for its attractive work toward those that are without. But it is also recognized as one of the most flexible and adaptable "arms of the service" for aggressive work, whether in great cities or on the frontier. It was about the year 1825 that this work began to be organized on a national scale. But it is since the war that it has sprung into vastly greater efficiency. The agreement upon uniform courses of biblical study, to be followed simultaneously by many millions of pupils over the entire continent, has given a unity and coherence before unknown to the Sunday-school system; and it has resulted in extraordinary enterprise and activity on the part of competent editors and publishers to provide apparatus for the thorough study of the text, which bids fair in time to take away the reproach of the term "Sunday-schoolish" as applied to superficial, ignorant, or merely sentimental expositions of the Scriptures. The work of the "Sunday-school Times," in bringing within the reach of teachers all over the land the fruits of the world's best scholarship, is a signal fact in history— the most conspicuous of a series of like facts. The tendency, slow, of course, and partial, but powerful, is toward serious, faithful study and teaching, in which "the mind of the Spirit" is sought in the sacred text, with strenuous efforts of the teachable mind, with all the aids that can be brought from whatever quarter. The Sunday-school system, coextensive with Protestant Christianity in America, and often the forerunner of church and ministry, and, to a less extent and under more scrupulous control of clergy, adopted into the Catholic Church, has become one of the distinctive features of American Christianity.

An outgrowth of the Sunday-school system, which, under the conduct of a man of genius for organization, Dr. John H. Vincent, now a bishop of the Methodist Church, has expanded to magnificent dimensions, is that which is suggested by the name "Chautauqua." Beginning in the summer of 1874 with a fortnight's meeting in a grove beside Chautauqua Lake for the study of the methods of Sunday-school teaching, it led to the questions, how to connect the Sunday-school more intimately with other departments of the church and with other agencies in society; how to control in the interest of religious culture the forces, social, commercial, industrial, and educational, which, for good or evil, are affecting the Sunday-school pupils every day of the week. Striking root at other centers of assembly, east, west, and south, and combining its summer lectures with an organized system of home studies extending through the year, subject to written examinations, "Chautauqua," by the comprehensive scope of its studies and by the great multitude of its students, is entitled to be called, in no ignoble sense of the word, a university.[363:1] A weighty and unimpeachable testimony to the power and influence of the institution has been the recent organization of a Catholic Chautauqua, under the conduct of leading scholars and ecclesiastics of the Roman Church.

Another organization of the unpaid service of private Christians is the Young Men's Christian

Association. Beginning in London in 1844, it had so far demonstrated its usefulness in 1851 as to attract favorable attention from visitors to the first of the World's Fairs. In the end of that year the Association in Boston was formed, and this was rapidly followed by others in the principal cities. It met a growing exigency in American society. In the organization of commerce and manufacture in larger establishments than formerly, the apprenticeship system had necessarily lapsed, and nothing had taken its place. Of old, young men put to the learning of any business were "articled" or "indentured" as apprentices to the head of the concern, who was placed in loco parentis, being invested both with the authority and with the responsibility of a father. Often the apprentices were received into the house of the master as their home, and according to legend and romance it was in order for the industrious and virtuous apprentice to marry the old man's daughter and succeed to the business. After the employees of a store came to be numbered by scores and the employees of a factory by hundreds, the word "apprentice" became obsolete in the American language. The employee was only a "hand," and there was danger that employers would forget that he was also a heart and a soul. This was the exigency that the Young Men's Christian Association came to supply. Men of conscience among employers and corporations recognized their opportunity and their duty. The new societies did not lack encouragement and financial aid from those to whom the character of the young men was not only a matter of Christian concern, but also a matter of business interest. In every considerable town the Association organized itself, and the work of equipment, and soon of building, went on apace. In 1887 the Association buildings in the United States and Canada were valued at three and a half millions. In 1896 there were in North America 1429 Associations, with about a quarter of a million of members, employing 1251 paid officers, and holding buildings and other real estate to the amount of nearly $20,000,000.

The work has not been without its vicissitudes. The wonderful revival of 1857, preëminently a laymen's movement, in many instances found its nidus in the rooms of the Associations; and their work was expanded and invigorated as a result of the revival. In 1861 came on the war. It broke up for the time the continental confederacy of Associations. Many of the local Associations were dissolved by the enlistment of their members. But out of the inspiring exigencies of the time grew up in the heart of the Associations the organization and work of the Christian Commission, coöperating with the Sanitary Commission for the bodily and spiritual comfort of the armies in the field. The two organizations expended upward of eleven millions of dollars, the free gift of the people at home. After the war the survivors of those who had enlisted from the Associations came back to their home duties, in most cases, better men for all good service in consequence of their experience of military discipline.

A natural sequel to the organization and success of the Young Men's Christian Association is the institution of the Young Women's Christian Association, having like objects and methods in its proper sphere. This institution, too, owes the reason of its existence to changed social conditions. The plausible arguments of some earnest reformers in favor of opening careers of independent self-support to women, and the unquestionable and pathetic instances by which these arguments are enforced, are liable to some most serious and weighty offsets. Doubtless many and many a case of hardship has been relieved by the general introduction of this reform. But the result has been the gathering in large towns of populations of unmarried, self-supporting young women, severed from home duties and influences, and, out of business hours, under no effective restraints of rule. There is a rush from the country into the city of applicants for employment, and wages sink to less than a living rate. We are confronted with an artificial and perilous condition for the church to deal with, especially in the largest cities. And of the various instrumentalities to this end, the Young Women's Christian Association is one of the most effective.

The development of organized activity among women has been a conspicuous characteristic of this period. From the beginning of our churches the charitable sewing-circle or "Dorcas Society" has been known as a center both of prayer and of labor. But in this period the organization of women for charitable service has been on a continental scale.

In 1874, in an outburst of zeal, "women's crusades" were undertaken, especially in some western towns, in which bands of singing and praying women went in person to tippling-houses and even worse resorts, to assail them, visibly and audibly, with these spiritual weapons. The crusades, so long as they were a novelty, were not without result. Spectacular prayers, offered with one eye on the heavens and the other eye watching the impressions made on the human auditor, are not in vain; they have their reward. But the really important result of the "crusades" was the organization of the "Women's Christian Temperance Union," which has extended in all directions to the utmost bounds of the country, and has accomplished work of undoubted value, while attempting other work the value of which is open to debate.

The separate organization of women for the support and management of missions began on an extensive scale, in 1868, with the Women's Board of Missions, instituted in alliance with the American Board of Commissioners for Foreign Missions of the Congregationalist churches. The example at once commended itself to the imitation of all, so that all the principal mission boards of the Protestant churches are in alliance with actively working women's boards.

The training acquired in these and other organizations by many women of exceptional taste and talent for the conduct of large affairs has tended still further to widen the field of their activity. The ends of the earth, as well as the dark places nearer home, have felt the salutary results of it.[367:1]

In this brief and most incomplete sketch of the origin of one of the distinguishing features of contemporary Christianity—the application of the systematized activity of private Christians—no mention has been made of the corps of "colporteurs," or book-peddlers, employed by religious publication societies, nor of the vastly useful work of laymen employed as city missionaries, nor of the houses and orders of sisters wholly devoted to pious and charitable work. Such work, though the ceremony of ordination may have been omitted, is rather clerical or professional than laical. It is on this account the better suited to the genius of the Catholic Church, whose ages of experience in the conduct of such organizations, and whose fine examples of economy and efficiency in the use of them, have put all American Christendom under obligation. Among Protestant sects the Lutherans, the Episcopalians, and the Methodists have (after the Moravians) shown themselves readiest to profit by the example. But a far more widely beneficent service than that of all the nursing "orders" together, both Catholic and Protestant, and one not less Christian, while it is characteristically American in its method, is that of the annually increasing army of faithful women professionally educated to the work of nursing, at a hundred hospitals, and fulfilling their vocation individually and on business principles. The education of nurses is a sequel of the war and one of the beneficent fruits of it.

Not the least important item in the organization of lay activity is the marvelously rapid growth of the "Young People's Society of Christian Endeavor." In February, 1881, a pastor in Portland, Me., the Rev. Francis E. Clark, organized into an association within his church a number of young people pledged to certain rules of regular attendance and participation in the association meetings and of coöperation in useful service. There seems to have been no particular originality in the plan, but through some felicity in arrangement and opportuneness in the time it caught like a forest fire, and in an amazingly short time ran through the country and around the world. One wise precaution was taken in the basis of the organization: it was provided that it should not interfere with any member's fidelity to his church or his sect, but rather promote it. Doubtless jealousy of its influence was thus in some measure forestalled and averted. But in the rapid spread of the Society those who were on guard for the interests of the several sects recognized a danger in too free affiliations outside of sectarian lines, and soon there were instituted, in like forms of rule, "Epworth Leagues" for Methodists, "Westminster Leagues" for Presbyterians, "Luther Leagues" for Lutherans, "St. Andrew's Brotherhoods" for Episcopalians, "The Baptist Young People's Union," and yet others for yet other sects. According to the latest reports, the total pledged membership of this order of associated young disciples, in these various ramifications, is about 4,500,000[369:1]—this in the United States alone. Of the Christian Endeavor Societies still adhering to the old name and constitution, there are in all the world 47,009, of which 11,119 are "Junior Endeavor Societies." The total membership is 2,820,540.[369:2]

Contemporary currents of theological thought, setting away from the excessive individualism which has characterized the churches of the Great Awakening, confirm the tendency of the Christian life toward a vigorous and even absorbing external activity. The duty of the church to human society is made a part of the required curriculum of study in preparation for the ministry, in fully equipped theological seminaries. If ever it has been a just reproach of the church that its frequenters were so absorbed in the saving of their own souls that they forgot the multitude about them, that reproach is fast passing away. "The Institutional Church," as the clumsy phrase goes, cares for soul and body, for family and municipal and national life. Its saving sacraments are neither two nor seven, but seventy times seven. They include the bath-tub as well as the font; the coffee-house and cook-shop as well as the Holy Supper; the gymnasium as well as the prayer-meeting. The "college settlement" plants colonies of the best life of the church in regions which men of little faith are tempted to speak of as "God-forsaken." The Salvation Army, with its noisy and eccentric ways, and its effective discipline, and its most Christian principle of setting every rescued man at work to aid in the rescue of others, is welcomed by all orders of the church, and honored according to the measure of its usefulness, and even of its faithful effort to be useful.

It is not to be supposed that this immense, unprecedented growth of outward activity can have been gained without some corresponding loss. The time is not long gone by, when the sustained contemplation of the deep things of the cross, and the lofty things in the divine nature, and the subtile and elusive facts concerning the human constitution and character and the working of the human will, were eminently characteristic of the religious life of the American church. In the times when that life was stirred to its most strenuous activity, it was marked by the vicissitude of prolonged passions of painful sensibility at the consciousness of sin, and ecstasies of delight in the contemplation of the infinity of God and the glory of the Saviour and his salvation. Every one who is conversant with the religious biography of the generations before our own, knows of the still hours and days set apart for the severe inward scrutiny of motives and "frames" and the grounds of one's hope. However truly the church of to-day may judge that the piety of their fathers was disproportioned and morbidly introspective and unduly concerned about one's own salvation, it is none the less true that the reaction from its excesses is violent, and is providing for itself a new reaction. "The contemplative orders," whether among Catholics or Protestants, do not find the soil and climate of America congenial. And yet there is a mission-field here for the mystic and the quietist; and when the stir-about activity of our generation suffers their calm voices to be heard, there are not a few to give ear.

An event of great historical importance, which cannot be determined to a precise date, but which belongs more to this period than to any other, is the loss of the Scotch and Puritan Sabbath, or, as many like to call it, the American Sabbath. The law of the Westminster divines on this subject, it may be affirmed without fear of contradiction from any quarter, does not coincide in its language with the law of God as expressed either in the Old Testament or in the New. The Westminster rule requires, as if with a "Thus saith the Lord," that on the first day of the week, instead of the seventh, men shall desist not only from labor but from recreation, and "spend the whole time in the public and private exercises of God's worship, except so much as is to be taken up in the works of necessity and mercy."[371:1] This interpretation and expansion of the Fourth Commandment has never attained to more than a sectarian and provincial authority; but the overmastering Puritan influence, both of Virginia and of New England, combined with the Scotch-Irish influence, made it for a long time dominant in America. Even those who quite declined to admit the divine authority of the glosses upon the commandment felt constrained to "submit to the ordinances of man for the Lord's sake." But it was inevitable that with the vast increase of the travel and sojourn of American Christians in other lands of Christendom, and the multitudinous immigration into America from other lands than Great Britain, the tradition from the Westminster elders should come to be openly disputed within the church, and should be disregarded even when not denied. It was not only inevitable; it was a Christian duty distinctly enjoined by apostolic authority.[372:1] The five years of war, during which Christians of various lands and creeds intermingled as never before, and the Sunday laws were dumb "inter arma" not only in the field but among the home churches, did perhaps even more to break the force of the tradition, and to lead in a perilous and demoralizing reaction. Some reaction was inevitable. The church must needs suffer the evil consequence of overstraining the law of God. From the Sunday of ascetic self-denial—"a day for a man to afflict his soul"—there was a ready rush into utter recklessness of the law and privilege of rest. In the church there was wrought sore damage to weak consciences; men acted, not from intelligent conviction, but from lack of conviction, and allowing themselves in self-indulgences of the rightfulness of which they were dubious, they "condemned themselves in that which they allowed." The consequence in civil society was alike disastrous. Early legislation had not steered clear of the error of attempting to enforce Sabbath-keeping as a religious duty by civil penalties; and some relics of that mistake remained, and still remain, on some of the statute-books. The just protest against this wrong was, of course, undiscriminating, tending to defeat the righteous and most salutary laws that aimed simply to secure for the citizen the privilege of a weekly day of rest and to secure the holiday thus ordained by law from being perverted into a nuisance. The social change which is still in progress along these lines no wise Christian patriot can contemplate with complacency. It threatens, when complete, to deprive us of that universal quiet Sabbath rest which has been one of the glories of American social life, and an important element in its economic prosperity, and to give in place of it, to some, no assurance of a Sabbath rest at all, to others, a Sabbath of revelry and debauch.

CHAPTER XXI. THE CHURCH IN THEOLOGY AND LITERATURE.

The rapid review of three crowded centuries, which is all that the narrowly prescribed limits of this volume have permitted, has necessarily been mainly restricted to external facts. But looking back over the course of visible events, it is not impossible for acute minds devoted to such study to trace the stream of thought and sentiment that is sometimes hidden from direct view by the overgrowth which itself has nourished.

We have seen a profound spiritual change, renewing the face of the land and leaving its indelible impress on successive generations, springing from the profoundest contemplations of God and his work of salvation through Jesus Christ, and then bringing back into thoughtful and teachable minds new questions to be solved and new discoveries of truth to be pondered. The one school of theological opinion and inquiry that can be described as characteristically American is the theology of the Great Awakening. The disciples of this school, in all its divergent branches, agree in looking back to the first Jonathan Edwards as the founder of it. Through its generations it has shown a striking sequence and continuity of intellectual and spiritual life, each generation answering questions put to it by its predecessor, while propounding new questions to the generation following. After the classical writings of its first founders, the most widely influential production of this school is the "Theology Explained and Defended in a Series of Sermons" of President Dwight. This had the advantage over some other systems of having been preached, and thus proved to be preachable. The "series of sermons" was that delivered to successive generations of college students at Yale at a time of prevailing skepticism, when every statement of the college pulpit was liable to sharp and not too friendly scrutiny; and it was preached with the fixed purpose of convincing and converting the young men who heard it. The audience, the occasion, and the man—a fervid Christian, and a born poet and orator—combined to produce a work of wide and enduring influence. The dynasty of the Edwardeans is continued down to the middle of the nineteenth century, and later, through different lines, ending in Emmons of Franklin, Taylor of New Haven, and

Finney of Oberlin, and is represented among the living by the venerable Edwards A. Park, of Andover, who adds to that power of sustained speculative thinking in a straight line which is characteristic of the whole school, a wide learning in the whole field of theological literature, which had not been usual among his predecessors. It is a prevailing trait of this theology, born of the great revival, that it has constantly held before itself not only the question, What is truth? but also the question, How shall it be preached? It has never ceased to be a revival theology.

A bold and open breach of traditionary assumptions and habits of reasoning was made by Horace Bushnell. This was a theologian of a different type from his New England predecessors. He was of a temper little disposed to accept either methods or results as a local tradition, and inclined rather to prefer that which had been "hammered out on his own anvil." And yet, while very free in manifesting his small respect for the "logicking" by syllogistic processes which had been the pride of the theological chair and even the pulpit in America, and while declining the use of current phraseologies even for the expression of current ideas, he held himself loyally subject to the canon of the Scriptures as his rule of faith, and deferential to the voice of the church catholic as uttered in the concord of testimony of holy men in all ages. Endowed with a poet's power of intuition, uplifted by a fervid piety, uttering himself in a literary style singularly rich and melodious, it is not strange that such a man should have made large contributions to the theological thought of his own and later times. In natural theology, his discourses on "The Moral Uses of Dark Things" (1869), and his longest continuous work, on "Nature and the Supernatural" (1858), even though read rather as prose-poems than as arguments, sound distinctly new notes in the treatment of their theme. In "God in Christ" (1849), "Christ in Theology" (1851), "The Vicarious Sacrifice" (1866), and "Forgiveness and Law" (1874), and in a notable article in the "New Englander" for November, 1854, entitled "The Christian Trinity a Practical Truth," the great topics of the Christian system were dealt with all the more effectively, in the minds of thoughtful readers in this and other lands, for cries of alarm and newspaper and pulpit impeachments of heresy that were sent forth. But that work of his which most nearly made as well as marked an epoch in American church history was the treatise of "Christian Nurture" (1847). This, with the protracted controversy that followed upon the publication of it, was a powerful influence in lifting the American church out of the rut of mere individualism that had been wearing deeper and deeper from the days of the Great Awakening.

Another wholesome and edifying debate was occasioned by the publications that went forth from the college and theological seminary of the German Reformed Church, situated at Mercersburg in Pennsylvania. At this institution was effected a fruitful union of American and German theology; the result was to commend to the general attention aspects of truth, philosophical, theological, and historical, not previously current among American Protestants. The book of Dr. John Williamson Nevin, entitled "The Mystical Presence: A Vindication of the Reformed or Calvinistic Doctrine of the Holy Eucharist," revealed to the vast multitude of churches and ministers that gloried in the name of Calvinist the fact that on the most distinctive article of Calvinism they were not Calvinists at all, but Zwinglians. The enunciation of the standard doctrine of the various Presbyterian churches excited among themselves a clamor of "Heresy!" and the doctrine of Calvin was put upon trial before the Calvinists. The outcome of a discussion that extended itself far beyond the boundaries of the comparatively small and uninfluential German Reformed Church was to elevate the point of view and broaden the horizon of American students of the constitution and history of the church. Later generations of such students owe no light obligation to the fidelity and courage of Dr. Nevin, as well as to the erudition and immense productive diligence of his associate, Dr. Philip Schaff.[377:1]

It is incidental to the prevailing method of instruction in theology by a course of prelections in which the teacher reads to his class in detail his own original summa theologiæ, that the American press has been prolific of ponderous volumes of systematic divinity. Among the more notable of these systems are those of Leonard Woods (in five volumes) and of Enoch Pond; of the two Drs. Hodge, father and son; of Robert J. Breckinridge and James H. Thornwell and Robert L. Dabney; and the "Systematic Theology" of a much younger man, Dr. Augustus H. Strong, of Rochester Seminary, which has won for itself very unusual and wide respect. Exceptional for ability, as well as for its originality of conception, is "The Republic of God: An Institute of Theology," by Elisha Mulford, a disciple of Maurice and of the realist philosophy, the thought of whose whole life is contained in this and his kindred work on "The Nation."

How great is the debt which the church owes to its heretics is frequently illustrated in the progress of Christianity in America. If it had not been for the Unitarian defection in New England, and for the attacks from Germany upon the historicity of the gospels, the theologians of America might to this day have been engrossed in "threshing old straw" in endless debates on "fixed fate, free will, foreknowledge absolute." The exigencies of controversy forced the study of the original documents of the church. From his entrance upon his professorship at Andover, in 1810, the eager enthusiasm of Moses Stuart made him the father of exegetical science not only for America, but for all the English-speaking countries. His not less eminent pupil and associate, Edward Robinson, later of the Union Seminary, New York, created out of nothing the study of biblical geography. Associating with himself the most accomplished living Arabist, Eli Smith, of the American mission at Beirût, he made those "Biblical Researches in Palestine" which have been the foundation on which all later explorers have built. Another American missionary, Dr. W. M. Thomson, has given the most valuable popular exposition of the same subject in his volumes on "The Land and the Book." With the exception of Dr. Henry Clay Trumbull in his determination of the site of Kadesh-barnea, the American successors to Robinson in the original exploration of the Bible lands have made few additions to our knowledge. But in the department of biblical archæology the work of Drs. Ward, Peters, and Hilprecht in the mounds of Babylonia, and of Mr. Bliss in Palestine, has added not a little to the credit of the American church against the heavy balance which we owe to the scholarship of Europe.

Monumental works in lexicography have been produced by Dr. Thayer, of Cambridge, on New Testament Greek; by Professor Francis Brown, of New York, in conjunction with Canon Driver, of Oxford, on the languages of the Old Testament; and by Dr. Sophocles, of Cambridge, on the Byzantine Greek.

In the work of the textual criticism of the Scriptures, notwithstanding its remoteness from the manuscript sources of study, America has furnished two names that are held in honor throughout the learned world: among the recent dead, Ezra Abbot, of Cambridge, universally beloved and lamented; and among the living, Caspar René Gregory, successor to the labors and the fame of Tischendorf. A third name is that of the late Dr. Isaac H. Hall, the successful collator of Syriac New Testament manuscripts.

In those studies of the higher criticism which at the present day are absorbing so much of the attention of biblical scholars, and the progress of which is watched with reasonable anxiety for their bearing on that dogma of the absolute inerrancy of the canonical Scriptures which has so commonly been postulated as the foundation of Protestant systems of revealed theology, the American church has taken eager interest. An eminent, and in some respects the foremost, place among the leaders in America of these investigations into the substructure, if not of the Christian faith, at least of the work of the system-builders, is held by Professor W. H. Green, of Princeton, whose painstaking essays in the higher criticism have done much to stimulate the studies of younger men who have come out at conclusions different from his own. The works of Professors Briggs, of Union Seminary, and Henry P. Smith, of Lane Seminary, have had the invaluable advantage of being commended to public attention by ecclesiastical processes and debates. The two volumes of Professor Bacon, of Yale, have been recognized by the foremost scholars of Great Britain and Germany as containing original contributions toward the solution of the problem of Pentateuchal analysis. The intricate critical questions presented by the Book of Judges have been handled with supreme ability by Professor Moore, of Andover, in his commentary on that book. A desideratum in biblical literature has been well supplied by Professor Bissell, of Hartford, in a work on the Old Testament Apocrypha. But the magnum opus of American biblical scholarship, associating with itself the best learning and ability of other nations, is the publication, under the direction of Professor Haupt, of Baltimore, of a critical text of the entire Scriptures in the original languages, with new translations and notes, for the use of scholars.

The undeniably grave theological difficulties occasioned by the results of critical study have given rise to a novel dogma concerning the Scriptures, which, if it may justly be claimed as a product of the Princeton Seminary, would seem to discredit the modest boast of the venerated Dr. Charles Hodge, that "Princeton has never originated a new idea." It consists in the hypothesis of an "original autograph" of the Scriptures, the precise contents of which are now undiscoverable, but which differed from any existing text in being absolutely free from error of any kind. The hypothesis has no small advantage in this, that if it is not susceptible of proof, it is equally secure from refutation. If not practically useful, it is at least novel, and on this ground entitled to mention in recounting the contributions of the American church to theology at a really perilous point in the progress of biblical study.

The field of church history, aside from local and sectarian histories, was late in being invaded by American theologians. For many generations the theology of America was distinctly unhistorical, speculative, and provincial. But a change in this respect was inevitably sure to come. The strong propensity of the national mind toward historical studies is illustrated by the large proportion of historical works among the masterpieces of our literature, whether in prose or in verse. It would seem as if our conscious poverty in historical monuments and traditions had engendered an eager hunger for history. No travelers in ancient lands are such enthusiasts in seeking the monuments of remote ages as those whose homes are in regions not two generations removed from the prehistoric wilderness. It was certain that as soon as theology should begin to be taught to American students in its relation to the history of the kingdom of Christ, the charm of this method would be keenly felt.

We may assume the date of 1853 as an epoch from which to date this new era of theological study. It was in that year that the gifted, learned, and inspiring teacher, Henry Boynton Smith, was transferred from the chair of history in Union Theological Seminary, New York, to the chair of systematic theology. Through his premature and most lamented death the church has failed of receiving that system of doctrine which had been hoped for at his hands. But the historic spirit which characterized him has ever since been characteristic of that seminary. It is illustrative of the changed tone of theologizing that after the death of Professor Smith, in the reorganization of the faculty of that important institution, it was manned in the three chief departments, exegetical, dogmatic, and practical, by men whose eminent distinction was in the line of church history. The names of Hitchcock, Schaff, and Shedd cannot be mentioned without bringing to mind some of the most valuable gifts that America has made to the literature of the universal church. If to these we add the names of George Park Fisher, of Yale, and Bishop Hurst, and Alexander V. G. Allen, of Cambridge, author of "The Continuity of Christian Thought," and Henry Charles Lea, of Philadelphia, we have already vindicated for American scholarship a high place in this department of Christian literature.

In practical theology the productiveness of the American church in the matter of sermons has been so copious that even for the briefest mention some narrow rule of exclusion must be followed. There is no doubt that in a multitude of cases the noblest utterances of the American pulpit, being unwritten, have never come into literature, but have survived for a time as a glowing memory, and then a fading tradition. The statement applies to many of the most famous revival preachers; and in consequence of a prevalent prejudice against the writing of sermons, it applies especially to the great Methodist and Baptist preachers, whose representation on the shelves of libraries is most disproportionate to their influence on the course of the kingdom of Christ. Of other sermons,—and good sermons,—printed and published, many have had an influence almost as restricted and as evanescent as the utterances of the pulpit improvisator. If we confine ourselves to those sermons that have survived their generation or won attention beyond the limits of local interest or of sectarian fellowship, the list will not be unmanageably long.

In the early years of the nineteenth century the Unitarian pulpits of Boston were adorned with every literary grace known to the rhetoric of that period. The luster of Channing's fame has outshone and outlasted that of his associates; and yet these were stars of hardly less magnitude. The two Wares, father and son, the younger Buckminster, whose singular power as a preacher was known not only to wondering hearers, but to readers on both sides of the ocean, Gannett and Dewey—these were among them; and, in the next generation, Henry W. Bellows, Thomas Starr King, and James Freeman Clarke. No body of clergy of like size was ever so resplendent with talents and accomplishments. The names alone of those who left the Unitarian pulpit for a literary or political career—Sparks, Everett, Bancroft, Emerson, Ripley, Palfrey, Upham, among them—are a constellation by themselves.

To the merely literary critic those earnest preachers, such as Lyman and Edward Beecher, Griffin, Sereno Dwight, Wayland, and Kirk, who felt called of God to withstand, in Boston, this splendid array of not less earnest men, were clearly inferior to their antagonists. But they were successful.

A few years later, the preëminent American writer of sermons to be read and pondered in every part of the world was Horace Bushnell; as the great popular preacher, whose words, caught burning from his lips, rolled around the world in a perpetual stream, was Henry Ward Beecher. Widely different from either of these, and yet in an honorable sense successor to the fame of both, was Phillips Brooks, of all American preachers most widely beloved and honored in all parts of the church.

Of living preachers whose sermons have already attained a place of honor in libraries at home and abroad, the name of Bishop F. D. Huntington stands among the foremost; and those who have been charmed by the brilliant rhetoric and instructed from the copious learning of his college classmate, Dr. Richard S. Storrs, must feel it a wrong done to our national literature that these gifts should be chiefly known to the reading public only by occasional discourses and by two valuable studies in religious history instead of by volumes of sermons. Perhaps no American pulpits have to-day a wider hearing beyond the sea than two that stand within hearing distance of each other on New Haven Green, occupied by Theodore T. Munger and Newman Smyth. The pulpit of Plymouth Church, Brooklyn, has not ceased, since the accession of Lyman Abbott, to wield a wide and weighty influence,—less wide, but in some respects more weighty, than in the days of his famous predecessor,—by reason of a well-deserved reputation for biblical learning and insight, and for candor and wisdom in applying Scriptural principles to the solution of current questions.

The early American theology was, as we have seen, a rhetorical and not a merely scholastic theology—a theology to be preached.[384:1] In like manner, the American pulpit in those days was distinctly theological, like a professor's chair. One who studies with care the pulpit of to-day, in those volumes that seem to command the widest and most enduring attention, will find that it is to a large extent apologetic, addressing itself to the abating of doubts and objections to the Christian system, or, recognizing the existing doubts, urging the religious duties that are nevertheless incumbent on the doubting mind. It has ceased to assume the substantial soundness of the hearer in the main principles of orthodox opinion, and regards him as one to be held to the church by attraction, persuasion, or argument. The result of this attitude of the preacher is to make the pulpit studiously, and even eagerly, attractive and interesting. This virtue has its corresponding fault. The American preacher of to-day is little in danger of being dull; his peril lies at the other extreme. His temptation is rather to the feebleness of extravagant statement, and to an overstrained and theatric rhetoric such as some persons find so attractive in the discourses of Dr. Talmage, and others find repulsive and intolerable.

A direction in which the literature of practical theology in America is sure to expand itself in the immediate future is indicated in the title of a recent work of that versatile and useful writer, Dr. Washington Gladden, "Applied Christianity." The salutary conviction that political economy cannot be relied on by itself to adjust all the intricate relations of men under modern conditions of life, that the ethical questions that arise are not going to solve themselves automatically by the law of demand and supply, that the gospel and the church and the Spirit of Christ have somewhat to do in the matter, has been settling itself deeply into the minds of Christian believers. The impression that the questions between labor and capital, between sordid poverty and overgrown wealth, were old-world questions, of which we of the New World are relieved, is effectually dispelled. Thus far there is not much of history to be written under this head, but somewhat of prophecy. It is now understood, and felt in the conscience, that these questions are for every Christian to consider, and for those undertaking the cure of souls to make the subject of their faithful, laborious professional study. The founding of professorships of social ethics in the theological seminaries must lead to important and speedy results in the efficiency of churches and pastors in dealing with this difficult class of problems.[386:1] But whatever advances shall be made in the future, no small part of the impulse toward them will be recognized as coming from, or rather through, the inspiring and most Christian humanitarian writings and the personal influence and example of Edward Everett Hale.

In one noble department of religious literature, the liturgical, the record of the American church is meager. The reaction among the early colonists and many of the later settlers against forms of worship imposed by political authority was violent. Seeking for a logical basis, it planted itself on the assumption that no form (unless an improvised form) is permitted in public worship, except such as are sanctioned by express word of Scripture. In their sturdy resolution to throw off and break up the yoke, which neither they nor their fathers had been able to bear, of ordinances and traditions complicated with not a little of debilitating superstition, the extreme Puritans of England and Scotland rejected the whole system of holy days in the Christian year, including the authentic anniversaries of Passover and Pentecost, and discontinued the use of religious ceremonies at marriages and funerals.[386:2] The only liturgical compositions that have come down to us from the first generations are the various attempts, in various degrees of harshness and rudeness, at the versification of psalms and other Scriptures for singing. The emancipation of the church from its bondage to an artificial dogma came, as we have already seen, with the Great Awakening and the introduction of Watts's "Psalms of David, Imitated in the Language of the New Testament."[387:1] After the Revolution, at the request of the General Association of Connecticut and the General Assembly of the Presbyterian Church, Timothy Dwight completed the work of Watts by versifying a few omitted psalms,[387:2] and added a brief selection of hymns, chiefly in the grave and solemn Scriptural style of Watts and Doddridge. Then followed, in successive tides, from England, the copious hymnody of the Methodist revival, both Calvinist and Wesleyan, of the Evangelical revival, and now at last of the Oxford revival, with its affluence of translations from the ancient hymnists, as well as of original hymns. It is doubtless owing to this abundant intermittent inflow from England that the production of American hymns has been so scanty. Only a few writers, among them Thomas Hastings and Ray Palmer, have written each a considerable number of hymns that have taken root in the common use of the church. Not a few names besides are associated each with some one or two or three lyrics that have won an enduring place in the affections of Christian worshipers. The "gospel hymns" which have flowed from many pens in increasing volume since the revival of 1857 have proved their great usefulness, especially in connection with the ministry of Messrs. Moody and Sankey; but they are, even the best of them, short-lived. After their season the church seems not unwilling to let them die.

Soon after the mid-point of the nineteenth century, began a serious study of the subject of the conduct of public worship, which continues to this day, with good promise of sometime reaching useful and stable results. In 1855 was published "Eutaxia, or the Presbyterian

Liturgies: Historical Sketches. By a Minister of the Presbyterian Church." The author, Charles W. Baird, was a man peculiarly fitted to render the church important service, such as indeed he did render in this volume, and in the field of Huguenot history which he divided with his brother, Henry M. Baird. How great the loss to historical theology through his protracted feebleness of body and his death may be conjectured, not measured. This brief volume awakened an interest in the subject of it in America, and in Scotland, and among the nonconformists of England. To American Presbyterians in general it was something like a surprise to be reminded that the sisterhood of the "Reformed" sects were committed by their earliest and best traditions in favor of liturgic uses in public worship. At about the same time the fruitful discussions of the Mercersburg controversy were in progress in the German Reformed Church. "Mercersburg found fault with the common style of extemporaneous public prayer, and advocated a revival of the liturgical church service of the Reformation period, but so modified and reproduced as to be adapted to the existing wants of Protestant congregations."[388:1] Each of these discussions was followed by a proposed book of worship. In 1857 was published by Mr. Baird "A Book of Public Prayer, Compiled from the Authorized Formularies of Worship of the Presbyterian Church, as Prepared by the Reformers, Calvin, Knox, Bucer, and others"; and in 1858 was set forth by a committee of the German Reformed Church "A Liturgy, or Order of Christian Worship." In 1855 St. Peter's Presbyterian Church of Rochester published its "Church-book," prepared by Mr. L. W. Bacon, then acting as pastor, which was principally notable for introducing the use of the Psalms in parallelisms for responsive reading—a use which at once found acceptance in many churches, and has become general in all parts of the country. Sporadic experiments followed in various individual congregations, looking toward greater variety or greater dignity or greater musical attractiveness in the services of public worship, or toward more active participation therein on the part of the people. But these experiments, conducted without concert or mutual counsel, often without serious study of the subject, and with a feebly esthetic purpose, were representative of individual notions, and had in them no promise of stability or of fruit after their kind. Only, by the increasing number of them, they have given proof of an unrest on this subject which at last is beginning to embody itself in organization and concerted study and enterprise. A fifty years of mere tentative groping is likely to be followed by another fifty years of substantial progress.

The influence of the Protestant Episcopal Church upon this growing tendency has been sometimes favorable, sometimes unfavorable, but always important. To begin with, it has held up before the whole church an example of prescribed forms for divine worship, on the whole, the best in all history. On the other hand, it has drawn to itself those in other sects whose tastes and tendencies would make them leaders in the study of liturgics, and thus while reinforcing itself has hindered the general advance of improvement in the methods of worship. Withal, its influence has tended to narrow the discussion to the consideration of a single provincial and sectarian tradition, as if the usage of a part of the Christians of the southern end of one of the islands of the British archipelago had a sort of binding authority over the whole western continent. But again, on the other hand, the broadening of its own views to the extent of developing distinctly diverse ways of thinking among its clergy and people has enlarged the field of study once more, and tended to interest the church generally in the practical, historical, and theological aspects of the subject. The somewhat timid ventures of "Broad" and "Evangelical" men in one direction, and the fearless breaking of bounds in the other direction by those of "Ritualist" sympathies, have done much to liberate this important communion from slavish uniformity and indolent traditionalism; and within a few years that has been accomplished which only a few years earlier would have been deemed impossible—the considerable alteration and improvement of the Book of Common Prayer.

It is safe to prognosticate, from the course of the history up to this point, that the subject of the conduct of worship will become more and more seriously a subject of study in the American church in all its divisions; that the discussions thereon arising will be attended with strong antagonisms of sentiment; that mutual antagonisms within the several sects will be compensated by affiliations of men like-minded across sectarian lines; and that thus, as many times before, particular controversies will tend to general union and fellowship.

One topic under this title of Liturgics requires special mention—the use of music in the church. It was not till the early part of the eighteenth century that music began to be cultivated as an art in America.[391:1] Up to that time "the service of song in the house of the Lord" had consisted, in most worshiping assemblies on this continent, in the singing of rude literal versifications of the Psalms and other Scriptures to some eight or ten old tunes handed down by tradition, and variously sung in various congregations, as modified by local practice. The coming in of "singing by rule" was nearly coincident with the introduction of Watts's psalms and hymns, and was attended with like agitations. The singing-school for winter evenings became an almost universal social institution; and there actually grew up an American school of composition, quaint, rude, and ungrammatical, which had great vogue toward the end of the last century, and is even now remembered by some with admiration and regret. It was devoted mainly to psalmody tunes of an elaborate sort, in which the first half-stanza would be sung in plain counterpoint, after which the voices would chase each other about in a lively imitative movement, coming out together triumphantly at the close. They abounded in forbidden progressions and empty chords, but were often characterized by fervor of feeling and by strong melodies. A few of them, as "Lenox" and "Northfield," still linger in use; and the productions of this school in general, which amount to a considerable volume, are entitled to respectful remembrance as the first untutored utterance of music in America. The use of them became a passionate delight to our grandparents; and the traditions are fresh and vivid of the great choirs filling the church galleries on three sides, and tossing the theme about from part to part.

The use of these rudely artificial tunes involved a gravely important change in the course of public worship. In congregations that accepted them the singing necessarily became an exclusive privilege of the choir. To a lamentable extent, where there was neither the irregular and spontaneous ejaculation of the Methodist nor the rubrical response of the Episcopalian, the people came to be shut out from audible participation in the acts of public worship.

A movement of musical reform in the direction of greater simplicity and dignity began early in this century, when Lowell Mason in Boston and Thomas Hastings in New York began their multitudinous publications of psalmody. Between them not less than seventy volumes of music were published in a period of half as many years. Their immense and successful fecundity was imitated with less success by others, until the land was swamped with an annual flood of church-music books. A thin diluvial stratum remains to us from that time in tunes, chiefly from the pen of Dr. Mason, that have taken permanent place as American chorals. Such pieces as "Boylston," "Hebron," "Rockingham," "Missionary Hymn," and the adaptations of Gregorian melodies, "Olmutz" and "Hamburg," are not likely to be displaced from their hold on the American church by more skilled and exquisite compositions of later schools. But the fertile labors of the church musicians of this period were affected by the market demand for new material for the singing-school, the large church choir, and the musical convention. The music thus introduced into the churches consisted not so much of hymn-tunes and anthems as of "sacred glees."[392:1]

Before the middle of the century the Episcopal Church had arrived at a point at which it was much looked to to set the fashions in such matters as church music and architecture. Its influence at this time was very bad. It was largely responsible for the fashion, still widely prevalent, of substituting for the church choir a quartet of professional solo singers, and for the degradation of church music into the dainty, languishing, and sensuous style which such "artists" do most affect. The period of "The Grace Church Collection," "Greatorex's Collection," and the sheet-music compositions of George William Warren and John R. Thomas was the lowest tide of American church music.

A healthy reaction from this vicious condition began about 1855, with the introduction of hymn-and-tune books and the revival of congregational singing. From that time the progressive improvement of the public taste may be traced in the character of the books that have succeeded one another in the churches, until the admirable compositions of the modern English school of psalmody tend to predominate above those of inferior quality. It is the mark of a transitional period that both in church music and in church architecture we seem to depend much on compositions and designs derived from older countries. The future of religious art in America is sufficiently well assured to leave no cause for hurry or anxiety. In glancing back over this chapter, it will be strange if some are not impressed, and unfavorably impressed, with a disproportion in the names cited as representative, which are taken chiefly from some two or three sects. This may justly be referred in part, no doubt, to the author's point of view and to the "personal equation"; but it is more largely due to the fact that in the specialization of the various sects the work of theological literature and science has been distinctively the lot of the Congregationalists and the Presbyterians, and preëminently of the former.[394:1] It is matter of congratulation that the inequality among the denominations in this respect is in a fair way to be outgrown.

Special mention must be made of the peculiarly valuable contribution to the liturgical literature of America that is made by the oldest of our episcopal churches, the Moravian. This venerable organization is rich not only in the possession of a heroic martyr history, but in the inheritance of liturgic forms and usages of unsurpassed beauty and dignity. Before the other churches had emerged from a half-barbarous state in respect to church music, this art was successfully cultivated in the Moravian communities and missions. In past times these have had comparatively few points of contact and influence with the rest of the church; but when the elements of a common order of divine worship shall by and by begin to grow into form, it is hardly possible that the Moravian traditions will not enter into it as an important factor.

A combination of conditions which in the case of other bodies in the church has been an effective discouragement to literary production has applied with especial force to the Roman Catholic Church in America. First, its energies and resources, great as they are, have been engrossed by absolutely prodigious burdens of practical labor; and secondly, its necessary literary material has been furnished to it from across the sea, ready to its hand, or needing only the light labor of translation. But these two conditions are not enough, of themselves, to account for the very meager contribution of the Catholic Church to the common religious and theological literature of American Christendom. Neither is the fact explained by the general low average of culture among the Catholic population; for literary production does not ordinarily proceed from the man of average culture, but from men of superior culture, such as this church possesses in no small number, and places in positions of undisturbed "learned leisure" that would seem in the highest degree promotive of intellectual work. But the comparative statistics of the Catholic and the Protestant countries and universities of Germany seem to prove conclusively that the spirit and discipline of the Roman Church are unfavorable to literary productiveness in those large fields of intellectual activity that are common and free alike to the scholars of all Christendom. It remains to be seen whether the stimulating atmosphere and the free and equal competitions of the New World will not show their invigorating effect in the larger activity of Catholic scholars, and their liberation from within the narrow lines of polemic and defensive literature. The republic of Christian letters has already shown itself prompt to welcome accessions from this quarter. The signs are favorable. Notwithstanding severe criticisms of their methods proceeding from the Catholic press, or rather in consequence of such criticisms, the Catholic institutions of higher learning are rising in character and in public respect; and the honorable enterprise of establishing at Washington an American Catholic university, on the upbuilding of which shall be concentrated the entire intellectual strength and culture of this church, promises an invigorating influence that shall extend through that whole system of educational institutions which the church has set on foot at immense cost, and not with wholly satisfactory results.

Recent events in the Catholic Church in America tend to reassure all minds on an important point on which not bigots and alarmists only, but liberal-minded citizens apostolically willing to "look not only on their own things but also on the things of others," have found reasonable ground for anxiety. The American Catholic Church, while characterized in all its ranks, in respect of loyal devotion to the pope, by a high type of ultramontane orthodoxy, is to be administered on patriotic American principles. The brief term of service of Monsignor Satolli as papal legate clothed with plenipotentiary authority from the Roman see stamped out the scheme called from its promoter "Cahenslyism," which would have divided the American Catholic Church into permanent alien communities, conserving each its foreign language and organized under its separate hierarchy. The organization of parishes to be administered in other languages than English is suffered only as a temporary necessity. The deadly warfare against the American common-school system has abated. And the anti-American denunciations contained in the bull and syllabus of December 8, 1864, are openly renounced as lacking the note of infallibility.[396:1]

Of course, as in all large communities of vigorous vitality, there will be mutually antagonist parties in this body; but it is hardly to be doubted that with the growth and acclimatization of the Catholic Church in America that party will eventually predominate which is most in sympathy with the ruling ideas of the country and the age.

CHAPTER XXII. TENDENCIES TOWARD A MANIFESTATION OF THE UNITY OF THE AMERICAN CHURCH.

The three centuries of history which we have passed under rapid review comprise a series of political events of the highest importance to mankind. We have seen, from our side-point of view, the planting, along the western coast of the Atlantic Ocean, without mutual concert or common direction, of many independent germs of civilization. So many of these as survived the perils of infancy we have seen growing to a lusty youth, and becoming drawn each to each by ties of common interest and mutual fellowship. Releasing themselves from colonial dependence on a transatlantic power, we find these several communities, now grown to be States, becoming conscious, through common perils, victories, and hopes, of national unity and life, and ordaining institutes of national government binding upon all. The strong vitality of the new nation is proved by its assimilating to itself an immense mass of immigrants from all parts of Europe, and by expanding itself without essential change over the area of a continent. It triumphs again and again, and at last in a struggle that shakes the world, over passions and interests that threaten schism in the body politic, and gives good reason to its friends to boast the solid unity of the republic as the strongest existing fact in the political world. The very great aggrandizement of the nation has been an affair of the last sixty years; but already it has recorded itself throughout the vast expanse of the continent in monuments of architecture and engineering worthy of the national strength.

The ecclesiastical history which has been recounted in this volume, covering the same territory and the same period of time, runs with equal pace in many respects parallel with the political history, but in one important respect with a wide divergence. As with civilization so with Christianity: the germs of it, derived from different regions of Christendom, were planted without concert of purpose, and often with distinct cross-purposes, in different seed-plots along the Atlantic seaboard. Varying in polity, in forms of dogmatic statement, and even in language, the diverse growths were made, through wonders of spiritual influence and through external stress of trial, to feel their unity in the one faith. The course of a common experience tended to establish a predominant type of religious life the influence of which has been everywhere felt, even when it has not been consented to. The vital strength of the American church, as of the American nation, has been subjected to the test of the importation of enormous masses of more or less uncongenial population, and has shown an amazing power of digestion and assimilation. Its resources have been taxed by the providential imposition of burdens of duty and responsibility such, in magnitude and weight, as never since the early preaching of the gospel have pressed upon any single generation of the church. Within the space of a single lifetime, at an expenditure of toil and treasure which it is idle to attempt to compute, the wide and desolate wilderness, as fast as civilization has invaded it, has been occupied by the church with churches, schools, colleges, and seminaries of theology, with pastors, evangelists, and teachers, and, in one way or another, has been constrained to confess itself Christian. The continent which so short a time ago had been compassionately looked upon from across the sea as missionary ground has become a principal base of supplies, and recruiting-ground for men and women, for missionary operations in ancient lands of heathenism and of a decayed Christianity.

So much for the parallel. The divergence is not less impressive. In contrast with the solid political unity into which the various and incongruous elements have settled themselves, the unity of the Christian church is manifested by oneness neither of jurisdiction nor of confederation, nor even by diplomatic recognition and correspondence. Out of the total population of the United States, amounting, according to the census of 1890, to 62,622,000 souls, the 57,000,000 accounted as Christians, including 20,000,000 communicant church-members, are gathered into 165,297 congregations, assembling in 142,000 church edifices containing 43,000,000 sittings, and valued (together with other church property) at $670,000,000; and are served in the ministry of the gospel by more than 111,000 ministers.[400:1] But this great force is divided among 143 mutually independent sects, larger and smaller. Among these sects is recognized no controlling and coördinating authority; neither is there any common leadership; neither is there any system of mutual counsel and concert. The mutual relations of the sects are sometimes those of respect and good will, sometimes of sharp competition and jealousy, sometimes of eager and conscientious hostility. All have one and the same unselfish and religious aim—to honor God in serving their fellow-men; and each one, in honestly seeking this supreme aim, is affected by its corporate interests, sympathies, and antipathies.

This situation is too characteristic of America, and too distinctly connected with the whole course of the antecedent history, not to be brought out with emphasis in this concluding chapter. In other lands the church is maintained, through the power of the civil government, under the exclusive control of a single organization, in which the element of popular influence may be wholly wanting, or may be present (as in many of the "Reformed" polities) in no small measure. In others yet, through government influence and favor, a strong predominance is given to one organized communion, under the shadow of which dissentient minorities are tolerated and protected. Under the absolute freedom and equality of the American system there is not so much as a predominance of any one of the sects. No one of them is so strong and numerous but that it is outnumbered and outweighed by the aggregate of the two next to it. At present, in consequence of the rush of immigration, the Roman Catholic Church is largely in advance of any single denomination besides, but is inferior in numerical strength and popular influence to the Methodists and Baptists combined—if they were combined.

And there is no doubt that this comminution of the church is frankly accepted, for reasons assigned, not only as an inevitable drawback to the blessings of religious freedom, but as a good thing in itself. A weighty sentence of James Madison undoubtedly expresses the prevailing sentiment among Americans who contemplate the subject merely from the political side: "In a free government the security for civil rights must be the same as that for religious rights. It consists, in the one case, in the multiplicity of interests, and, in the other, in the multiplicity of sects. The degree of security in both cases will depend on the number of interests and sects."[402:1] And no student of history can deny that there is much to justify the jealousy with which the lovers of civil liberty watch the climbing of any sect, no matter how purely spiritual its constitution, toward a position of command in popular influence. The influence of the leaders of such a sect may be nothing more than the legitimate and well-deserved influence of men of superior wisdom and virtue; but when reinforced by the weight of official religious character, and backed by a majority, or even a formidable minority, of voters organized in a religious communion, the feeling is sure to gain ground that such power is too great to be trusted to the hands even of the best of men. Whatever sectarian advantage such a body may achieve in the state by preponderance of number will be more than offset by the public suspicion and the watchful jealousy of rival sects; and the weakening of it by division, or the subordination of it by the overgrowth of a rival, is sure to be regarded with general complacency.

It is not altogether a pleasing object of contemplation—the citizen and the statesman looking with contentment on the schism of the church as averting a danger to the state. It is hardly more gratifying when we find ministers of the church themselves accepting the condition of schism as being, on the whole, a very good condition for the church of Christ, if not, indeed, the best possible. It is quite unreservedly argued that the principle, "Competition is the life of business," is applicable to spiritual as well as secular concerns; and the "emulations" reprobated by the Apostle Paul as "works of the flesh" are frankly appealed to for promoting the works of the spirit. This debasing of the motive of church work is naturally attended by a debasement of the means employed. The competitive church resorts to strange business devices to secure its needed revenue. "He that giveth" is induced to give, not "with simplicity," but with a view to incidental advantages, and a distinct understanding is maintained between the right hand and the left. The extent and variety of this influence on church life in America afford no occasion for pride, but the mention of them could not rightly be omitted. It remains for the future to decide whether they must needs continue as an inevitable attendant on the voluntary system.

Sectarian divisions tend strongly to perpetuate themselves. The starting of schism is easy and quick; the healing of it is a matter of long diplomatic negotiations. In a very short time the division of the church, with its necessary relations to property and to the employment of officials, becomes a vested interest. Provision for large expenditure unnecessary, or even detrimental, to the general interests of the kingdom of Christ, which had been instituted in the first place at heavy cost to the many, is not to be discontinued without more serious loss to influential individuals. Those who would set themselves about the healing of a schism must reckon upon personal and property interests to be conciliated.

This least amiable characteristic of the growth of the Christian church in America is not without its compensations. The very fact of the existence, in presence of one another, of these multitudinous rival sects, all equal before the law, tends in the long run, under the influence of the Holy Spirit of peace, to a large and comprehensive fellowship.[404:1] The widely prevalent acceptance of existing conditions as probably permanent, even if not quite normal, softens the mutual reproaches of rival parties. The presumption is of course implied, if not asserted, in the existence of any Christian sect, that it is holding the absolute right and truth, or at least more nearly that than other sects; and the inference, to a religious mind, is that the right and true must, in the long run, prevail. But it is only with a high act of faith, and not as a matter of reasonable probability, that any sect in America can venture to indulge itself in the expectation of a supremacy, or even a predominance, in American Christendom. The strongest in numbers, in influence, in prestige, however tempted to assert for itself exclusive or superior rights, is compelled to look about itself and find itself overwhelmingly outnumbered and outdone by a divided communion—and yet a communion—of those whom Christ "is not ashamed to call his brethren"; and just in proportion as it has the spirit of Christ, it is constrained in its heart to treat them as brethren and to feel toward them as brethren. Its protest against what it regards as their errors and defects is nowise weakened by the most unreserved manifestations of respect and good will as toward fellow-Christians. Thus it comes to pass that the observant traveler from other countries, seeking the distinctive traits of American social life, "notes a kindlier feeling between all denominations, Roman Catholics included, a greater readiness to work together for common charitable aims, than between Catholics and Protestants in France or Germany, or between Anglicans and nonconformists in England."[405:1]

There are many indications, in the recent history of the American church, pointing forward toward some higher manifestation of the true unity of the church than is to be found in occasional, or even habitual, expressions of mutual good will passing to and fro among sharply competing and often antagonist sects. Instead of easy-going and playful felicitations on the multitude of sects as contributing to the total effectiveness of the church, such as used to be common enough on "anniversary" platforms, we hear, in one form and another, the acknowledgment that the divided and subdivided state of American Christendom is not right, but wrong. Whose is the wrong need not be decided; certainly it does not wholly belong to the men of this generation or of this country; we are heirs of the schisms of other lands and ages, and have added to them schisms of our own making. The matter begins to be taken soberly and seriously. The tender entreaty of the Apostle Paul not to suffer ourselves to be split up into sects[405:2] begins to get a hearing in the conscience. The nisus toward a more manifest union among Christian believers has long been growing more and more distinctly visible, and is at the present day one of the most conspicuous signs of the times.

Already in the early history we have observed a tendency toward the healing, in America, of differences imported from over sea. Such was the commingling of Separatist and Puritan in New England; the temporary alliance of Congregationalist and Presbyterian to avert the imposition of a state hierarchy; the combination of Quaker and Roman Catholic to defeat a project of religious oppression in Maryland; the drawing together of Lutheran and Reformed Germans for common worship, under the saintly influence of the Moravian Zinzendorf; and the "Plan of Union" by which New Englander and Scotch-Irishman were to labor in common for the evangelization of the new settlements.[406:1] These were sporadic instances of a tendency that was by and by to become happily epidemic. A more important instance of the same tendency was the organization of societies for charitable work which should unite the gifts and personal labors of the Christians of the whole continent. The chief period of these organizations extended from 1810, the date of the beginning of the American Board of Commissioners for Foreign Missions, to 1826, when the American Home Missionary Society was founded.[406:2] The "catholic basis" on which they were established was dictated partly by the conscious weakness of the several sects as they drew near to undertakings formidable even to their united forces, and partly by the glow of fraternal affection, and the sense of a common spiritual life pervading the nation, with which the church had come forth from the fervors of "the second awakening."[406:3] The societies, representing the common faith and charity of the whole church as distinguished from the peculiarities of the several sects, drew to themselves the affection and devotion of Christian hearts to a degree which, to those who highly valued these distinctions, seemed to endanger important interests. And, indeed, the situation was anomalous, in which the sectarian divisions of the Christian people were represented in the churches, and their catholic unity in charitable societies. It would have seemed more Pauline, not to say more Christian, to have had voluntary societies for the sectarian work, and kept the churches for Christian communion. It is no wonder that High-church champions, on one side and another, soon began to shout to their adherents, "To your tents, O Israel!" Bishop Hobart played not in vain upon his pastoral pipe to whistle back his sheep from straying outside of his pinfold, exhorting them, "in their endeavors for the general advancement of religion, to use only the instrumentality of their own church."[407:1] And a jealousy of the growing influence of a wide fellowship, in charitable labors, with Christians of other names, led to the enunciation of a like doctrine by High-church Presbyterians,[407:2] and contributed to the convulsive and passionate rending of the Presbyterian Church, in 1837, into nearly equal fragments. So effective has been the centrifugal force that of the extensive system of societies which from the year 1810 onward first organized works of national beneficence by enlisting the coöperation of "all evangelical Christians," the American Bible Society alone continues to represent any general and important combination from among the different denominations.

For all the waning of interest in the "catholic basis" societies, the sacred discontent of the Christian people with sectarian division continued to demand expression. How early the aspiration for an ecumenical council of evangelical Christendom became articulate, it may not be easy to discover[408:1] In the year 1846 the aspiration was in some measure realized in the first meeting of the Evangelical Alliance at London. No more mistakes were made in this meeting than perhaps were necessarily incident to a first experiment in untried work. Almost of course the good people began with the question, What good men shall we keep out? for it is a curious fact, in the long and interesting history of efforts after Christian union, that they commonly take the form of efforts so to combine many Christians as to exclude certain others. In this instance, beginning with the plan of including none but Protestant Christians, they proceeded at once to frame a platform that should bar out that "great number of the best and holiest men in England who are found among the Quakers," thus making up, "designedly and with their eyes open, a schismatic unity—a unity composed of one part of God's elect, to the exclusion of another; and this in a grand effort after the very unity of the body of Christ."[409:1] But in spite of this and other like mistakes, or rather because of them (for it is through its mistakes that the church is to learn the right way), the early and unsuccessful beginnings of the Evangelical Alliance marked a stage in the slow progress toward a "manifestation of the sons of God" by their love toward each other and toward the common Lord.

It is in large part the eager appetency for some manifestation of interconfessional fellowship that has hastened the acceptance of such organizations as the Young Men's Christian Association and the Young People's Society of Christian Endeavor; just as, on the other hand, it is the conscientious fear, on the part of watchful guardians of sectarian interests, that habitual fellowship across the boundary lines of denominations may weaken the allegiance to the sect, which has induced the many attempts at substituting associations constituted on a narrower basis. But the form of organization which most comprehensively illustrates the unity of the church is that "Charity Organization" which has grown to be a necessity to the social life of cities and considerable towns, furnishing a central office of mutual correspondence and coördination to all churches and societies and persons engaged in the Christian work of relieving poverty and distress. This central bureau of charitable coöperation is not the less a center of catholic fellowship for the fact that it does not shut its door against societies not distinctively Christian, like Masonic fraternities, nor even against societies distinctively non-Christian, like Hebrew synagogues and "societies of ethical culture." We are coming to discover that the essence of Christian fellowship does not consist in keeping people out. Neither, so long as the apostolic rubric of Christian worship[410:1] remains unaltered, is it to be denied that the fellowship thus provided for is a fellowship in one of the sacraments of Christian service.

A notable advance in true catholicity of communion is reported from among the churches and scattered missions in Maine. Hitherto, in the various movements of Christian union, it was common to attempt to disarm the suspicions of zealous sectarians by urgent disclaimers of any intent or tendency to infringe on the rights or interests of the several sects, or impair their claim to a paramount allegiance from their adherents. The Christians of Maine, facing tasks of evangelization more than sufficient to occupy all their resources even when well economized and squandering nothing on needless divisions and competitions, have attained to the high grace of saying that sectarian interests must and shall be sacrificed when the paramount interests of the kingdom of Christ require it.[410:2] When this attainment is reached by other souls, and many other, the conspicuous shame and scandal of American Christianity will begin to be abated.

Meanwhile the signs of a craving for larger fellowship continue to be multiplied. Quite independently of practical results achieved, the mere fact of efforts and experiments is a hopeful fact, even when these are made in directions in which the past experience of the church has written up "No Thoroughfare."

I. No one need question the sincerity or the fraternal spirit with which some important denominations have each proposed the reuniting of Christians on the simple condition that all others should accept the distinctive tenet for which each of these denominations has contended against others. The present pope, holding the personal respect and confidence of the Christian world to a higher degree than any one of his predecessors since the Reformation (to name no earlier date), has earnestly besought the return of all believers to a common fellowship by their acceptance of the authority and supremacy of the Roman see. With equal cordiality the bishops of the Protestant Episcopal Church have signified their longing for restored fellowship with their brethren on the acceptance by these of prelatical episcopacy. And the Baptists, whose constant readiness at fraternization in everything else is emphasized by their conscientious refraining from the sacramental sign of communion, are not less earnest in their desire for the unification of Christendom by the general acceptance of that tenet concerning baptism, the widespread rejection of which debars them, reluctant, from unrestricted fellowship with the general company of faithful men. But while we welcome every such manifestation of a longing for union among Christians, and honor the aspiration that it might be brought about in one or another of these ways, in forecasting the probabilities of the case, we recognize the extreme unlikeliness that the very formulas which for ages have been the occasions of mutual contention and separation shall become the basis of general agreement and lasting concord.

II. Another indication of the craving for a larger fellowship is found in the efforts made for large sectarian councils, representing closely kindred denominations in more than one country. The imposing ubiquity of the Roman Church, so impressively sustaining its claim to the title Catholic, may have had some influence to provoke other denominations to show what could be done in emulation of this sort of greatness. It were wiser not to invite comparison at this point. No other Christian organization, or close fellowship of organizations, can approach that which has its seat at Rome, in the world-wideness of its presence, or demand with so bold a challenge,

Quæ regio in terris non nostri plena laboris?

The representative assembly of any other body of Christians, however widely ramified, must seem insignificant when contrasted with the real ecumenicity of the Vatican Council. But it has not been useless for the larger sects of Protestantism to arrange their international assemblies, if it were for nothing more than this, that such widening of the circle of practical fellowship may have the effect to disclose to each sect a larger Christendom outside to which their fellowship must sooner or later be made to reach.

The first of these international sectarian councils was that commonly spoken of as "the Pan-Anglican Synod," of Protestant Episcopal bishops gathered at Lambeth by invitation of the Archbishop of Canterbury in 1867 and thrice since. The example was bettered by the Presbyterians, who in 1876 organized for permanence their "Pam-Presbyterian Alliance," or "Alliance of the Reformed Churches throughout the world holding the Presbyterian System." The first of the triennial general councils of this Alliance was held at Edinburgh in 1877, "representing more than forty-nine separate churches scattered through twenty-five different countries, and consisting of more than twenty thousand congregations."[413:1] The second council was held at Philadelphia, and the third at Belfast. The idea was promptly seized by the Methodists. At the instance of the General Conference of the United States, a Pam-Methodist Council was held in London in 1881,—"the first Ecumenical Methodist Conference,"—consisting of four hundred delegates, representing twenty-eight branches of Methodism, ten in the eastern hemisphere and eighteen in the western, including six millions of communicants and about twenty millions of people.[413:2] Ten years later, in 1891, a second "Methodist Ecumenical Conference" was held at Washington.

Interesting and useful as this international organization of sects is capable of being made, it would be a mistake to look upon it as marking a stage in the progress toward a manifest general unity of the church. The tendency of it is, on the whole, in the opposite direction.

III. If the organization of "ecumenical" sects has little tendency toward the visible communion of saints in the American church, not much more is to be hoped from measures for the partial consolidation of sects, such as are often projected and sometimes realized. The healing of the great thirty years' schism of the Presbyterian Church, in 1869, was so vast a gain in ecclesiastical economy, and in the abatement of a long-reeking public scandal and of a multitude of local frictions and irritations, that none need wonder at the awakening of ardent desires that the ten Presbyterian bodies still surviving might "find room for all within one fold"[413:3] in a national or continental Presbyterian Church. The seventeen Methodist bodies, separated by no differences of polity or of doctrine that seem important to anybody but themselves, if consolidated into one, would constitute a truly imposing body, numbering nearly five millions of communicants and more than fifteen millions of people; and if this should absorb the Protestant Episcopal Church (an event the possibility of which has often been contemplated with complacency), with its half-million of communicants and its elements of influence far beyond the proportion of its numbers, the result would be an approximation to some good men's ideal of a national church, with its army of ministers coördinated by a college of bishops, and its plebs adunata sacerdoti. Consultations are even now in progress looking toward the closer fellowship of the Congregationalists and the Disciples. The easy and elastic terms of internal association in each of these denominations make it the less difficult to adjust terms of mutual coöperation and union. Suppose that the various Baptist organizations were to discover that under their like congregational government there were ways in which, without compromising or weakening in the slightest their protest against practices which they reprobate in the matter of baptism, they could, for certain defined purposes, enter into the same combination, the result would be a body of nearly five millions of communicants, not the less strong for being lightly harnessed and for comprehending wide diversities of opinion and temperament. In all this we have supposed to be realized nothing more than friends of Christian union have at one time or another urged as practicable and desirable. By these few and, it would seem, not incongruous combinations there would be four powerful ecclesiastical corporations,—one Catholic and three Protestant,—which, out of the twenty millions of church communicants in the United States, would include more than seventeen and one half millions.[415:1]

The pondering of these possibilities is pertinent to this closing chapter on account of the fact that, as we near the end of the nineteenth century, one of the most distinctly visible tendencies is the tendency toward the abatement of sectarian division in the church. It is not for us simply to note the converging lines of tendency, without some attempt to compute the point toward which they converge. There is grave reason to doubt whether this line of the consolidation or confederation of sects, followed never so far, would reach the desired result.

If the one hundred and forty-three sects enumerated in the eleventh census of the United States[415:2] should by successful negotiation be reduced to four, distinguished each from the others by strongly marked diversities of organization and of theological statement, and united to each other only by community of the one faith in Jesus Christ, doubtless it would involve some important gains. It would make it possible to be rid of the friction and sometimes the clash of much useless and expensive machinery, and to extinguish many local schisms that had been engendered by the zeal of some central sectarian propaganda. Would it tend to mitigate the intensity of sectarian competition, or would it tend rather to aggravate it? Is one's pride in his sect, his zeal for the propagation of it, his jealousy of any influence that tends to impair its greatness or hinder its progress, likely to be reduced, or is it rather likely to be exalted, by the consciousness that the sect is a very great sect, standing alone for important principles? Whatever there is at present of asperity in the emulous labors of the competing denominations, would it not be manifold exasperated if the competition were restricted to four great corporations or confederations? If the intestine conflict of the church of Christ in America should even be narrowed down (as many have devoutly wished) to two contestants,—the Catholic Church with its diversity of orders and rites, on the one hand, and Protestantism with its various denominations solidly confederated, on the other,—should we be nearer to the longed-for achievement of Christian union? or should we find sectarian animosities thereby raised to the highest power, and the church, discovering that it was on the wrong track for the desired terminus, compelled to reverse and back in order to be switched upon the right one? Questions like these, put to be considered, not to be answered, raise in the mind the misgiving that we have been seeking in diplomatic negotiations between high contracting parties that which diplomacy can do only a little toward accomplishing. The great aim is to be sought in humbler ways. It is more hopeful to begin at the lower end. Not in great towns and centers of ecclesiastical influence, but in villages and country districts, the deadly effects of comminuted fracture in the church are most deeply felt. It is directly to the people of such communities, not through the medium of persons or committees that represent national sectarian interests, that the new commandment is to be preached, which yet is no new commandment, but the old commandment which they have had from the beginning. It cannot always be that sincere Christian believers, living together in a neighborhood in which the ruinous effects of division are plain to every eye, shall continue to misapprehend or disregard some of the tenderest and most unmistakable counsels of their Lord and his apostles, or imagine the authority of them to be canceled by the authority of any sect or party of Christians. The double fallacy, first, that it is a Christian's prime duty to look out for his own soul, and, secondly, that the soul's best health is to be secured by sequestering it from contact with dissentient opinions, and indulging its tastes and preferences wherein they differ from those of its neighbor, must sometime be found out and exposed. The discovery will be made that there is nothing in the most cherished sermons and sacraments and prayers that is comparable in value, as a means of grace, with the giving up of all these for God's reign and righteousness—that he who will save his soul shall lose it, and he who will lose his soul for Christ and his gospel shall save it to life eternal. These centuries of church history, beginning with convulsive disruptions of the church in Europe, with persecutions and religious wars, present before us the importation into the New World of the religious divisions and subdivisions of the Old, and the further division of these beyond any precedent in history. It begins to look as if in this "strange work" God had been grinding up material for a nobler manifestation of the unity of his people. The sky of the declining century is red with promise. Hitherto, not the decay of religious earnestness only, but the revival of it, has brought into the church, not peace, but division. When next some divine breathing of spiritual influence shall be wafted over the land, can any man forbid the hope that from village to village the members of the disintegrated and enfeebled church of Christ may be gathered together "with one accord in one place" not for the transient fervors of the revival only, but for permanent fellowship in work and worship? A few examples of this would spread their influence through the American church "until the whole was leavened."

The record of important events in the annals of American Christianity may well end with that wholly unprecedented gathering at Chicago in connection with the magnificent celebration of the four hundredth anniversary of the discovery of America by Columbus—I mean, of course, the Parliament of Religions. In a land which bears among the nations the reproach of being wholly absorbed in devotion to material interests, and in which the church, unsupported and barely recognized by the state, and unregulated by any secular authority, scatters itself into what seem to be hopelessly discordant fragments, a bold enterprise was undertaken in the name of American Christianity, such as the church in no other land of Christendom would have had the power or the courage to venture on. With large hospitality, representatives of all the religions of the world were invited to visit Chicago, free of cost, as guests of the Parliament. For seventeen days the Christianity of America, and of Christendom, and of Christian missions in heathen lands, sat confronted—no, not confronted, but side by side on the same platform—with the non-Christian religions represented by their priests, prelates, and teachers. Of all the diversities of Christian opinion and organization in America nothing important was unrepresented, from the authoritative dogmatic system and the solid organization of the Catholic Church (present in the person of its highest official dignitaries) to the broadest liberalism and the most unrestrained individualism. There were those who stood aloof and prophesied that nothing could come of such an assemblage but a hopeless jangle of discordant opinions. The forebodings were disappointed. The diverse opinions were there, and were uttered with entire unreserve. But the jangle of discord was not there. It was seen and felt that the American church, in the presence of the unchristian and antichristian powers, and in presence of those solemn questions of the needs of humanity that overtask the ingenuity and the resources of us all combined, was "builded as a city that is at unity with itself." That body which, by its strength of organization, and by the binding force of its antecedents, might have seemed to some most hopelessly isolated from the common sympathies of the assembly, like all the rest was faithful in the assertion of its claims, and, on the other hand, was surpassed by none in the manifestation of fraternal respect toward fellow-Christians of other folds. Since those seventeen wonderful September days of 1893, the idea that has so long prevailed with multitudes of minds, that the only Christian union to be hoped for in America must be a union to the exclusion of the Roman Catholic Church and in antagonism to it, ought to be reckoned an idea obsolete and antiquated.

The theme prescribed for this volume gives no opportunity for such a conclusion as the literary artist delights in—a climax of achievement and consummation, or the catastrophe of a decline and fall. We have marked the sudden divulging to the world of the long-kept secret of divine Providence; the unveiling of the hidden continent; the progress of discovery, of conquest, of colonization; the planting of the church; the rush of immigration; the occupation of the continent with Christian institutions by a strange diversity of sects; the great providential preparations as for some "divine event" still hidden behind the curtain that is about to rise on the new century,—and here the story breaks off half told.

To so many of his readers as shall have followed him to this last page of the volume, the author would speak a parting word. He does not deprecate the criticisms that will certainly be pronounced upon his work by those competent to judge both of the subject and of the style of it. He would rather acknowledge them in advance. No one of his critics can possibly have so keen a sense as the author himself of his incompetency, and of the inadequacy of his work, to the greatness of the subject. To one reproach, however, he cannot acknowledge himself justly liable: he is not self-appointed to a task beyond his powers and attainments, but has undertaken it at the instance of eminent men to whose judgment he was bound to defer. But he cannot believe that even his shortcomings and failures will be wholly fruitless. If they shall provoke some really competent scholar to make a book worthy of so great and inspiring a theme, the present author will be well content.

CPSIA information can be obtained
at www.ICGtesting.com
Printed in the USA
LVHW082259020320
648805LV00020B/1096